MW00447812

"We all need a friend who doesn't just say 'get your sh*t together' but 'here's how.' From page one, Shira offers actionable systems, suggestions, and shifts with zero shame and a whole lot of love. What a gift!"

—SAMARA BAY, author of *Permission to Speak*

"Shira Gill's *LifeStyled* is an indispensable guide to creating a beautiful life centered on what matters most. It's a must-read for anyone who wants to feel more grounded and more purposeful in daily life."

—INGRID FETELL LEE, author of *Joyful*

"The life-organizing handbook everyone needs to build healthy lifestyle habits, streamline routines, delete the excess, and save time—all with style and ease."

—JULIA ROCKWELL, author of *Mothering Earth: The Busy Family's Guide to Saving the Planet*

"Step into a more purposeful life with Shira Gill's *LifeStyled*. This powerful guide cuts through mental clutter to help you simplify your daily routines and cultivate a life of ease and freedom. *LifeStyled* equips you to transform your world, one small step at a time."

—SHIRIN ETESSAM, author of *Free to Be: A Six Week Guide to Reclaiming Your Soul*

Life
Styled

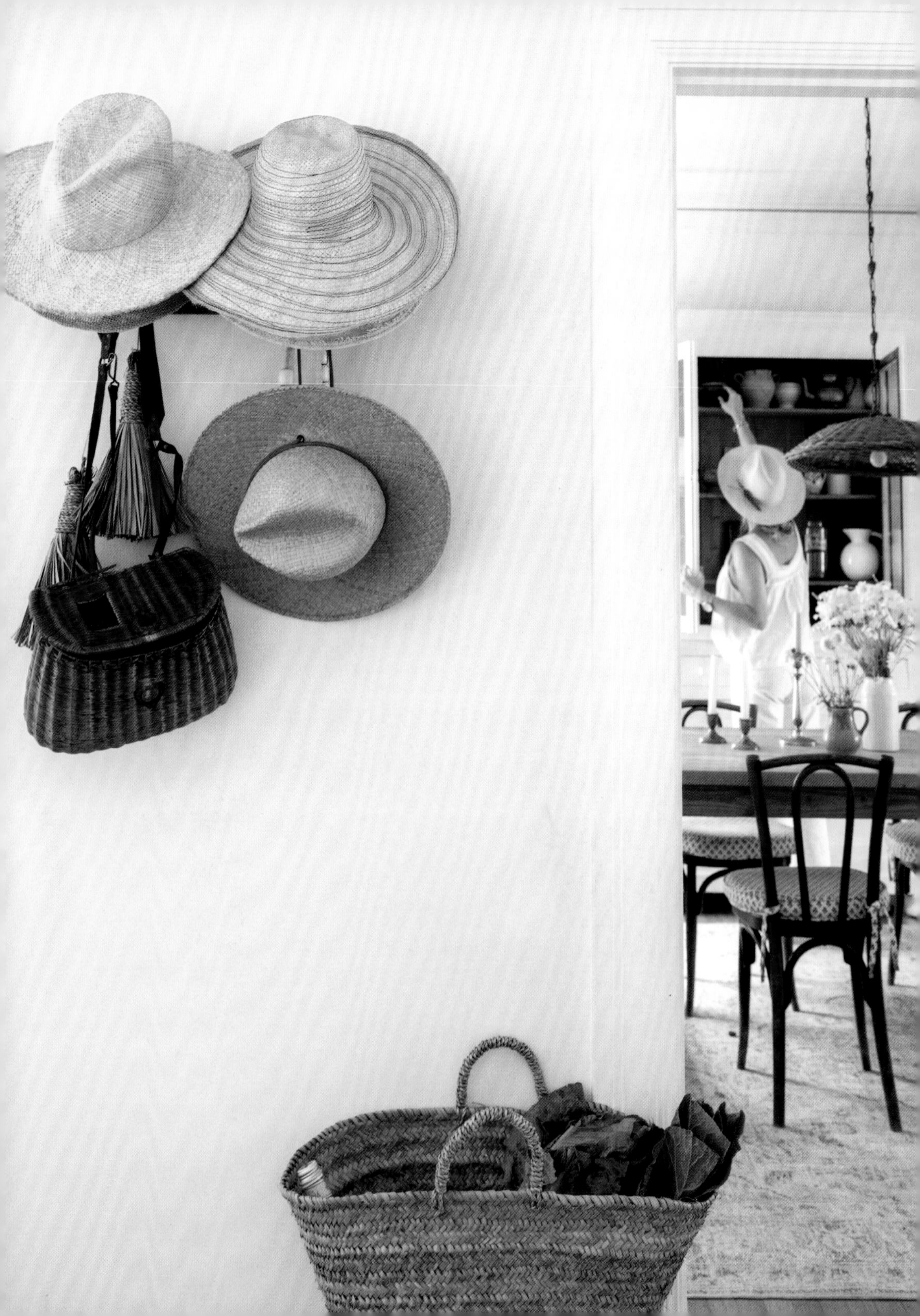

Life Styled

Your Guide to a More Organized & Intentional Life

Shira Gill

author of *Minimalista*

Photographs by Vivian Johnson

TEN SPEED PRESS
California | New York

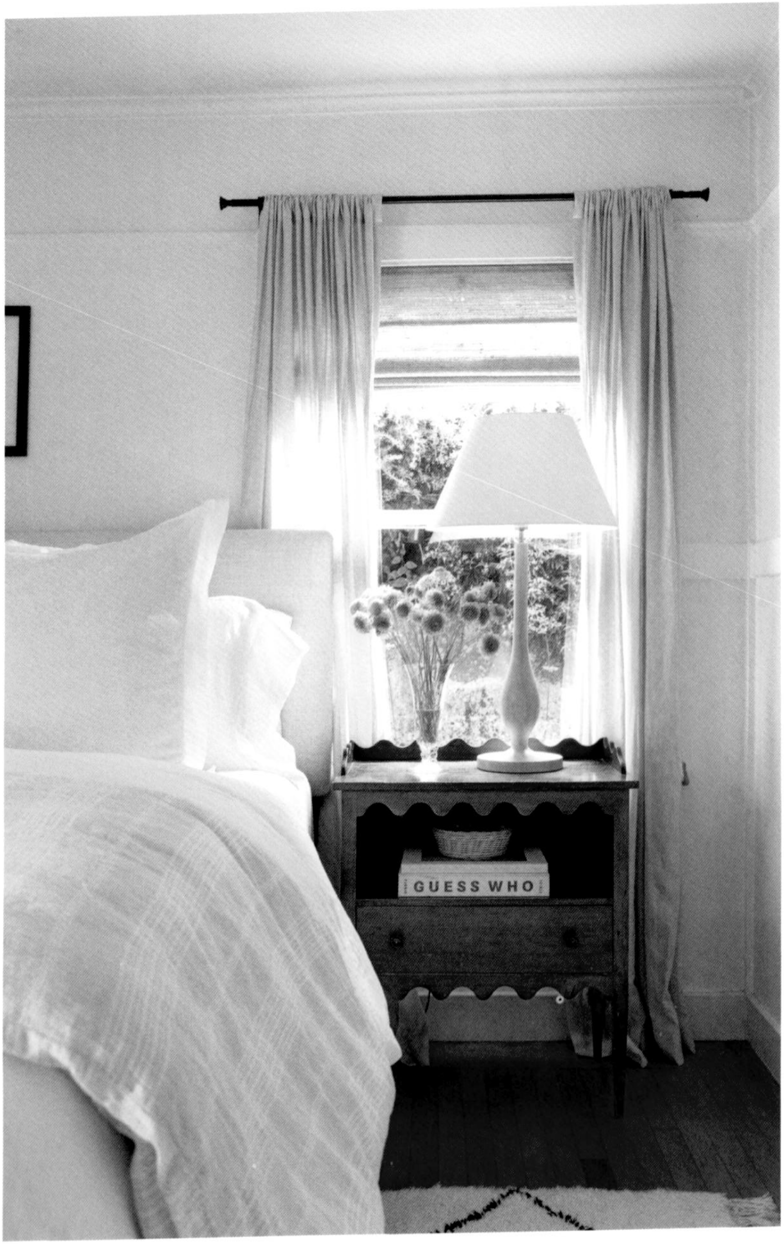
GUESS WHO

CONTENTS

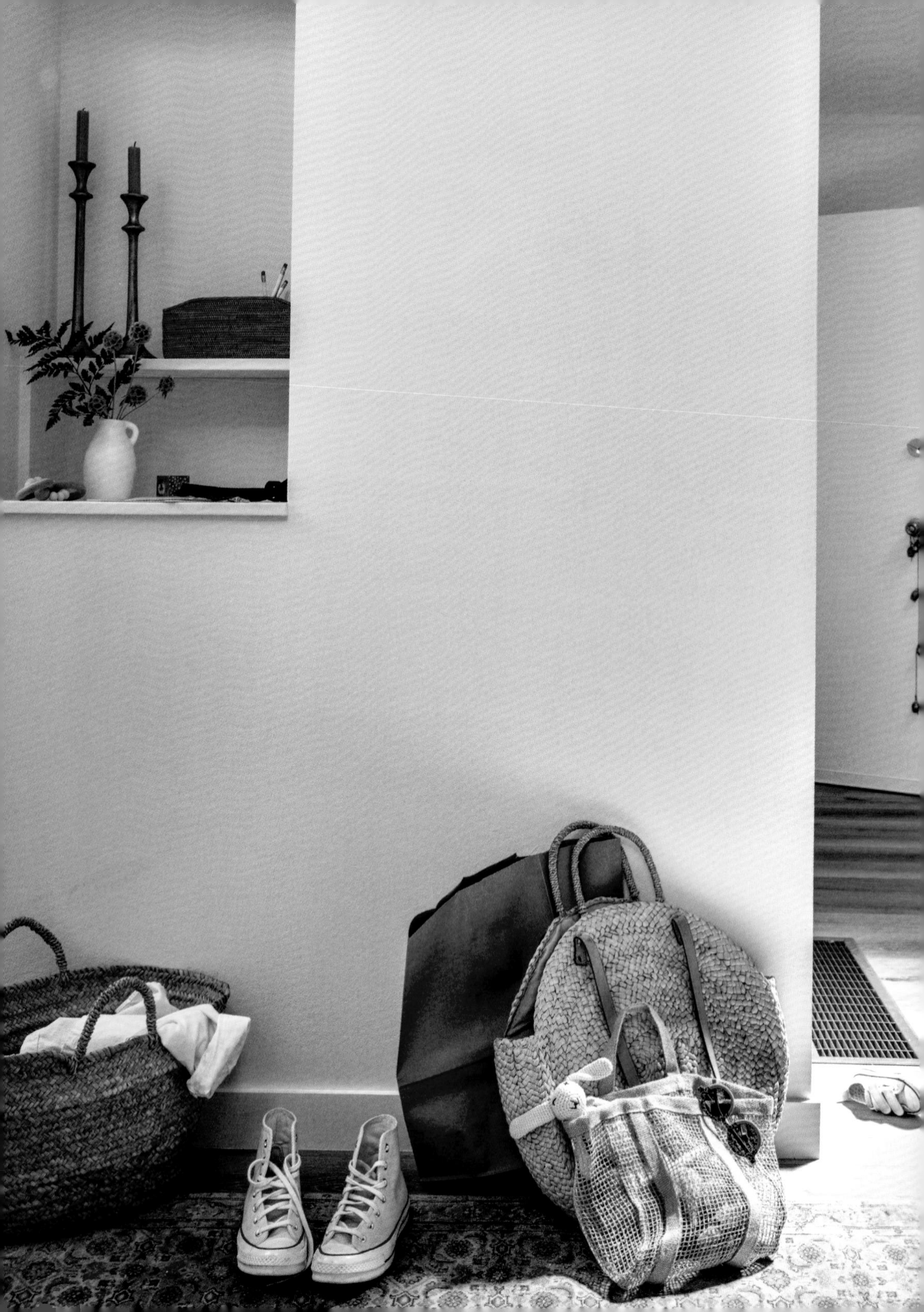

INTRODUCTION

This is a book about living intentionally and taking responsibility for creating the life you want. It is also a book about what happens when your dog throws up on the carpet and your back inexplicably goes out, and both of your kids come home from school with lice the day before you're hosting a holiday party (true story).

But let's back up. I've dedicated much of my life and work to solving the challenge of *too-muchness*, using principles of minimalism as my guide. I'll admit that while it's always been easy for me to keep clutter out of my home, balancing all the moving parts of my life has proven to be far more daunting. As a wife, mother, daughter, friend, entrepreneur, and author, it's easy to feel like I'm always falling short or failing in one area or another, and I often find myself yearning for more hours in the day. And I'm not alone.

Over the course of my lengthy career helping thousands of people organize their homes and lives, I've gained an inside perspective on what people are struggling with. Here's what I've learned: So many of us are teetering right on the edge of total burnout, riddled with imposter syndrome, trying to figure out how to continue to do it all while barely keeping it together. If you're feeling like it's all too much to manage successfully, that's probably because it is.

In America, as well as most other Western cultures, we are oversaturated, overstimulated, overextended, overscheduled, and exhausted. The cumulative effects of a cluttered home and life can lead to anxiety, depression, and other serious mental health challenges. Lost passports, missed medical appointments, and cluttered calendars are more than just a minor inconvenience. I've been inside the homes of some of the most successful people on the planet, and I've been witness to every type of breakdown and tearful confession you can imagine–people at the top of their industries who've confessed they can't even think about getting their house in order because they're completely depleted, overwhelmed, and underwater in their lives.

Amy, a successful attorney and mother of three, told me she fantasized about getting sick just so she could get a break from her frenetic schedule and spend the day in bed. Elena, a producer in Hollywood, confessed that she sometimes neglected to eat, or even *go to the bathroom*, because she was so overscheduled. My client Holly only semi-jokingly asked if I could accidentally set her garage on fire so she wouldn't have to deal with it. Between daily household responsibilities, family and career obligations, and the seemingly endless buzzing of emails, texts, and news notifications clamoring for our attention, it's only natural to feel a bit like we're drowning.

Fortunately, there is an actionable antidote to an overextended life, and it involves making better and more intentional decisions about how to invest our precious time, energy, and resources. Since it is impossible to do everything well all at once, it's up to us to decide what matters most at any given time. Using principles of minimalism to get more intentional about where we place our attention, and simple systems of organization and habit formation to ensure that our priorities get met, we can create more spaciousness, ease, and joy for ourselves, and radically alter the course of our lives–and we can start today!

In my first book, *Minimalista*, I taught readers how to edit, elevate, and maintain their homes using a minimalist mindset and my five-step process. In my second book, *Organized Living*, I brought people inside the homes of twenty-five organizing experts across the globe to illuminate how organization can be leveraged as a tool to create more order, ease, freedom, and joy. In *LifeStyled*, I will share how you can take these same principles and use them to transform your *entire life*. I'll share specific examples from my work with clients as well as my

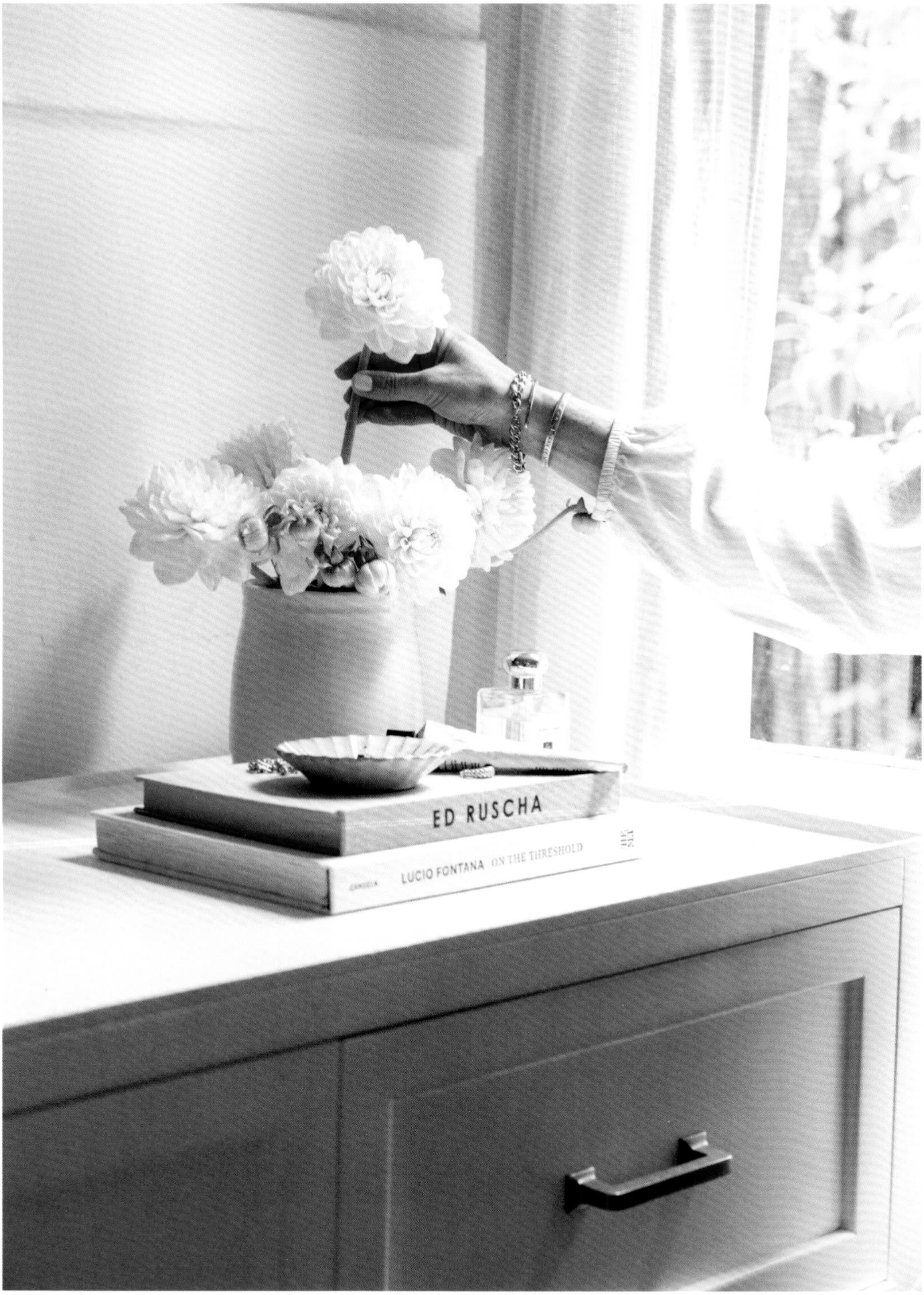
ED RUSCHA
LUCIO FONTANA ON THE THRESHOLD

own experiences (we're in this together!), and provide small, actionable steps you can take to improve every part of your life—from community and relationships to health and wellness, career and finance, and personal development.

Throughout the book, you'll discover lots of quick and impactful things you can do to make progress—even when you don't have a lot of time. The methods I teach are approachable, practical, and for everyone.

In part one, I'll share a simple tool kit and framework you can use to reduce mental clutter and transform how you approach your home, schedule, and life. In part two, I'll break down specific prompts and strategies to improve every aspect of your life, choose-your-own-adventure style. Throughout the chapters ahead, you'll see "Try It" or "Quick Win" to cue you when it's time to reflect, jot down some notes, or take action. Also look out for "Fifteen-Minute Wins," tiny things you can integrate or practice to start seeing results now. Little effort, big reward. This entire book is designed so you can revisit individual chapters any time to recalibrate as your values and priorities shift and evolve. I want to help you activate your best self, even if you're short on time or capacity. If you're one of those people who's like, "Just cut to the chase and tell me what to *do*" (I am that person, too.), I've provided a concise roundup of small, actionable prompts you can pick and choose from to get started right away on page 236.

Before we get started, I want to acknowledge that crafting an intentional life can feel more possible—both intellectually and functionally—depending on your access to resources and privilege. This pursuit is made more challenging by very real cultural and systemic obstacles, including poverty, racism, sexism, homophobia, transphobia, and other forms of discrimination. The philosophy and perspective shared in this book are informed by my own lived experience (one of a decent amount of privilege with some challenges woven in), but guided primarily by my intention to share methods and strategies that will be universally applicable and useful. The goal is to empower you to take specific and consistent actions toward a more aligned, authentic, and fulfilling life—*whatever that may look like for you.*

I truly believe that no matter who you are, and how you're feeling right now, you're only a few decisions away from beginning to completely transform your life. I promise you this: If you commit to completing even a fraction of the steps outlined ahead, you will see real and powerful changes start to occur. Relief is on the way.

MINIMALISM: A NEW DEFINITION

The term *minimalism* gets a bad rap, often conjuring up images of stark white rooms, scarcity, and deprivation, or a rigid or proscriptive protocol. Not on my watch! I define *minimalism* as being radically intentional—not just with the things you own, but with how you spend your time, resources, and energy. It's about clarifying what's important to *you* and cutting the clutter and distractions that stand in the way. To me, minimalism doesn't refer to the lack or absence of something—it's about having the *perfect* amount. Just enough without the excess. More specifically, I mean the exact right number of something for *you*. I preach a philosophy of minimalism that confronts excess, not one that deprives you of the things you actually enjoy. I'll never tell you exactly how many coffee mugs or handbags you should own because we are all different. My version of minimalism is about defining your own version of *enough*. I've coached hundreds of people through this process, and they've all arrived at their own answers. For me, six coffee mugs is more than enough (I don't even drink coffee!). For my client Nikki, who lives in a big home, and frequently hosts huge family gatherings, two dozen coffee mugs makes sense. Fine! My brand of minimalism is flexible and customizable. It's a tool that can help you live in greater alignment with your values. If the term or idea of *minimalism* makes you squirm, just replace it with *intentionalism*. Deal? Good. Now let's get into it!

PART ONE

The Tool Kit

Start your engines and get ready to step on the gas! I'm going to break down how to organize your home, life, and mind by leveraging three simple tools: **adjusting volume, creating systems, and implementing habits**. I've used these tools consistently over the course of my career as a professional organizer, and, when used in tandem, they are magic.

You'll learn how to cut the clutter and get to the good stuff (volume), create new structure and processes (systems), and shift your behavior to create new results (habits). By adjusting volume, creating simple and intuitive systems, and shifting your daily habits, you'll be able to reclaim control over your home, life, and mind. The best news is you can apply this tool kit to literally anything—from your overflowing closets to your jam-packed calendar. Introducing: The Tool Kit.

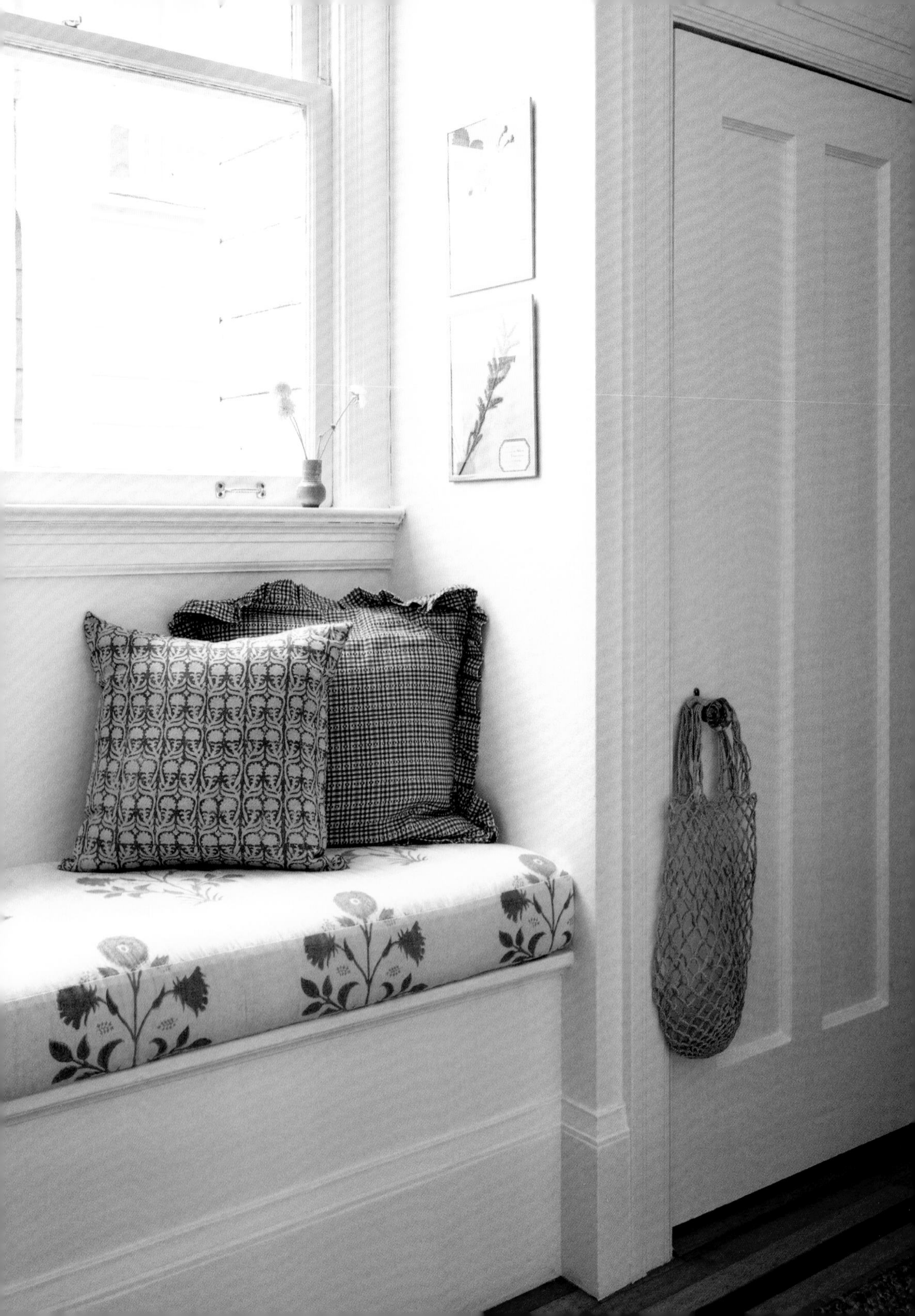

TOOL ONE
Adjusting Volume

VOLUME:
an amount, quantity, or capacity of something

If you're feeling busy but not productive, on the edge of exhaustion, or simply stretched too thin, the volume tool is about to become your new BFF. A simple analogy: Imagine your life is represented by a single cup. You can only pour so much into it before it starts to overflow and make a big mess. If you've ever spilled a cup of coffee or a fruit smoothie in your car, you'll know that the stakes are high here—avoid that mess at all costs! Instead, if you carefully monitor the quantity as you're pouring, you'll arrive at just the right amount—full enough without spilling over. In my experience, most problems are a volume problem; that is, a *too much* problem. People think they need elaborate, color-coded systems or the latest apps or gadgets to get organized, when, really, they almost always just need to have less to manage. In this chapter, we'll thoughtfully and methodically edit your life, eliminating everything that's not essential. What can you reduce, or get rid of completely, to simplify and improve your days? We'll consider how your cup can be full (a rich life, enough friends, a meaningful career) without becoming unmanageable (an overflowing schedule, too many events and commitments, buzzing apps and notifications that feel relentless).

In *Minimalista* I talked about being a gatekeeper, the bouncer at the front door of your house who decides which items get to enter and which items won't gain admission past the red rope. Just as every single item we allow into our homes instantly becomes our responsibility (and potentially burden) to manage, we must set up similar boundaries to curb the inflow of meetings, events, social plans, even people (!) entering our lives. By clarifying your values and then strategically cutting the clutter, you'll be able to reclaim a sense of peace and control over your life.

THE MORE OF LESS

I've learned firsthand that the best way to maximize efficiency, creativity, and productivity is not to do more, but rather to commit to doing radically, intentionally less. How liberating! The foundational principle of minimalism is to first clarify what is most essential and then strip away the extra clutter. With this remarkably simple but powerful philosophy as my guide, I've tested the less-but-better principle in every aspect of my life and career—from buying fewer, but better things, to investing in fewer, but more meaningful relationships, to taking on fewer, but more impactful career opportunities. To ensure that you edit your life ruthlessly, but not recklessly, you'll need to start by clarifying your deepest priorities, values, and intentions so you can filter out whatever isn't in alignment with that vision. It's always easier to say *no* when you've already defined what you're saying *yes* to.

TRY IT

Start by clarifying your priorities in response to these prompts (it's totally normal if this takes you some time and deeper reflection):

- One thing I deeply care about that's being neglected
- One new result I want to create in my life
- One thing I really want to create more space for
- One thing I want to start doing more of
- One thing I want to start doing less of

- One big thing I'd like to accomplish by the end of next year
- One thing I would really regret not doing
- One boundary I can set up to minimize distractions

Once you've clarified the things you want most, it will be remarkably easy to cut the clutter and reduce the things that don't move you closer to your goals.

THE ART OF THE EDIT

Editing is simply the process of deciding what you want to keep and what you want to let go of. For many people this practice is challenging, even paralyzing. Why?

First, decision-making requires lots of mental energy if you don't have a clear process for doing so. Second, letting go can feel grueling and painful, especially when you focus on what you are subtracting. Here's how to make it easier:

Simplify Decision-Making

To make clear, confident decisions, define clear criteria, constrain your options, and set a decision-making time frame. A few examples:

EXAMPLE ONE

You want to reduce your packed social calendar, so you have more free time for yourself.

Define Your Criteria: I will commit to no more than two social plans per week for the next month.

Limit Your Options: I will only make social plans with people I love spending time with and who add value to my life (no more optional work happy hours or preschool socials).

Set a Time Frame: I will commit to this plan for a month and then reevaluate, if necessary.

EXAMPLE TWO

You want to buy a new couch but don't want to make yourself crazy browsing every store, reading every consumer report, or boring your friends with incessant couch chatter.

Define Your Criteria: I want a comfortable blue couch that costs less than $2,000 and is available for shipping within three months.

Limit Your Options: I will go to three local shops to test comfort and select my favorite couch from one of those stores.

Set a Time Frame: I will order my couch by March 1 and never think about couch buying again.

By defining your criteria, limiting your options, and setting a time frame, decision-making becomes less arduous and time-consuming. The final step is to banish the word *regret* from your vocabulary. There is no upside to regret, but you can always learn from your mistakes and do better next time. One time when I got particularly ruthless editing my clothes (goodbye skirts, shorts, and dresses), I realized that I had absolutely nothing to wear to an upcoming event. I could have beat myself up over it (what was I thinking getting rid of so many clothes?), but instead I just borrowed a dress from a friend and committed to being a little more thoughtful during my next closet rampage.

Focus On What You Are Adding Instead of What You Are Subtracting

When editing, if you focus on what you are letting go of, you will remain distracted and stuck in mental limbo. Instead, commit to focusing your attention on what you are *adding* or *creating*.

Scenario 1: When I reduce the volume of social activities I participate in, I create more quality time to spend with my closest friends and family.

Scenario 2: When I edit my wardrobe and donate a massive bag of clothes, I create a curated and spacious closet that's lovely to look at.

Scenario 3: When I decline unnecessary social plans, I free up time to read, relax, and work on creative projects.

Saying *no* to some things directly equates to saying *yes* to other things. Consider: What do you want to edit in your life to make space for more personally satisfying passions or pursuits?

When you feel stuck, ask yourself the following clarifying questions:

- Could I happily live without this thing?
- Am I operating out of pressure or guilt?
- Is this thing moving me closer to the life I want?

FIVE THINGS TO LET GO OF NOW (LIKE, RIGHT NOW)

1. Other People's Opinions

Oof, this one is a toughie. But, try as we might, we will just never be able to control what other people think of us. As one of my mentors used to say, "You can be the juiciest peach in the patch, but some people just don't like peaches." Allowing people to judge or dislike you (as if we had a choice) can be one of the most liberating pursuits of your life.

2. Comparing and Despairing (see also *Instagram Doom-Scrolling*)

As the old saying goes, "Comparison is the thief of joy." In the age of the seemingly endless social media scroll, it's far too easy to compare your own vulnerabilities and challenges with other people's glossy highlight reels. The truth is that the shiny, happy images we see on social media (and even sometimes in real life) are a mere sliver of reality. I've personally witnessed many an influencer filming themselves beaming, in a spotless, styled corner of their bedroom and then returning to a screaming toddler, a work crisis, or a house full of dirty laundry and dishes, just like the rest of us. Since everyone has their own private struggles and realities you probably know nothing about, it's best to stay in your lane, show up fully, do your best work, and try to celebrate and derive inspiration (not envy) from the success and accomplishments of others. When you do notice the little green monster cropping up, use it as information: What are you craving in your own life that you can start to activate more?

3. The I'm-Too-Old Fallacy

We have been conditioned to believe that once we reach a certain age we're dried up, and we should no longer dream big, start a new career, move to a new city, whatever. Nonsense! As I've hit middle age, I've started looking for evidence to debunk this silly myth, which is everywhere: Vera Wang designed her first dress at age forty. Toni Morrison received her Nobel Prize in literature at sixty-two. Gladys Burrill became the oldest woman to complete a marathon at ninety-two!

4. Imposter Syndrome

I've coached so many brilliant, highly capable women who all have one thing in common: They're not sure they're good enough. Having imposter syndrome is human nature, and it's also useless. Knowing that some of the greatest achievers in the world are also plagued by self-doubt can help normalize this very human tendency. Here's a strategy that can help: Remind yourself that our brains are wired to protect us, and fear anything new or unknown. Experiencing fear, anxiety, self-doubt, or even panic as we venture out in pursuit of new things is completely normal, and to be expected. I've found myself in the fetal position more times than I can count on the way toward conquering a big, scary goal like writing a book or giving a talk to thousands of people. Now when my brain tells me to *pack it up and quietly retreat*, I just remind myself that fear and self-doubt are all part of the process: "Oh, here's the part where I just want to curl up in a ball and plow through a pint of ice cream. That's just my brain trying to keep me safe. Onward!" When you choose to stay the course even though you're feeling self-doubt, you will build resilience and confidence and trust with yourself. Stepping out into the arena is super brave, and we all need to be kinder to ourselves on the way. If you need to hear it from anyone, you can hear it from me: Imposter syndrome is just your reminder that you're doing something brave. You've got this.

5. Complaining

I once tried to abstain from complaining for a week and barely made it one hour. Yikes. Once you start paying attention, you'll likely be shocked at how easy it is to walk through life pointing out the negative (My drink is too cold, I'm exhausted, My kids left crumbs all over the counter again). Are there things to complain about? One thousand percent. Is there an upside to complaining? Not that I can find. Challenge yourself to become more aware of your personal complaining habits so you can dial it down. Try this: Every time you find yourself stuck in complaint mode, think about something in your life that you are truly grateful for and watch your complaint melt away.

WHEN IT ALL FEELS LIKE TOO MUCH

When things feel out of whack, assessing volume in the various areas of your life can be used as a helpful diagnostic tool. Do you need to crank up the dial or turn it down? There are times when you'll want to turn the volume up, perhaps putting more effort or energy into cultivating friendships, investing in your health, or working toward a goal, but I'm guessing that more often than not it will greatly benefit you to strategically turn the volume down and *quiet that noise.*

Your Digital Life

I recently did a survey on Instagram asking which areas of life felt the most overwhelming, and I was surprised to learn that (in addition to cluttered garages and paper piles) digital clutter led the pack. Technology is such a massive part of modern life that it's imperative to create clear boundaries when it comes to what we allow in and give our attention to. If we want to spend our time on the most meaningful pursuits and achievements, instead of the most trivial distractions, we must ruthlessly edit our digital life.

EMAIL

There have been entire books and courses created on how to edit and organize your inbox, so I'll make this brief.

1. If you have more than five hundred emails in your inbox, I suggest archiving (not deleting) all but the fifty most recent and starting from scratch. Using this strategy, you can clear out your inbox in seconds, and make it manageable to reply to, delete, or file the most recent. Exhale!

2. Decide which brands, services, subscriptions, and companies you would like to receive email communication from and unsubscribe from the rest. Your time and attention are your most precious resources. Do you really want to surrender them to learn about a sale on something called *The Miracle Egg Cracker*? Methinks not.

Quick Win

You can sign up for a service like unroll.me to efficiently unsubscribe from all the junk and promotional emails in one fell swoop. You can also click unsubscribe each time you receive an unwanted email, which takes a second and will dramatically lighten your inbox over time. Whenever I'm engaged in a massive work project, I set up an email response indicating that response times will be delayed. My friend Holly once set up an auto-response that simply read "Happy holidays! I'm taking a break from email for the next month to focus on spending quality time with my family." Wait. You can do that? Yes, you can.

Set Clear Professional Boundaries

Leverage your email signature to set expectations about your work hours and response times. My client Molly's reads: "Emails will be responded to within 72 hours, between the hours of 9 a.m. and 4 p.m., Monday through Thursday only." Clear, direct messages are best.

Bonus: Taming Social Media Messaging

If your social media inboxes are creating additional mental clutter, consider setting up an auto-response directing people elsewhere: "Thanks for reaching out. I don't check messages here—if you'd like to get in touch, please [insert preferred method of communication here]."

SOCIAL MEDIA APPS

Chances are you have a bunch of random social media apps cluttering up your phone and your brain. As social scientist and author Arthur Brooks cautions, "Social media is the junk food of social life." Social media can provide you with short bursts of pleasure, like eating your favorite chips or candy, but it can't keep you feeling nourished or satisfied for long. Even though I use social media as a business and marketing tool, I've decided to delete and unsubscribe from all apps aside from Instagram. One social media app is all my brain can manage. Bonus: It makes it super easy for others to find and engage with me.

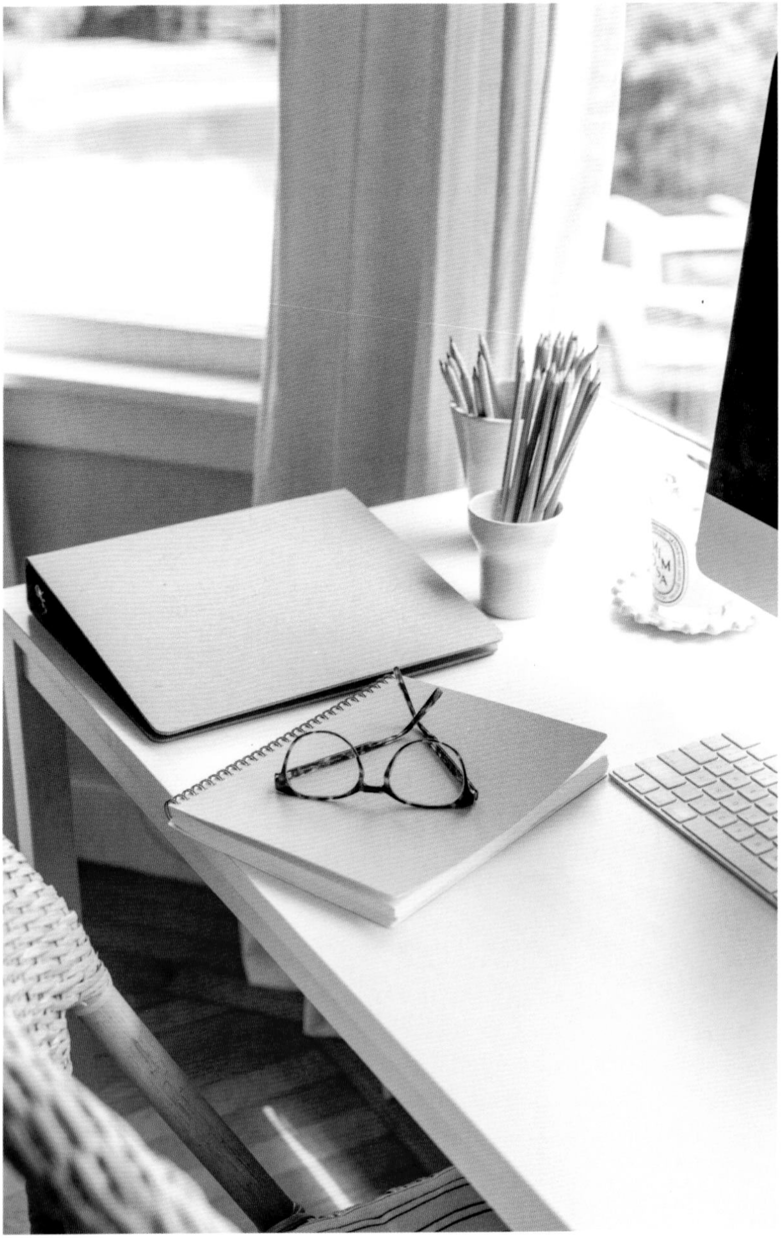

Quick Win

Take fifteen minutes to delete all apps that you don't use or recognize (what even is *Cat Paint*?). I suggest keeping no more than ten total if you can swing it. I recently did this and it was so deeply cleansing that I felt like I had just been to the spa. Bonus: You can organize the remaining apps into neat little folders and move them to the second page of your screen, so your home screen is just a photo of whatever makes you the happiest.

SUBSCRIPTIONS AND MEMBERSHIPS

Hard truth: The subscription business model counts on the fact that most people opt in on a whim and then totally lose track of what they've signed up for. It pays to get clear on which subscriptions and memberships you use so you can cancel the rest and reallocate your spending. Case in point: I recently helped a client unsubscribe from nine different streaming services and five memberships she never used for a total savings of over $12,000 per year. Win!

Quick Win

Identify and cancel all of your unwanted subscription and membership services. Apps like rocketmoney.com or scribeup.io can make this daunting process relatively quick and painless. Ka-ching! Your bank account is smiling already.

YOUR COMPUTER DESKTOP

I've seen quite a few computer desktops in my day, and I will confess that most of them make me a little dizzy.

Quick Win

Delete all the random downloads, screenshots, and photos from your desktop. This should take no more than five minutes and will make you feel very accomplished. For extra credit, move the documents you want to keep into neat, labeled folders divided into broad categories like Tax Documents, Work Projects, or School Forms.

DIGITAL PHOTOS AND VIDEOS

Confession: As I write this, I currently have 33,690 photos and videos saved on my phone, and they are not organized. There—I said it. Off-brand, I know, but the truth is I've decided I just can't be bothered to edit and organize this part of my life. If you want to reduce volume in this department, here are a few easy action steps.

Quick Wins

- You can merge duplicates with the push of a button on most phones, or by using an app like Smart Cleaner, Flic, or Cleanup.

- Transfer photos and videos to an external hard drive, or online storage host like Google, Dropbox, or iCloud, and then remove them from your personal devices to clear up space.

- Select your favorites, delete the rest, and don't look back. Freedom!

PUSH NOTIFICATIONS

One word. Why? Unless you're POTUS, opt out, mute, do whatever you have to do to silence that noise.

NEWS UPDATES

Now that news updates and notifications are available 24/7, the barrage of information can feel relentless and distracting. If you burst into tears or existential panic every time you see anything remotely sad, I suggest being very selective about when and how you consume your news.

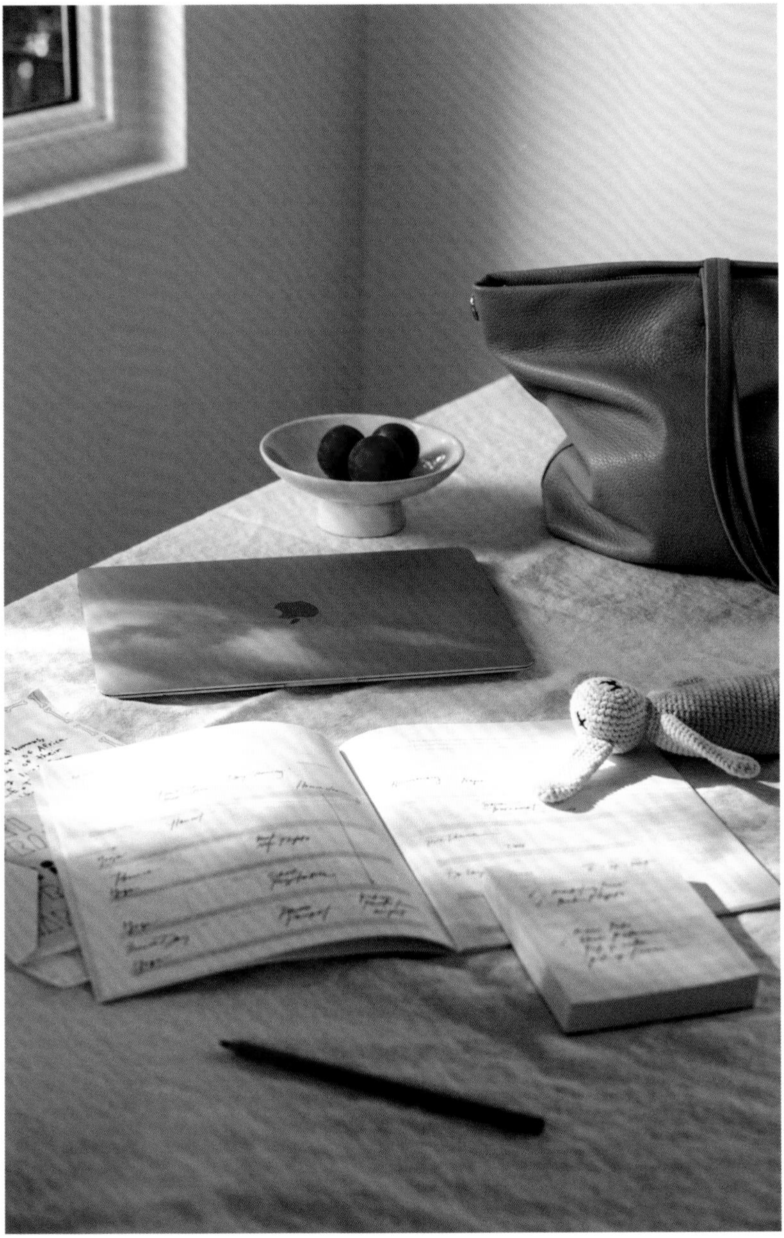

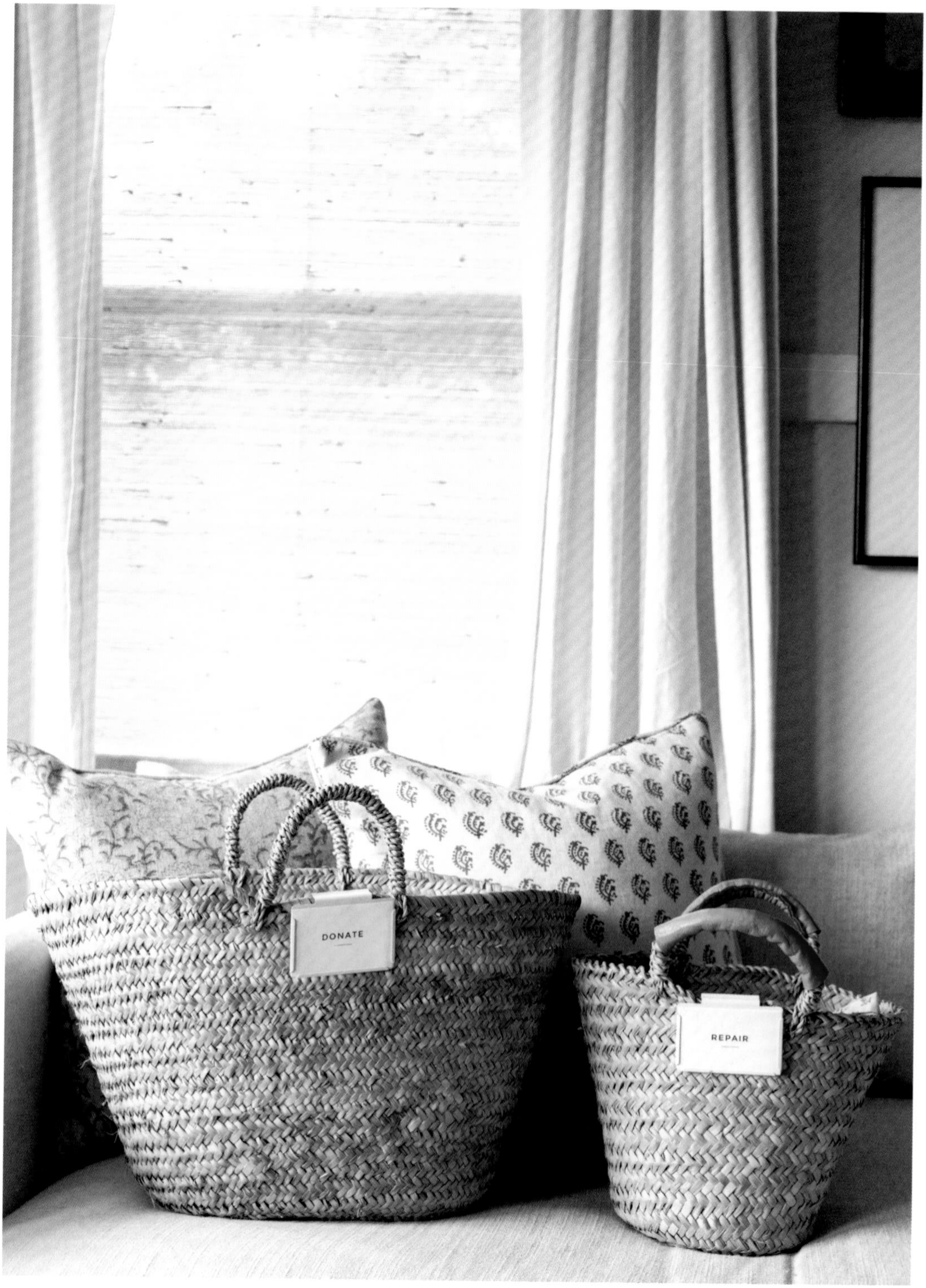
DONATE
REPAIR

Quick Win

Identify a few trusted sources you'd like to receive news updates from and decide exactly when and how you will view them. Delete, unsubscribe, or mute everything else.

Your Environment

When it comes to your physical environment, visual and physical clutter can take quite a toll, not just on overall productivity, but also on your mental health and sense of well-being. I already detailed exactly how to edit and organize every room in your home in *Minimalista*, so for our purposes here I'll just outline some super-quick volume-reducing wins.

Quick Wins

- Clear your surfaces. Set a timer for fifteen minutes and give the cluttered surfaces in your home a good sweep. Goodbye aspirational books on your nightstand, bills by your bedside, and junk mail on the counter.

- Make it easy to donate. Identify a few local resources that accept donations (community centers, nonprofits, parenting groups, and buy-nothing groups are great resources). Hang a tote in your entry area, and once it's full, drop it off and give yourself a well-deserved high five. Rinse and repeat as necessary.

- Try a purchase pause: One way to reduce physical clutter is to simply stop buying more stuff. As obvious as this sounds, halting all nonessential purchases for a set period can be a total game changer, resulting in more money in your pocket, more gratitude for what you do have, even more contentment, ease, and clarity in your day-to-day life. Hot tip: Now that we live in a world where you can order dish soap, dinner, or even *a car* with the touch of your fingertip, you may want to disable the autofill feature and saved credit card info that enables one-click ordering online. Creating friction will help halt frivolous or unnecessary purchases in their tracks.

Your Wardrobe

Fun fact: My brother wears the exact same thing every single day. His uniform consists of a black T-shirt, black pants, black sneakers, and occasionally a black sweatshirt or jacket when the weather calls for it. Shorts? Nope. He just rolls up his pants on the beach or in warm weather. His all-black uniform is even acceptable in top restaurants around the world, no questions asked. I've also arrived at my own minimalist uniform, albeit a bit more varied: high-waisted jeans, airy white blouse, high-top sneakers, done! In both cases, we've both found the same benefits of paring down our wardrobes—less decision fatigue getting dressed, more brainpower and mental energy for other pursuits, a great way to refine and embrace your personal style . . . the list goes on and on.

TRY IT

Identify which silhouette and colors you feel best in. Do you prefer structured, tailored, layered outfits, or a more casual or flowy vibe? Are you a bold pop-of-color person, or do you love a more neutral look? Where is the intersection of what you love and what's practical for your lifestyle, climate, and career? You can also play around with a basic uniform, coupled with a bold accessory, to keep things interesting. My friend Tiffany never leaves the house without a hat and bright red lipstick. My client Nora dresses simply but always has incredible shoes and bags. Get yourself a signature look and embrace what you feel like your best self in.

Define your wardrobe criteria so you can avoid shopping mishaps. Maybe you want to shop small and avoid the big box stores. You might want to skip synthetic fabrics, like acrylic or polyester, in favor of natural linen or cotton. Perhaps you're sick of wearing shoes that make you walk like a baby deer and it's time to embrace comfort town. Take note of your likes and dislikes and own them; intentionality is the name of the game. It's better to build your dream wardrobe slowly over time than to waste your hard-earned cash on items that just don't measure up to your standards or preferences.

Quick Win

Ready to reduce the volume of garments taking up real estate in your closet? Grab your donation bag and start fresh by ditching the following items:

- Aspirational pieces that make zero sense for your actual life (I'm looking at you, ski pants, sequin dresses, and four-inch stilettos!)
- Big-ticket items or splurges that just never worked out
- Duplicates (unless you're rocking a uniform, why do you have ten identical black T-shirts?)
- Conference swag and freebies (or random corporate-logoed T-shirts!)
- I've-given-up-on-life loungewear and super-sad pajamas
- Items that don't fit or flatter your body (bye!)

Courses, Classes, and Activities

I have a personal rule that I only enroll in one class, workshop, or activity at a time. This way I can give whatever I'm doing my all and get the most out of each investment. The same rule holds true for my daughters. They are each allowed to pick *one* activity outside of school (a fact that made a client's brains explode–her three kids were enrolled in five different activities each and she had become a glorified chauffeur, finishing her workday in parking lots and drowning in logistics). This decision has been a win-win for our entire family (and for my client, who partnered with her kids to trim their activities to save her sanity and theirs). My husband and I can divide and conquer without moving into our cars, and the kids learn the benefit of fully focusing on one commitment at a time. Set limits and determine the volume of activities each kid can participate in, but allow them to take the wheel and select which pursuits they want to focus on.

TRY IT

Are you enrolled in more activities than you can keep up with?
If so, ask yourself:

- Why am I doing this activity?
- Is this activity adding value to or detracting from my life?
- Is this activity moving me closer to the life I want to create?
- Would it be a relief to let it go, postpone it, or find a way to make it easier (say, with an online class or a single workshop)?

IDENTIFY YOUR TIME WASTERS

In a quest to create more time and spaciousness in our lives, we must increase awareness of our "time wasters." These are the activities that keep us distracted and fail to add value to our lives or move us toward our bigger goals. Step one is identifying these time wasters. Here's my quick list:

- Doom-scrolling the news
- Social media rabbit holes
- Mindless TV watching
- Worrying about things in the future that I can't control
- Googling which specialty ice cream shops deliver nationwide

Step two is to counter each time waster with an activity you'd like to do instead. For example, instead of doom-scrolling the news, I'd like to donate time, money, and energy to nonprofits that are doing good work to make the world a better place. My client Lisa decided that every time she had the urge to shop online, she would step outside for some fresh air and take a brisk walk. My friend Naomi now chooses to read for fifteen minutes each morning when she wakes up instead of heading straight for her phone. *Feels so much better.*

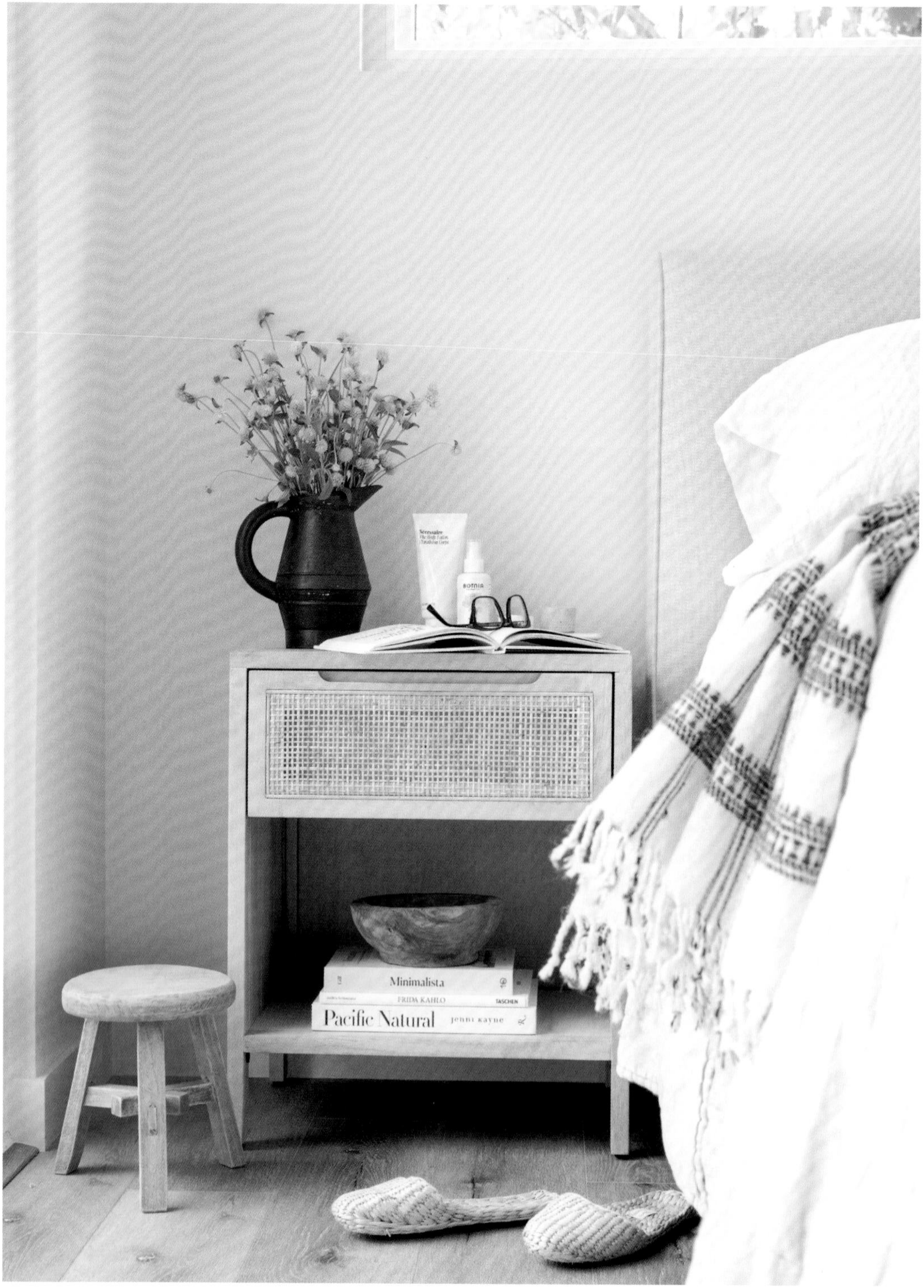
Minimalista
FRIDA KAHLO
TASCHEN
Pacific Natural
jenni kayne

YOUR BELIEF SYSTEM

In the realm of things that clutter up our lives, mental clutter may have the most impact of all. When I was certified as a life coach, one of the many life-changing things I learned was this: *A belief is just a thought you've practiced a lot.* And not only that—our thoughts create our feelings, which prompt our actions and create our results. Want to change your life? Start by shifting your mindset. It turns out that we are capable of altering and transforming our beliefs and our perspective at any time. Yep, it's true. You're that powerful. One of the most impactful exercises you can do is to examine your belief system and then decide which thoughts or beliefs you want to hold on to on purpose, and which beliefs you want to let go of and release.

TRY IT

Consider the following (you might want to jot down a list):

- What do you believe about yourself?
- What do you believe about your past?
- What do you believe about your future?
- What do you believe about others?
- What do you believe about the world?

Then ask:

- Which beliefs are serving you, adding value to your life?
- Which beliefs are detracting from your quality of life or overall happiness?
- Which beliefs would you like to shift or let go of completely?

In my work, I've coached clients through this process and seen powerful, life-altering results. Jen decided to stop believing that she was not an organized person (or capable of becoming one). She started practicing the belief that organizing might be easier than she thought. Sasha started catching herself every time she started complaining about her husband's laziness and began pointing out all the things he was doing right instead. This single adjustment helped her remember what she loved about him, and completely shifted the trajectory of their relationship.

Amanda realized that she had spent a lifetime believing that most people were the actual worst (and looking for evidence to prove it). That's certainly not the most useful belief system to cultivate while embarking on dating after divorce. Instead, she decided to look for evidence that people are mainly well-intentioned despite being flawed. Our brains are wired to find evidence for our beliefs, so we may as well seek out what serves us.

Here's a very personal example to explain how I've used this tool in my own life. At nine months pregnant, I woke up to find my once smooth stomach stretched taught like a torpedo and speckled with hundreds of purple stretch marks. Fortunately, all was well, and shortly thereafter I gave birth to a beautiful, healthy baby girl. The skin across my stomach, and the muscles beneath, didn't exactly bounce back (diastasis, party of one). I started having not-so-friendly thoughts, and while I kept telling myself it was perfectly normal for a woman's body to change after childbirth, I felt like I had a shameful secret (and the stomach of a very wrinkly elephant–as I said, not nice). Friends, while I'd like to tell you that I eventually let it go, I actually became obsessed with thinking about it. I even tried bargaining with reality: "I don't need a supermodel's stomach; I just want mine back. Can I go back in time and just have my smooth stomach back? Put me in a time machine!" Now, here's where the volume tool comes into play: While I still haven't completely made peace with my postpartum body (work in progress!), I have decided that I refuse to spend any more mental energy being distracted by it. Life is just too short. I made a deal with myself: I will never make disparaging comments about my body again–to myself or anyone else. I will focus on the things I *can* control: showing up in the world, doing good work, being a good friend, wife, and parent. As the mother of two girls, I take this pledge very seriously. The last thing I want to teach my girls is to be preoccupied or obsessed with their bodies. By shifting my focus and turning up the volume on positive thoughts, I finally turned the volume down on the "stomach drama."

TRY IT

Time to rewire those neural pathways, friends!

- What personal belief would you like to shift or alter in your own life?
- What would you like to focus on believing instead?
- What evidence can you find that this new belief could be true?

JUST SAY NO: YOUR BOUNDARY-SETTING CHEAT SHEET

Setting clear and firm boundaries is one of the most loving things you can do for yourself and others. I've had to become super good at setting and maintaining boundaries because I'm an emotional sponge and a recovering people pleaser. Here's what I've learned: Even the most well-intentioned people will take as much of you as you will give them. If you set clear, confident boundaries, you'll not only improve your relationships, but also have more authentic connections. If you're someone who always says yes, saying no and setting limits can feel super awkward at first, but it will get more effortless with practice. Here are some easy formulas for setting healthier boundaries.

Start with the Love Part

I love you so much, and I know you have the best of intentions, but I really don't want any parenting advice. If you continue to email me articles and resources, I'll just delete them. Mkay, bye Mom!

Offer an Alternative

It's so generous of you to offer us your hand-me-downs, but we're already well-stocked with kids' clothes! I've heard our local charity is accepting donations right now and they have an easy drop-off system.

Make It Clear and Unapologetic

I need to prioritize my health right now. I'll be slow to reply to texts and emails.

Make It Direct and Specific

I've got a hard stop today at 2 p.m., so let's hop on a call tomorrow to finish our conversation.

Make It Non-Negotiable

I'm at full capacity and unable to add anything to my plate right now, but I wish you the best of luck with the event. Sidenote: When I declined to chair my kids' school auction, I was informed that a woman with *three kids and a full-time corporate job* had accepted the position last year. I rejected the effort to mom-shame me by simply replying, "Wow, good for her! Not possible for me." And that was that.

Boundaries can be difficult to form but are guaranteed to help prioritize your health and your sanity.

Be confident, use clear, direct, and loving language, and get comfortable with "no." If you are feeling maxed out in your home, life, and schedule, this life skill should be non-negotiable. Practice saying "no" in your everyday life. "No" to buy-one-get-one-free deals, "no" to the new streaming service everyone is talking about, "no" to hand-me-downs you don't want or need, "no" to new responsibilities you can't take on. I promise you this: Renewal, peace, and freedom are on the other side of "no."

THE BOTTOM LINE

You can use the volume tool at any time to adjust where you place your time, energy, and attention. It is always within your power to constrain your choices and reduce physical, mental, digital, and emotional clutter. You get to decide how many credit cards you open, how many apps you use, how many friendships you pursue, how many plans you make, what you watch or don't watch, and even what you think and believe. Using the volume tool takes nothing more than the desire to make a change, the time to objectively assess, and a little practice and experimentation. Turn it up, dial it down, until you find just the right amount of everything for you.

TAME YOUR TO-DO LIST

If your schedule and to-do list are feeling less than manageable, it's time to get out your favorite pen and start making some tough cuts.

Write down everything that is taking up real estate in your brain. Every. Single. Thing. Nagging to-do's, errands, chores, meetings, invitations—you get the picture. Keep writing until your brain feels cleansed. Take a minute and enjoy that feeling. Now, let's look at your list with an editor's eye. I often have things on my list that feel very pressing and urgent to my brain but turn out to be totally silly and unnecessary once I really think about them. Look at your list and do the following:

- Slash anything that's not urgent or necessary.
- Identify anything that can be delegated and then get it off your plate immediately.
- Identify anything that can be batched or simplified.
- Schedule the rest on your calendar.

This simple practice will help you trim down your list and make it more manageable in fifteen minutes or less. Want a real-life example? Here's a peek at my to-do list for this week:

- Hem pants
- Drop off donations
- Return sweater
- Buy vitamins
- Finish next chapter of book
- Write keynote for an upcoming conference
- Buy tickets to Ohio for fall conference
- Get groceries for the week
- Give dog a bath
- Confirm clients for the week

- Prepare opening activities for retreat
- Set up an orthodontist appointment to replace Emilie's retainer (the dog ate it; I wish I was kidding)
- Fill out forms for Chloe's school trip

Now that everything is out of my head and on the page, I can clearly see what I can cut, delegate, and schedule. The dog doesn't urgently need to be bathed (sorry, Patches!) and I can throw the sweater I need to return, my donation bag, and the pants for hemming in my trunk for whenever it's convenient on my route. The other tasks do need to be completed this week, but I can get some support. I can ask my assistant to confirm my clients and book me a flight to Ohio. I can ask my kids to bring in and put away groceries (and vitamins) if I place an order online. Suddenly my list is looking much more manageable. Here's what's left to schedule and complete:

- Finish next chapter of book
- Write keynote for upcoming conference
- Prepare opening activities for retreat
- Set up orthodontist appointment
- Fill out forms for Chloe's school trip

As you can see, this edited list is a fraction of my original list, and now I can wrap my brain around it. Setting up an orthodontist appointment and signing a school form will take less than five minutes, and the remaining items can be scheduled on my calendar for the workweek ahead. Sweet relief.

GET DOWN: THE UPSIDE OF LOWERING THE BAR

None of us are capable of doing All of the Things at once. With lives that are filled with obligations and opportunities, it's up to us to determine where we want to invest our limited time, energy, and resources. Lowering the bar on purpose (as opposed to dropping the ball by accident) can feel both liberating and empowering. I believe in setting and achieving goals, showing up fully for the people I love, and living up to my fullest potential. I have very high standards for myself, but I also believe that lowering the bar on certain activities can be a compassionate and productive form of self-care and a way to free up energy for more important pursuits. Here are some areas where I've decided to intentionally lower the bar in my own life.

Home-Cooked Meals

I'm lucky enough to have married a man who truly loves cooking, but sometimes he's busy or tired (because, he's human) or out of town and I'm in charge of family dinner. I don't love cooking or meal planning and I used to get incredibly stressed out about this task, but I've decided that life is too short to fret about dinner, so I just focus on making it as easy as possible. Sometimes I boil fresh pasta and top it with loads of Parmesan cheese and fresh cracked pepper. Sometimes we'll do "breakfast for dinner" or improvise a picnic supper. Sometimes I just order a pizza. Kids are happy and I get to reroute that effort elsewhere.

Folding Laundry

Surprise! I don't take tremendous pride in perfectly folding my, or anyone else's, clothes into neat little packages. I've put my girls in charge of putting away their own laundry (and have accepted that sometimes that means their clothes will be shoved into their dressers in twisted little balls). If they want to go to school in wrinkled clothes, that's fine by me. Ditto for the bed linens, which I simply plop into bins so our linen closet looks tidy (just don't look too closely at the fold on the fitted sheets, which I will never ever master).

Keeping Plants Alive

My family has a special talent: We unintentionally kill nearly all plants. We've tried lovingly potting baby tomatoes and strawberries and little clusters of basil. We tried to grow a pear tree. We've picked out pale pink flowers to spruce up our porch. All of these plants have one thing in common: They've died almost instantly. Instead of beating myself up about this, I've decided to acknowledge that I don't care much for gardening and should probably stop planting things. We now have just a handful of very, very drought-tolerant potted olive trees scattered across our patio, and that works just fine for us.

A Well-Trained Dog

Our pup is the love of our lives, but well-trained she is not. After a handful of failed attempts to have her listen to us, we tried our hand at a group class. The result: One of our daughters fell asleep on the floor (no joke) and we had to borrow other people's treats because we're not good at following instructions. Ultimately, we realized that none of us could muster the time, energy, or consistency required to properly train our dog, so we threw in the towel. Some shoes and rugs were sacrificed along the way, but she's a gentle angel who mainly sleeps all day so we're happy to live without the party tricks and perfect behavior.

Refrigerator Organization

Confession: Even though I have the skill of artfully arranging a color-coded and magazine-worthy refrigerator, I've decided that the "fridge arts" just aren't how I want to invest my time. On the rare occasions when I have taken the time to meticulously style our family fridge, I'll return hours later to find a whole host of items—a giant bowl of raw cookie dough, a whole marinating chicken, a pitcher of homemade lemonade—shoved in haphazardly. My family loves to cook and bake and snack and eat, and it's fine that most of the time our fridge is more functional than photo worthy.

I choose to lower the bar on these things not because I'm lazy, but because they don't align with my current goals and priorities. I choose not to judge myself when I order takeout or let my kids wear wrinkled clothes because I know that my family and I feel loved, happy, and safe and that's what really matters. The more we can make intentional decisions about where we want to place our time, energy, and resources (and, conversely, where we don't), the better.

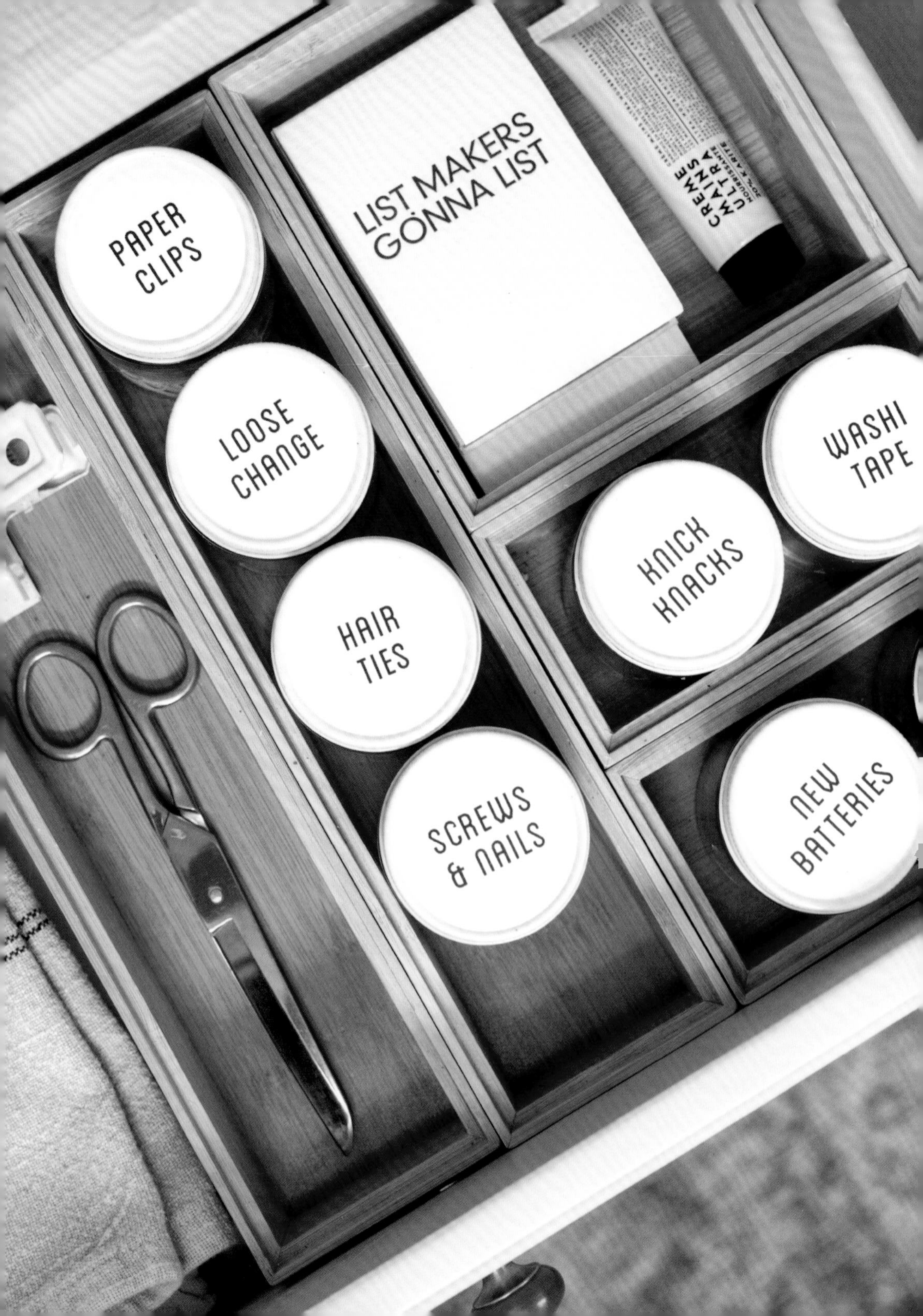
PAPER CLIPS
LIST MAKERS GONNA LIST
LOOSE CHANGE
WASHI TAPE
HAIR TIES
KNICK KNACKS
SCREWS & NAILS
NEW BATTERIES

TOOL TWO
Creating Systems

SYSTEM:
an organized framework or method. A set of processes, tools, and
strategies that work together to solve a problem or achieve a goal.

During the height of the 2020 Covid-19 pandemic, our neighbor Jenny confessed that she was nervous about things going back to normal. An unexpected positive by-product of the worldwide health crisis was the forced pause. Jenny loved the weekly drinks outside with friends in lawn chairs, the quiet time alone with her kids, the slower pace. She didn't trust herself not to get sucked back into a frenetic lifestyle once things opened up again. Which brings us to the big question: How do you make sure you craft the life you want when there are so many things calling for your attention? Through careful planning and intentionality. Through *systems*. Effective systems will help you to be proactive, not *reactive*. Smart systems will help you integrate, automate, and simplify the things that are important. Intuitive systems provide practical solutions that are easy to maintain.

We've already reviewed how to adjust volume so you can cut the clutter and minimize distraction or add energy or effort when necessary. In this chapter I'll teach you how to create systems that solve problems and simplify your life. I'll take you behind the scenes of my own life and share the systems I use to manage my busy calendar, business, and family life. I'll also provide examples from my work with clients. But, first, back to my neighbor Jenny. Once the stay-at-home orders were lifted, Jenny returned to her full-time job (and eventually her kids returned to school and activities). To retain some of the things she had loved about the forced pause, Jenny integrated a few simple systems into her life. She continued ordering groceries and household items online once a week, a practice that saved her time shopping and enabled her to spend a bit more relaxed time with her family. She set up a standing weekly cocktail hour with friends to ensure that she continued having consistent quality time with them (minus all the back-and-forth text coordination), and she convinced her boss to restructure her schedule so she could work from home three days a week, a simple move that saved her six hours a week of commute time! Go Jenny, go!

Systems should have a clearly defined purpose and accomplish something specific or solve a problem. Here's my three-step process for how to create your own home or life improvement systems:

1. Clarify the goal, objective, or challenge you're trying to solve.
2. Identify the *simplest* action you can take to create the most impactful outcome.
3. Test, evaluate, and tweak or adjust, if necessary.

A real-life example: A few years ago, my husband Jordan decided to buy a new camera and try his hand at photography. The only issue was that his camera came with a whole bunch of accessories, manuals, cords, and attachments that were suddenly strewn *all over our house*. Once we identified the challenge (lots of camera gear that didn't have a designated storage spot in our small home), the solution was easy. I found a spare bin, labeled it CAMERA STUFF, and centralized all things camera-related into this single bin that now lives in our entryway credenza. Out of sight, but still easy to access. Let the victory dance commence!

Here are some other real-life examples of successful systems in action. Make sure to pay attention to how *simple* they are.

EXAMPLE ONE:
THE CASE OF "STUFF MOUNTAIN"

The Problem: My client Sarah (an attorney and mother of three) was tired of staring at the piles that were always dumped by the front door—a combination of mail, shop returns, library books, and jackets.

The Solution: Once we reduced the volume (one coat by the door per family member, instead of five), we set up a basic entryway system. We installed additional hooks at arm's reach for her kids so they could hang up their own coats instead of tossing them on the floor (they weren't lazy, they just couldn't reach the high hooks before!). We added a basket on her entry table to corral incoming mail, bills, and packages, and another, larger basket to stow anything that needed to exit her home: library books to be returned, shop returns that needed to be sent back, the gardening gloves borrowed from the neighbor—you get the idea. A few hooks and baskets saved the day! These systems were simple and intuitive enough that Sarah's whole family (ranging from four to forty-six) could easily use and maintain them, eliminating the random piles in the entryway for good. High five!

EXAMPLE TWO:
THE CASE OF "CALL YOUR MOTHER!"

The Problem: My client Aviva felt guilty because she rarely called or visited her aging mother, despite her best intentions to do so. The call just got lost in the shuffle.

The Solution: I suggested that Aviva pick a regular time to visit her mother and schedule it as a repeating appointment on her calendar so it would be "baked into" her schedule. Since she had weekends off, she picked the first Sunday of each month as her visiting day. She also decided that she would call her mother on the other Sundays at 5 p.m. (aside from the in-person date) to check in and catch up. By automating both calls and visits, she could spare herself the scheduling back-and-forth drama—and the side of guilt.

EXAMPLE THREE:
THE CASE OF LOWERING YOUR STANDARDS— LITERALLY

The Problem: My client Charlotte wanted her kids to be more helpful setting up for mealtimes, but realized that they couldn't reach the plates, bowls, or glassware to set the table or take clean dishes from the dishwasher.

The Solution: Charlotte cleared out a low drawer in her kitchen and set up a little station stocked with enough plates, bowls, cups, and utensils for daily table setting. A new system was born, and the kids loved that they could access everything without heavy stools or precarious tiptoes! Lining your drawers with a sheet of felt or cork will ensure that items won't shift around or break. Game changer.

TRY IT

- Identify one simple system you can set up in your home. What can you corral, stash in a bin, or find a "home" for? (Like my husband Jordan's camera paraphernalia!)
- What can you contain, batch, or automate to create more ease in your life? Like a get-it-done day where you knock out all of your errands in one fell swoop.

THE LIFE-CHANGING MAGIC OF AUTOMATION

The average person makes 35,000 decisions a day. My brain hurts just thinking about that. With all the stimulation of modern life, coupled with daily work and family responsibilities, it's a wonder we get anything done at all. I'll be transparent with you: Even as an organizing expert who's built a life and career around minimalism and simplicity, I still find it challenging to remember when my quarterly taxes are due, or the car needs to be serviced. I just found out after nine years of owning a home that we're supposed to be regularly cleaning out our

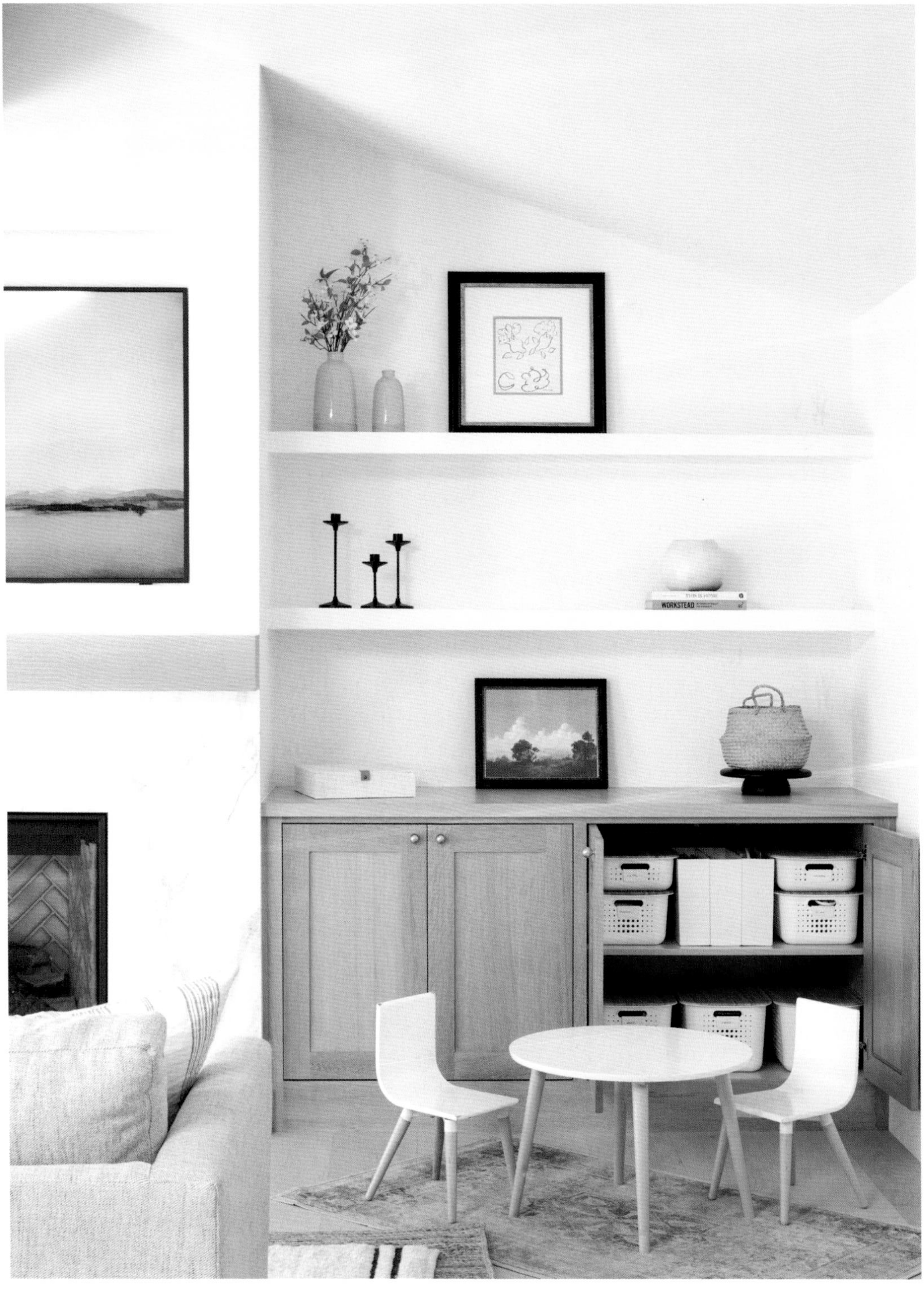
WORKSTEAD

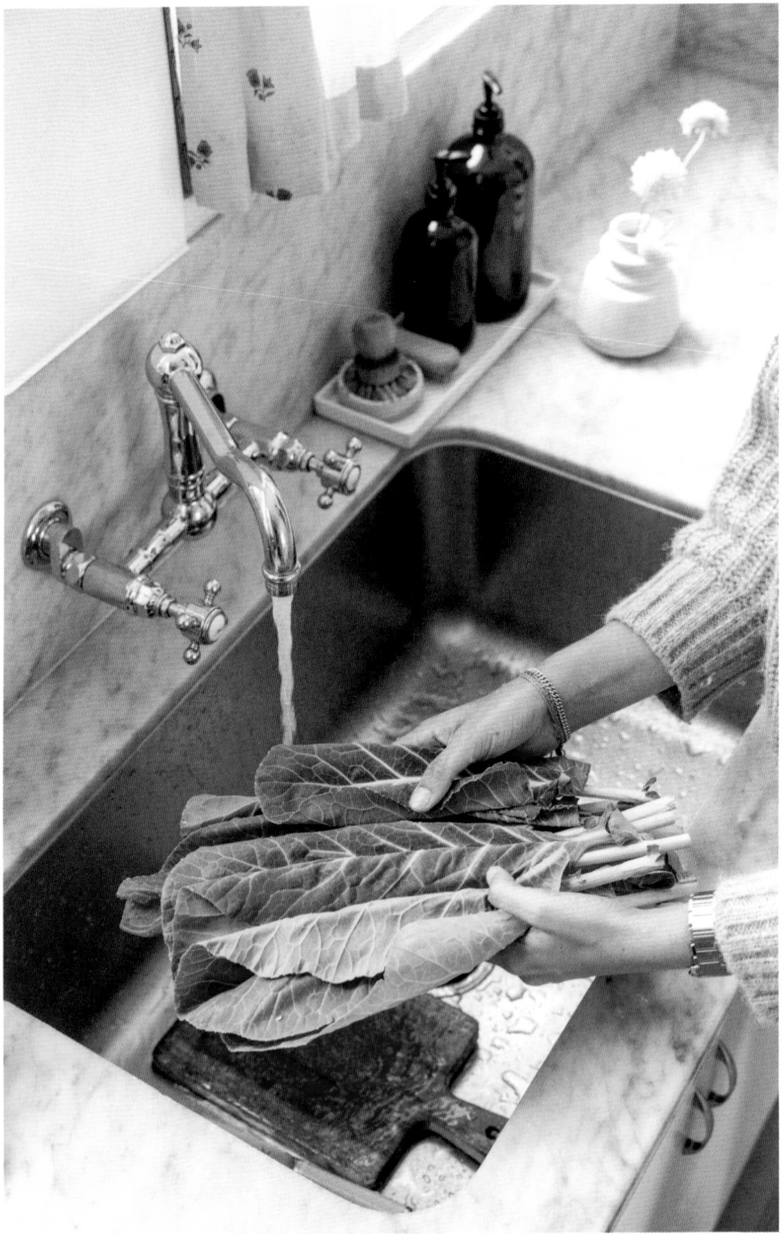

gutters and checking and changing our heating and cooling filters (I also just found out that we have said filters). *Who has time for this?* With so much constantly competing for our attention, it's up to us to constrain our choices (adjust the volume) and prioritize in advance what we want to spend our precious time and energy on. One surefire way to feel less overwhelmed is to find ways to automate and reduce your daily decision-making. Automating the things that are important can help reduce decision fatigue and ensure that you save time and energy for the things that matter. Sound good? Let's get into it.

Meal Planning

For years, at roughly five o'clock every day I would ask my husband Jordan, who cooks most of our meals, "What are we doing for dinner?" He would reply "I don't know, what do you feel like?" and I would respond by experiencing every single phase of grief while holding my head in my hands, whimpering "No, no, no." I'm not being hyperbolic when I tell you that we've tried *All of the Things*. We've experimented with meal planning apps, mail-order meal kits, recipe exchanges, crowdsourcing ideas from friends, giving up and ordering takeout—you name it. What to eat for dinner has been a constant pain point for our busy family, but after years of frustration I've finally sorted out a simpler method after having a meltdown where I may have shrieked, "I NEVER WANT TO TALK ABOUT WHAT WE'RE DOING FOR DINNER AGAIN."

Ready? Once a week, on Sunday, I go to the store (I prefer shopping in person) and I pick out five proteins, five bases (rice, tortillas, pasta), and five veggies. We always stock basics like eggs, herbs, garlic, cheese, and seasonings, so this enables us to shop once and have five easy improvisational meals for the week—no planning required! The best part is that shopping like this is a breeze and requires *zero* planning, and we can mix it up each week to create new and creative combinations. **Boom!**

TRY IT

How can you automate and simplify meal planning and grocery shopping? I've spoken with a lot of busy parents who swear by a weekly collection of themed nights (Monday is Mediterranean, Tuesday is taco night, and so on), and my friend Leila has been able to streamline her grocery list into a repeatable online delivery order. She clicks a button and everything she needs to feed her family for the week arrives on her porch the next day. If eating the same thing on repeat feels like a snooze, you can also try setting up a meal swap with friends or neighbors. We teamed up with our neighbors to take turns hosting dinner every Wednesday. It's been great to have a built-in social plan and know that we don't have to think about dinner every other Wednesday. Two birds, one stone. Try experimenting to see what system works best for you. You might also want to keep a note on your phone that includes all your household and pantry staples so you can restock or reorder easily. This will also help eliminate decision fatigue when confronted with twenty-two varieties of milk at the supermarket—*Ooh, I didn't know hemp milk was a thing. Is it delicious?* Supermarket paralysis is real. Pick your staples and put the hemp milk down.

HOUSEHOLD RESPONSIBILITIES

It took Jordan and me years before we tired of the daily "Who's doing what?" check-in dance and started clearly dividing and delegating our household chores and responsibilities. Hello, marriage saver! To streamline our process, we both have clearly designated jobs now. He's the trash man (even though he doesn't love when I call him that), while I stock the house with household supplies and groceries, and handle all things having to do with planning, organization, and social events. Jordan also does the cooking, pays the bills, and oversees a million other things I've now happily lost track of. Our teenage girls oversee feeding the dog, doing the dishes, and packing their own lunches, and we are each responsible for our own laundry—including folding and putting away our clothes. I knock mine out every Sunday, and Jordan and I take turns with the sheets and towels. I'll admit that I've lowered my standards when it comes to teaching my children the *folding arts*, which they (and, frankly, I) could care less about. I'd rather have them dump their messy piles in their respective dressers than spend my life folding laundry. Freedom!

> **TRY IT**
>
> Consider how you can automate household responsibilities in your own home. You might want to consider a divide-and-conquer approach, a weekly "get-it-done day," or assigning yourself a few small tasks you do weekly on specific days. I personally prefer to batch all household tasks and laundry, and implement a full-blown "Sunday Reset," so I can feel more carefree during the week. Play around and figure out what works for you.

Family Logistics

While we limit how many activities our kids can participate in at once, they are social creatures and there still seem to be endless rides, carpools, and logistics to coordinate. We've implemented a weekly family meeting every Sunday after dinner (incentivized with treats!) to review the week ahead. Jordan and I divide up the driving assignments or coordinate carpools with other parents when one of us is out of town to make sure all logistics are covered. We also use this time to sign school forms, and order birthday presents for upcoming parties. This brief check-in session spares us a whole lot of headaches later in the week.

> **TRY IT**
>
> Consider a weekly check-in with your family members, roommates, or just yourself, to make sure all plans and logistics are sorted for the week ahead.

Home Maintenance

The New York Times recently published a home-maintenance checklist that was helpful and comprehensive (and made me feel very, very sleepy). If you want to take good care of your home, consider giving that checklist a skim and adding annual or biannual maintenance appointments to your calendar. Ditto for your vehicle(s). I plan to get right on this now that I've learned all the things we've been neglecting for years. Better late than never!

TRY IT

Make a list of your key household-maintenance items, from deep cleaning to painting to home upkeep and repairs, and schedule them on your calendar annually.

Email Responses

It only took me about 457 times of sending the exact same email to realize that I could create an auto-response and spare myself from writing the exact same thing again and again for the rest of my life. Three cheers for templated emails! I now have a whole host of templated responses set up so I can swiftly reply to similar inquiries within seconds flat.

TRY IT

Pay attention to the information you tend to send again and again and create templated email responses. My brother, who is a chef, even batched his personal restaurant recs for the cities he's visited to simplify sharing resources with friends and other travelers.

Fitness

The only way I work out is if I schedule it. Period. End of story. I walk every single morning as soon as I wake up, and now I've also scheduled three weekly yoga classes on repeat. I used to search for classes

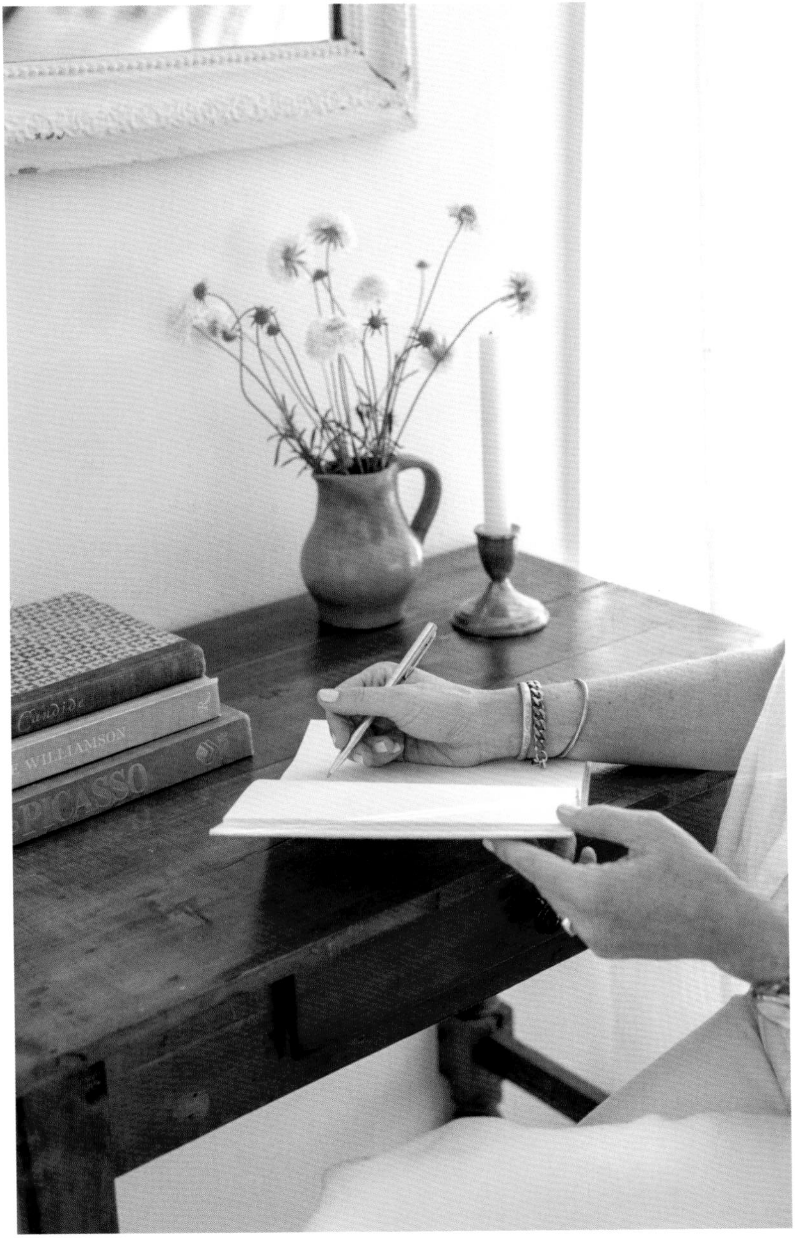
Candide
WILLIAMSON
PICASSO

each week when I was tired and then give up because it all seemed too complicated. Having weekly classes scheduled ahead of time ensures that I get up and go. Bonus: I get to know the teachers and repeat students, which adds more accountability and support for working out, and makes it more fun.

TRY IT

Whether you want to start small like me with a daily stroll, enroll in classes, or train for a legit marathon, solidify your weekly fitness schedule in advance and schedule it in your calendar.

Finances

In an effort to reduce paper clutter, I've signed up for digital invoices and auto-bill pay for everything under the sun. When we're really on track, Jordan and I review finances and pay bills together and we also schedule an annual "tax date" in February so we can prep taxes for our CPA well before the April deadline.

TRY IT

When it comes to finances, consider setting up auto-bill pay for any bills that will let you, an annual tax date, and anything else that will keep you on track.

Wellness and Self-Care

This one tends to fall low on the list, but it might be the most important of all. Scheduling annual physicals, dentist appointments, gynecology exams, and more is no one's idea of a good time, but, alas, they must be done. I've started scheduling annual or biannual reminders in my calendar, so I'm cued to take care of business. You can also automate personal appointments like haircuts, facials, manicures, or waxes.

TRY IT

Do a quick audit of the health practitioners you see and make sure you have regular appointments or reminders set up. Ditto for the fun stuff like your bimonthly pedicure or quarterly trip to get your eyebrows waxed or your highlights refreshed.

While it may seem like a drag to do all this preplanning and scheduling, automating your life can actually free up more time for creativity, spontaneity, and freedom.

Quick Win: The Idea Bank

One of the most common questions I receive from clients is how to organize all the *information overload* taking up real estate in our brains. This might include specific resources like travel tips, restaurant recommendations, or beauty hacks, as well as broader creative ideas, goals, or projects. Sure, there are a million apps designed to meticulously store and organize information, but they can feel overwhelming or time-consuming to set up. When it comes to organization and productivity, tech is my kryptonite and simplifying is my superpower. So, here's what I suggest: Ditch the sticky notes and stacks of half-filled notebooks and set up *one* designated place to park all your ideas. My friend Jill refers to this as "the parking lot." I call it "the idea bank." I use the Notes app on my phone to capture and centralize all of the gazillion ideas that are swarming around in my busy brain. My best ideas seem to fall from the sky and into my brain at the most random times, and my phone is compact and with me all day. Within the Notes app I set up a handful of broad folders like *Book Notes*, *Content Ideas*, and *Restaurant Recs*. I also keep a stack of index cards by my bed so I can jot down ideas that come to me just before I go to sleep or when I wake up and then I transfer them into my phone later. Some people love to batch and organize their ideas on a more granular level so they are easily searchable, but I'll be honest—I just dump my ideas and know they are safe.

TRY IT

Create a centralized place to store and capture your best (and even worst) ideas. It could be an app on your phone, an old-fashioned legal pad, or even a dry-erase board in your shower. If you want to, you can opt for one digital and one analog system, just promise me you'll say goodbye to the stacks of old notebooks and memo pads that just create more clutter in your life and mind.

TAKE THE TIME TO MAKE THE TIME

The other day, I got nothing done. I didn't work out. I didn't run errands, respond to work emails, or even think about meal planning. I ended up eating birthday cake and nachos for dinner because that was all we had in the house. In short, I ended the day feeling frustrated and defeated (and a touch nauseous). When I reflected on what happened, one singular idea jumped out at me: I had failed to plan my day. Sure, it's challenging to integrate planning and scheduling into your life when you already feel tight on time, but with just a little planning ahead of time, I could have had a completely different day. Here's the key, folks: Planning takes time but also *makes* time. Here is the planning protocol I now use on a regular basis to take control over my time for the year, season, week, and even day.

Step One: Clarify and Prioritize

FOR THE YEAR

I always like to have a broad mission statement for my year. For example, by the end of this year, I will have finished my manuscript, gone on one big family trip to a new country, and maintained my weekly health and wellness goals.

TRY IT

Create a mission statement for the year ahead. No matter where you are right now, you can always set new goals and effect positive change in your life. I'm a bit of a goal-setting junkie because I love the thrill of accomplishment and the feeling of making myself proud, but it's just as valuable to set goals centered on *rest* or *spaciousness*. Yours might be: In the next year I will take off one week each season. I will save up money to invest in monthly massages, and I will commit to taking weekends off to rest, read, and relax. Reflect on what you are craving more of and less of in your life, and make sure your annual goals are specific, measurable, and actionable. If you're stuck, ask yourself the following clarifying questions:

- What do I want to create space for in the coming year?
- What would I like to prioritize and accomplish?
- What would I like to be different or better by the end of the year?

FOR THE SEASON

There's something lovely about breaking down your year into distinct seasons and mapping out each season ahead of time. There's a reason most companies set quarterly goals and employee reviews.

TRY IT

Ask yourself: What would I like to prioritize this *season*? Consider social plans with friends and family, including holidays, vacations, and celebrations, as well as career or personal goals. Depending on your circumstances you may want to prioritize your health, or a big life transition like having a baby or being present for someone who's sick or struggling. Make sure your goals align with your core values and don't contain the word *should*. These are for you!

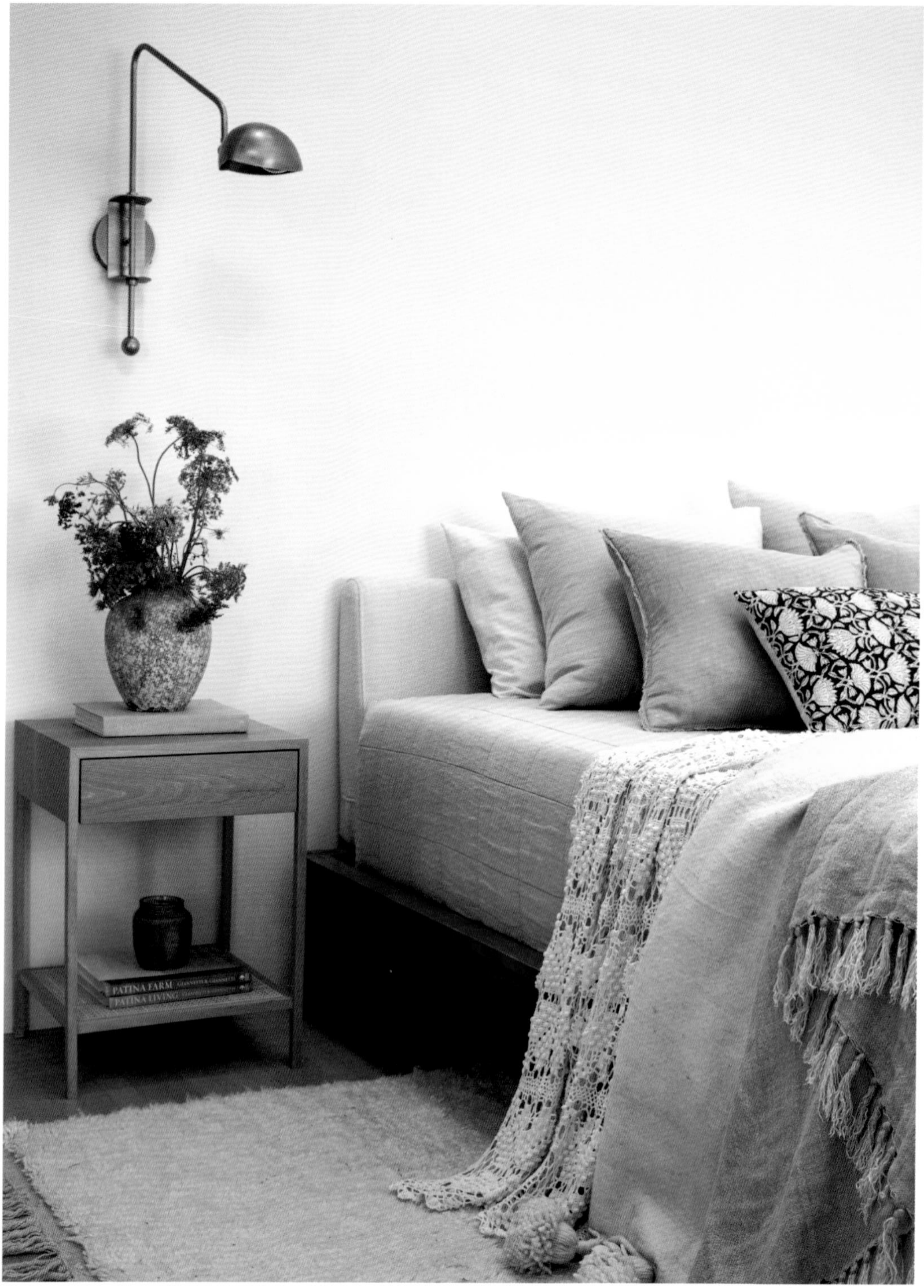
PATINA FARM
PATINA LIVING

FOR THE WEEK

I love to write down on Sundays what I want to accomplish by the end of the week to help anchor my schedule. If I limit myself to just a handful of personal and professional mile markers, I end up feeling more focused and less overwhelmed by my seemingly endless to-do list.

TRY IT

Consider a few personal and professional wins you'd like to prioritize for the week ahead. They can be *tiny*: Finish that nagging email, pick up the dry cleaning, be nicer to Susan in accounting—you get the picture.

FOR EACH DAY

Spend a few minutes before you go to bed thinking about the next day. What do you want to get done? Which tasks are the most important? What would make tomorrow a fulfilling and successful day?

TRY IT

Make sure your goals are specific, measurable, and actionable, and then circle the top three highest-priority items. I generally focus on one work-related goal, one personal goal like spending time with my family, and one health-related goal like scheduling a workout, or signing up for a spin class. It is crucial to map out your priorities *ahead of time* before you're inside of your day swatting away distractions like flies. If you find yourself getting pulled into something new, you can refer back to your list of goals and either swap one out or pull your focus back to what you were trying to accomplish.

Step Two: Plan and Schedule

Here's the part where you plan the most important things first. Before you get lost in errands and phone calls and social media and binge-ing on your favorite TV shows (*White Lotus* directly into my veins, please!), schedule your priorities. Give each item a specific amount of time and lock it down in your little black book or online calendar. Make sure to schedule time for research, phone calls, and even distractions or interruptions. You'll be shocked at how much more you can get done if you simply plan and schedule each hour of your day—this includes scheduling time to relax or hang out with friends or just lie down outside and stare at the sky. If it's a priority, put it on the calendar. Below you'll find an outline of my typical day when I use this time-blocking approach:

7 a.m.–8 a.m. Drink a full water bottle / take forty-five-minute walk with dog

8 a.m.–9 a.m. Shower, get dressed, breakfast

9 a.m.–Noon Focused work time / complete chapter seven and submit to editor

Noon–1 p.m. Lunch break / check emails

1 p.m.–3 p.m. Client meetings

3 p.m. Drop kids at activities

4 p.m.–6 p.m. Work wrap-up: client invoicing, submit invoicing to bookkeeper, finish new press kit

6 p.m. Make dinner for kids

7 p.m.–9 p.m. Dinner out with friends

9 p.m. Evening tidy, prep for tomorrow, skin-care routine, brush teeth

10 p.m. Reading in bed

10:30 p.m. Lights out!

Note that this schedule includes a broad mix of activities, including personal goals like exercise and reading, values-based goals like social time with friends and family, and even a touch of personal care (I moisturized!). As you create your own time-blocked daily calendars, give them a skim to make sure you are integrating things you care about and value that normally get lost in the shuffle.

Conversely, when I don't map out my day ahead of time here's what it ends up looking like:

7 a.m.–9 a.m. Social media rabbit hole

9 a.m.–Noon Randomly knock out laundry and chores

Noon–1 p.m. Lunch (I never skip lunch!)

1 p.m. Consume the tray of brownies my girls baked while searching for new Netflix specials

2 p.m.–5 p.m. Get lost in a black hole of emails

5 p.m.–6 p.m. Accomplish absolutely nothing

6 p.m. Order takeout because didn't plan dinner

7 p.m.–10 p.m. Mindless TV viewing until pass out

I share this rather mortifying example to illustrate how crucial planning is. I think you get it.

Step Three: Honor the Calendar

Here's my most important rule: Whatever the calendar says, I do. This is because I have thoughtfully planned and scheduled my calendar, based on my priorities and goals. If I ignore the calendar, I will end up totally sidetracked and have an unfocused, unproductive day, month, and year (see example above). Remember, scheduling ensures that you create space for the things you care about and can allow for spontaneity and flexibility. It's your *friend*. Treat the calendar like your new boss / friend / partner you want to impress and remember: *The things that get scheduled are the things that will get done.* Activity batching helps improve productivity by grouping similar tasks together to reduce context switching (brain fatigue!) and increase efficiency. Try consolidating all of your annoying errands into a single afternoon or get-it-done-day. Knock out emails during dedicated hours. Batch work meetings into one part of your day or week instead of scheduling them sporadically. You get the idea.

THE BOTTOM LINE

We wake up each day with limited mental capacity. It's up to us to craft systems that will help make the very best use of our time, energy, and resources and enable us to focus on the things we value most. Through automation, planning and scheduling, activity batching, and systems of organization, we can exert control over our time and move closer to our big goals. Creating simple and streamlined systems is a tool you can always call on to solve a specific problem or achieve a goal.

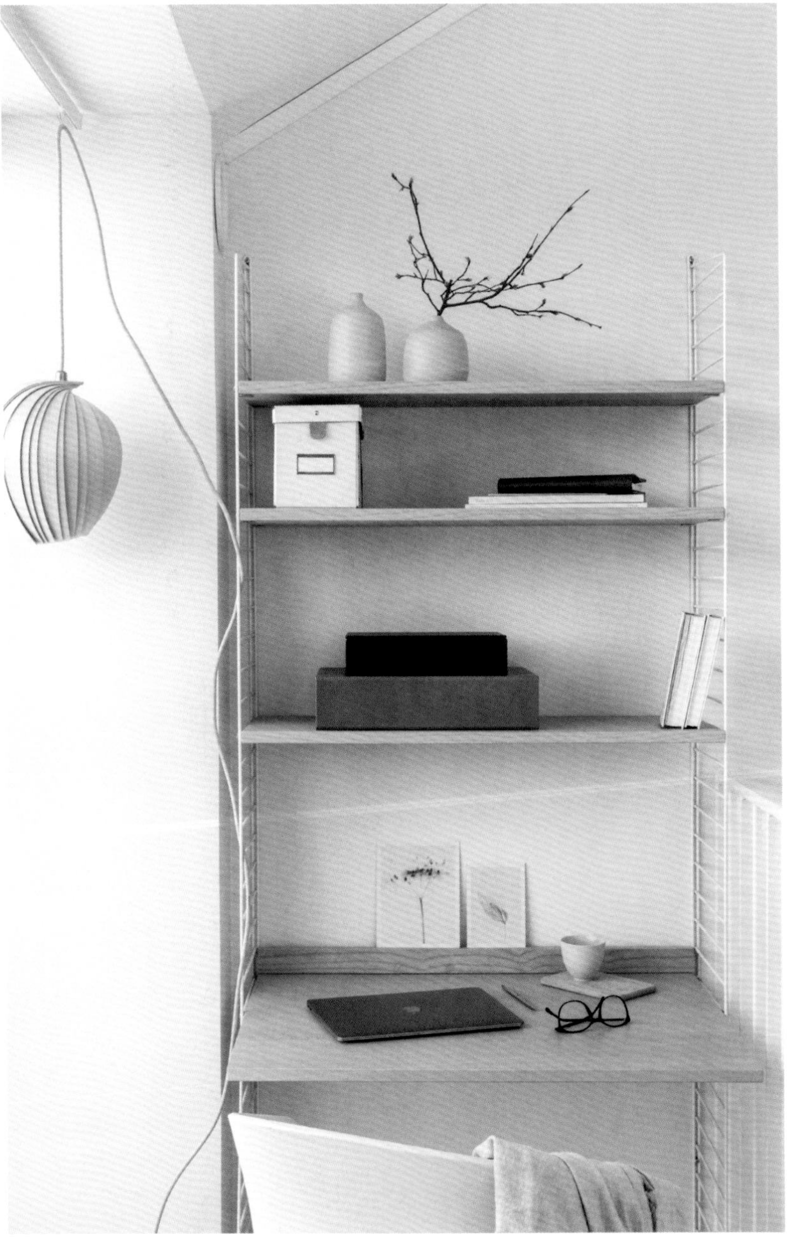

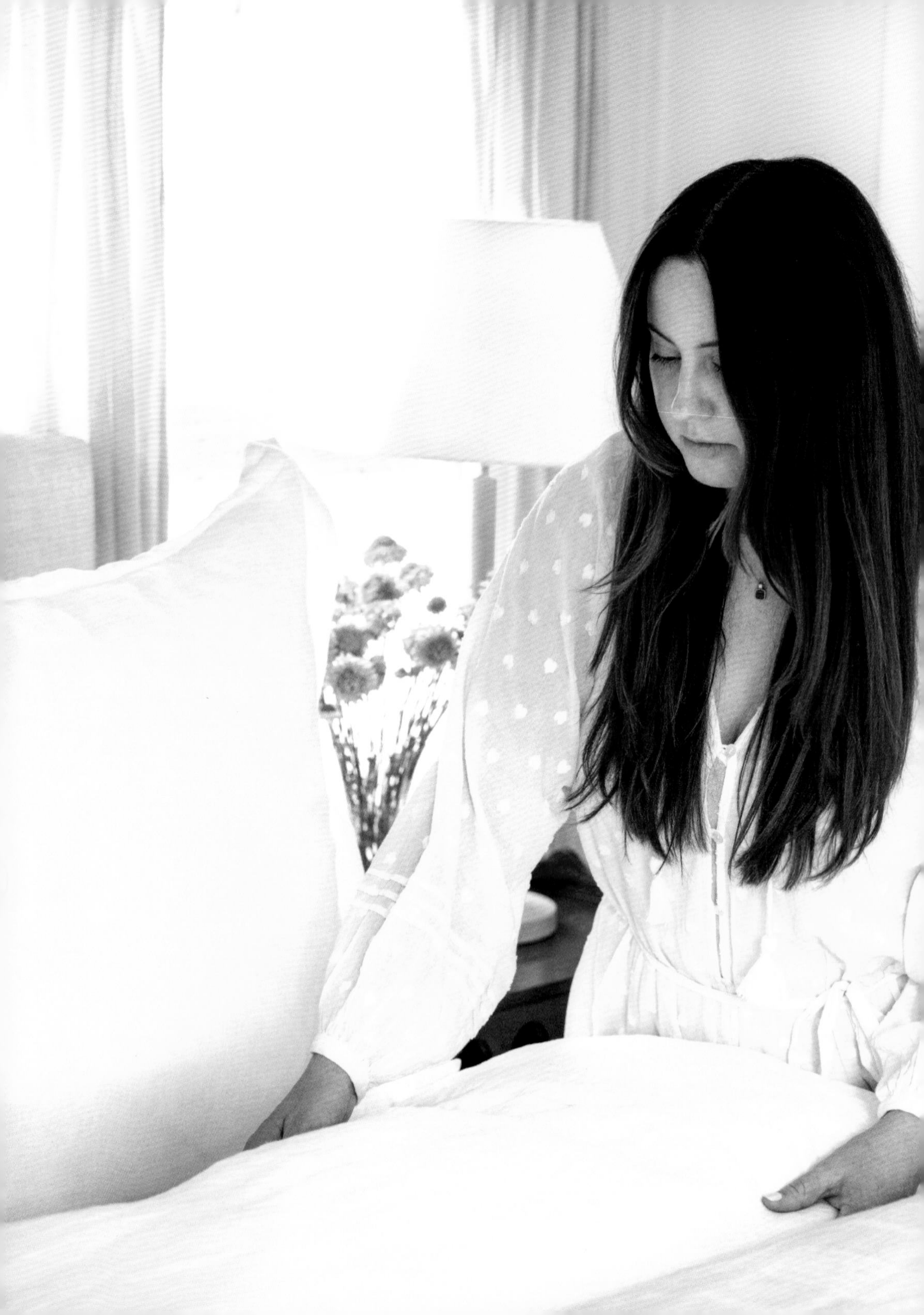

TOOL THREE
Implementing Habits

HABIT:
A regular tendency, routine, or practice that has become automatic.

My client Emme was frustrated. She had hired me—just a few weeks before—to help edit and organize her home in Los Angeles and it was in great shape when I left. We had hauled off two entire truckloads of donations and set up thoughtful systems to contain items by both type and usage, but the dreaded piles had returned. Her teenage sons had continued dumping their shoes, hoodies, and backpacks on the floor by the front door—even though we had set up cubbies and hooks a mere two feet away. Her husband kept tossing his mail and keys on the kitchen counter, even though there was a newly designated mail bin set up in the entryway. Even Emme found herself staring at a fresh stack of work projects piling up on her nightstand, even though we had agreed that she would keep anything stressful or work-related out of her bedroom. When I returned to her home again, Emme was filled with shame as she escorted me around, pointing out her "failure piles." We had already reduced the volume of stuff, so there was much less to manage, and we had set up beautiful, seemingly intuitive systems for her and her family throughout the home. What was the missing link that was leading to the piles?

We had employed the first two tools in my tool kit (reducing volume and creating systems) but there was a third key tool that was not being employed yet: Emme and her family had not yet started implementing new *habits*. Adjusting *volume* will reduce unnecessary clutter and distraction and create more focus and clarity of purpose. *Systems* are vital for streamlining and creating a sense of order and efficiency. But without the implementation of smart, consistent habits, even the most brilliant system will fall flat—and this is what had happened in Emme's home. Even with less stuff to wrangle and clearly labeled organizing systems, the *habits* necessary to maintain the systems were not being implemented consistently. Once we had clarified the missing link, we were able to create a plan to make it easier for Emme and her family to implement new habits by making them obvious, intentional, and reward-based. Her teenage sons started hanging up their backpacks and hoodies by the front door because they were granted permission to play their favorite video game immediately afterward. Emme's husband smartly asked that we move the mail and key drop station from the entryway to the kitchen nook where he was already acclimated to leaving his mail and keys. Emme decided to be more intentional about her boundaries and keep her stack of work projects in her off-site office so her bedroom could feel like more of a retreat. These simple habit shifts proved successful almost immediately and enabled Emme to have the tidy spaces she craved with minimal effort.

In this chapter, I'll teach you how to build better routines and integrate habits that stick. You'll learn how to set yourself up for success, and make your desired daily habits feel less like a chore and more like a ritual. Onward!

WHAT IS A HABIT?

A *habit* is just a repeated routine or behavior that has become second nature, typically including a specific cue, routine, and reward. Positive habits can help ensure that our desired results are achieved, whereas poor habits can lead to undesirable outcomes, like the piles left all over Emme's home. For better or for worse, our habits shape our lives. Because of this, it's critical that we increase awareness of our existing habits and make them more strategic and intentional. Let's get to it!

WHY ARE HABITS TRICKY TO CHANGE?

If you've ever tried to build a new habit, or break an existing habit, you've probably encountered at least a bit of resistance. Our well-intentioned brains are designed to keep us safe and protect us from harm at all costs (even when there is no actual threat). Because of this tendency, our own brain can work against our best interests by trying desperately to prevent us from doing anything new that it perceives as risky business. Thanks, brain. But also, *work with us, please*! We are biologically wired to seek pleasure and avoid pain and discomfort. Our brain is designed to do things that feel good (how did I end up eating an entire *sleeve* of Girl Scout cookies?) and reject the things that require discomfort (getting out of a warm cozy bed to stretch or work out). This kept us safe back in the day but here's the rub: In order to get new results in your life, you have to overcome discomfort. It is impossible to grow, change, or evolve without it. We must learn new strategies to move through discomfort to get the results we want. Luckily, there are plenty of proven strategies to help us overcome resistance and build great habits that stick.

HABIT HELPERS

I've rounded up a whole host of success strategies below to make it as easy as possible to follow through on building or breaking habits. You can try one at a time or layer them together for the best results.

Start with Why

I once joined an experimental habit lab led by a PhD psychologist with the goal of reducing my ice cream intake. When the head of the program asked me to share my compelling reason for quitting my ice cream habit, I realized that I didn't have one. Funny as it may sound, I just really love ice cream. Consuming it brings me so much joy, and so far (knocking on wood) there have been no major health ramifications due to my frequent consumption of this frozen treat. In a world full of more damaging vices, I realized that it's one I can live with. I ended up changing my goal to strength training three times a week. The reason? All of the older women on the maternal side of my family have weak, brittle bones and have developed osteoporosis, leading to pain, injury, and mobility limitations. I want to avoid the same genetic fate at all costs, and I know that strength training is one of the most impactful things I can do to achieve that goal. When I don't feel like heading to a workout class (um, every single time), I can call on this compelling reason to help me stay on track. Resistance and inertia are hard to overcome—even the most thoughtful, research- and science-based plans will not work if you're not committed to change. Motivation is the foundational force necessary to overcome resistance when trying to implement a new habit.

> **TRY IT**
>
> Pick any habit that you want to work on and answer the following questions: What is your primary motivation for making this change? What will change for the *worse* if you don't make this change? What will change for the *better* if you are successful? Make sure you clearly define your *why* before taking any action.

Set Habits So Your Future Self Will Thank You

We all have habits that are so unconscious and second nature that they require minimal planning or effort–brushing our teeth, brewing our morning coffee, or taking a shower, to name a few. The goal of this chapter is to help you start implementing habits that are conscious, intentional, and directly linked to your goals in life. Using this strategy, we can leverage the power of habit implementation to get us closer to the lives we crave. Some examples:

> Goal One: A tidy workspace
>
> Habit: A five-minute desk tidy before leaving the office for the day
>
> Goal Two: Saving for a solo trip to Paris
>
> Habit: Transferring 10 percent of your income into a travel fund each pay period
>
> Goal Three: Getting eight hours of sleep a night
>
> Habit: Committing to being in bed and unplugged by 10 p.m. each evening

TRY IT

Identify a specific goal you want to achieve and then identify and jot down at least one specific habit shift that will help get you there. Bada bing, bada boom.

Make It Micro

The number one mistake I see in my work is shooting too high too fast and missing altogether. For example, trying to organize an entire home all at once instead of starting with one drawer. If you want to succeed at implementing a new habit, make it as ridiculously tiny as possible to start, and then build on your success. Remember, you must design your habits to be simple, repeatable, and most of all *sustainable*. Consistency is the most important factor in successful habit formation, and tiny victories will create momentum, build your confidence, and compound to create massive transformation over time.

TRY IT

Jot down a new habit you'd like to implement and then identify how you can start as small as possible. If you want to run for an hour every day, start by putting on your running shoes and running (or even walking) for five minutes. If you want to be tidier at home, start by just putting your mail in your inbox every day for a week. If you want to eat healthier at home, pick one vegetable to add to your weekly shopping list. Small but mighty changes will help ensure your ultimate success.

Make It Easy

Since new habits are so difficult to integrate, you'll want to make it as easy and effortless to succeed as possible. For example, I lay out my workout gear and fill up my water bottle the night before if I want to make it to a workout class in the morning. My friend Nadia places a book on her pillow to encourage reading before bedtime instead of watching TV. I even have a client who's synced the timer on her coffee maker with her alarm clock. She knows that the smell of freshly brewed coffee helps motivate her to get out of bed and start her day, even on the laziest mornings.

TRY IT

What can you do to make your new habit as *obvious* and as *easy* as possible to integrate into your daily routine? Consider visual cues, activating the senses, and prepping in advance.

Make It Consistent

There's a reason most of us brush our teeth first thing in the morning and right before bedtime. The less time we have to think about *when* to implement a habit the better. This is why kids are trained to tidy up every day at school before recess and right before the final school bell. What's done consistently becomes intuitive and automatic. My husband Jordan literally can't start his day without a morning shower and coffee. My friend Hedy completes her skin-care routine right after dinner each night (otherwise she's too tired to do it right before bed). My girls make school lunches right after dinner each night, so they don't forget. My daughter Chloe gulps down a massive glass of water when she wakes up because she tends to forget to hydrate at school. When I wrote my first book, I wrote every single morning from 7 a.m. to 9 a.m. for months on end so I never had to think about when I was writing. The less work your brain has to do, the better!

> **TRY IT**
>
> Pick one new habit you'd like to work on and identify how you can make it part of your routine. Can you batch it with another well-established habit? Complete it at the same time each day, week, month, or year?

Do the Important Stuff First

The way you kick off your day can dramatically influence how the rest of it unfolds. Even a tiny task like making the bed can set the tone for your day and be a major mood booster. Our brain's mental capacity and focus decrease throughout the day as distractions mount and fatigue sets in. Even if you don't consider yourself a "morning person," it will greatly benefit you to knock out the most difficult or important tasks of your day bright and early. Work out in the morning. Make the hard phone call. Take care of the annoying errand. Finish the project. Spend the rest of the day basking in the glow of your accomplishments.

> **TRY IT**
>
> Start each day with a simple task completed. For example, drink water, move your body, write, meditate, take your vitamins, floss. I promise any one of these low-lift activities will feel so good to complete.

Get an Accountability Partner

While some rare unicorns among us are 100 percent intrinsically motivated, most humans are wired to seek approval, validation, and support from others. We can take advantage of this natural tendency by creating structures that reinforce outer accountability.

> **TRY IT**
>
> Buddy up with a friend and keep each other accountable. Tell your inner circle of friends about the new habit you're working on building or breaking so they can cheer you on. Join or start a goal-setting group.

Have a Backup Plan

What's that saying about the best-laid plans? The hard truth is that life is full of surprises and disruptions, so we must plan for them ahead of time. Consider all the variables that could get in the way of your success (traffic, kids requiring attention, illness, to name a few), and create a backup plan so you don't get derailed. When I was working with Berkeley Habit Lab (a cool company that helps people build or break habits), I set the goal of taking a workout class four times a week. We then brainstormed all the various things that could get in the way and made a plan for each one. For example, when I was traveling or logistically couldn't get to a class, I would take a one-hour power walk instead. This enabled me to stay on track with my goal of being healthier and stronger even if life got in the way.

TRY IT

Fill in the blank: If X happens, I will do Y.

Make It Fun

If you're struggling to integrate a new habit into your life, making your desired habit more fun and satisfying to complete is guaranteed to boost your success rate. Sign up for a dance class series with your BFF if you're tired of dragging yourself to the gym. Challenge your partner to a water-drinking competition if you want to stay hydrated (not to brag, but I did this and won). Crank up your favorite playlist and dance around the kitchen while you unload the dishwasher or whistle while you work—you get the idea.

TRY IT

Ask yourself, "How can I make this activity more fun and enjoyable?" Try pairing it with another activity you love, bring in a friend, or incorporate a treat or reward. Confession: Ben & Jerry's Coffee Heath Bar Crunch got me through tax season last year. And remember how I told you Jordan can't start his day without coffee? Well, I roped him into doing the habit challenge with me, and his fail-safe hack for making sure he does his morning workout is that he makes his morning coffee a reward.

Optimize Your Environment

Environmental design can be a game changer when it comes to making desired habits easier to implement. Dirty towels getting dumped on the bathroom floor? Place a laundry basket where they normally get dumped. Tired of the dog tracking in mud after each walk? Place a few towels or paw wipes by the front door. Want to watch less TV before you go to sleep? Get the TV out of the bedroom! The idea is just to consider how you can leverage your environment to make it easier to lock in the habits you want to implement and discourage the ones you don't.

TRY IT

How can you alter your physical environment to encourage the habits you most want to integrate? What small changes would help encourage (or discourage) your desired actions?

Try an Identity Shift

Changing your habits on some level always necessitates a bit of an identity shift, so it's important to consider who you want to become or the identity you want to inhabit: a healthy person? an organized person? a productive person? a person who always arrives on time? It can be hugely motivating to identify the *type* of person you want to become as you work on establishing new habits, and then ask yourself what that type of person would do in any situation. When you wake up and don't want to make your bed, ask yourself, "What would a tidy person do?" If you find yourself getting distracted, ask yourself, "What would a focused person do?" Don't want to commit to your workout plan? Ask, "What would a fit person do?" These simple prompts can serve to get you back on track and help you follow through on your desired actions.

TRY IT

Pick a specific identity that aligns with the new habit you want to integrate into your life. Ask yourself, "What would a healthy / wealthy / organized / productive / fill-in-the-blank person do?" before taking action.

Create Friction

We talked about how to make your desired habits *easier* to implement, but if there is a sticky habit you're struggling to break, you'll want to make it more *difficult by adding friction*. Delete the apps on your phone that tend to become a time suck if you're trying to be more productive. Remove your credit card info from sites that have one-click

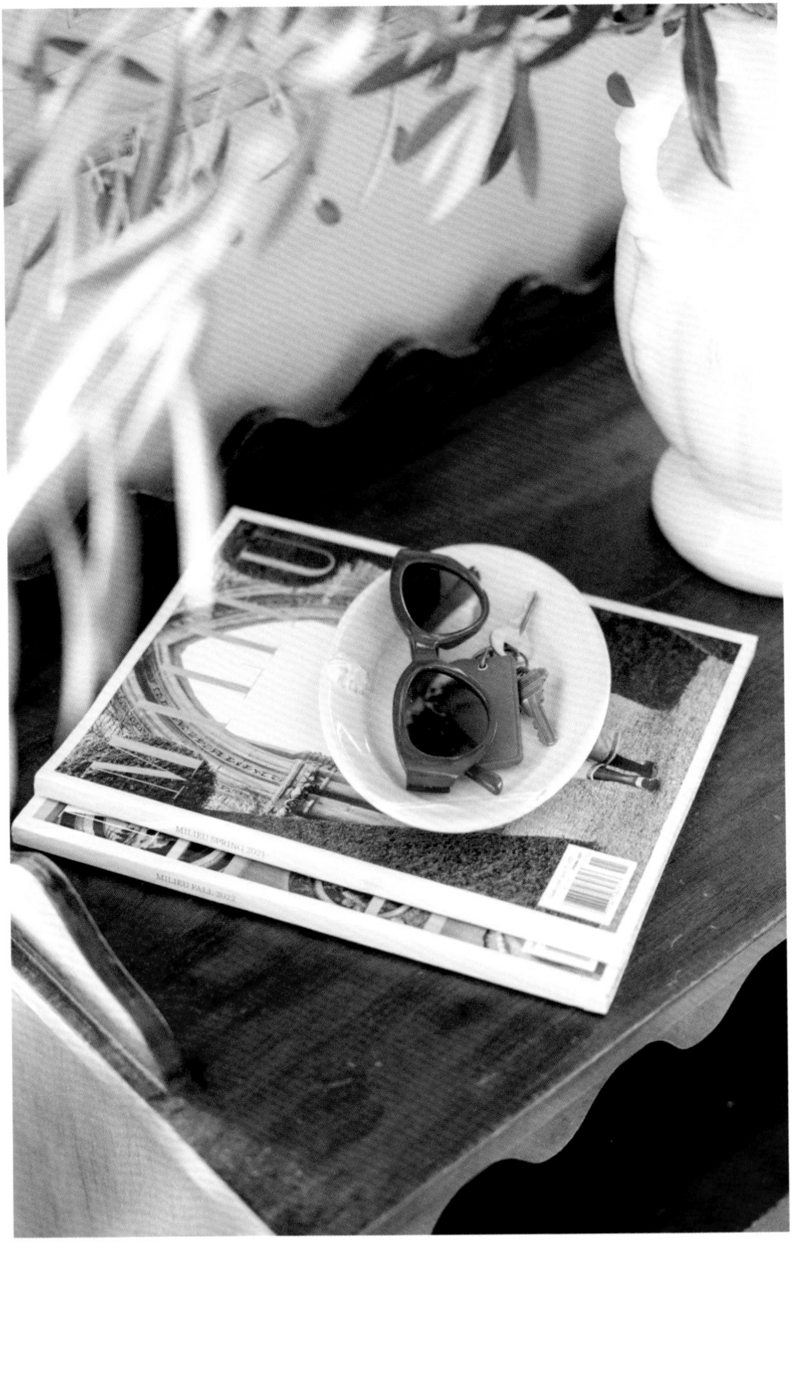
MILIEU SPRING 2021
MILIEU FALL 2022

ordering if you want to reduce impulse buying and save money. Relocate the tempting snacks to a hard-to-reach shelf or stop buying them altogether if you're trying to lose weight. I started leaving my phone downstairs in our kitchen each night (instead of on my bedroom nightstand), in order to break my morning scrolling habit.

TRY IT

How can you make the specific habits you want to stop doing more inconvenient? Experiment by adding friction—change your environment, add an extra layer of difficulty.

Quick Win

Pick *one* tiny habit you would like to implement over the next week. This is not a forever goal, but just a chance to practice following through on a new habit and strengthening your habit-forming muscle. Anticipate that you will run into resistance (you're human) and refer to the success strategies outlined in this chapter when you hit a roadblock. Most people thrive with accountability and structure, so write down your new habit, tell your inner circle about it, and schedule the actions you need to take on your calendar. You never know where this experiment might take you. I started with the goal of a fifteen-minute solo walk every morning for a week. I enjoyed these mini walks so much I ended up expanding my route into a forty-five-minute loop and have now been walking each morning religiously for three years. If I can do it, you can do it.

And Another Thing!

There is simply no upside to beating yourself up for past failures. As any personal trainer will tell you, doing something is always better than doing nothing and it is never too late to start. If you have a history of letting yourself down or not following through on your goals, make sure to start with micro changes by setting tiny, achievable habit shifts.

THE BOTTOM LINE

The tiny, seemingly insignificant actions we take each day, like putting away the mail, folding the laundry, or taking a brisk morning walk, create our bigger outcomes and results. If you want to transform your life, start by transforming your daily habits. You can make it easier to build new habits by making them small, intuitive, consistent, satisfying, and fun. You can discourage bad habits by adding friction or making them more difficult to follow through on. Focus on building or breaking just one new habit at a time so you can fully master your new routine before adding another habit into the mix.

PART ONE WRAP-UP

Congrats, you tool-kit graduate, you! The next time you're stuck or struggling I hope you will call on these tools to help you identify specific and actionable solutions. Ask yourself in any situation, "Do I need to *adjust volume, create a new system,* or *shift my habits*?" Remember: It's quite difficult to *think* your way into acting differently, and much easier to *act* your way into thinking differently. Now that we've laid the foundation, it's time to start applying these tools to every area of your life. Big improvements are just around the corner. Let's go!

PART TWO

The Practice

Let's start with this simple truth: *You cannot do all the things.* Personally, I find this news to be both wildly liberating and also a huge bummer. Inevitably, when given the directive to practice constraint by turning down plans, offers, or opportunities, our brain will have a bit of a fit. It's common to feel that we should all be able to keep unlimited numbers of balls in the air at the same time, and that it's not only possible, but expected, to maintain thriving relationships, a successful career, and a sparkly clean home all at once. This unhealthy belief system can lead to feelings of deep shame and imposter syndrome, especially for women.

So, instead of encouraging you to lean in to as many things as you can handle without having a breakdown, I want to do the opposite. I want to promote the idea that you should really lean in to a few things (only the most important) and dramatically lower the bar on the rest. Someone once told me that people can either have a super tidy home or be great at cooking dinner, but never both. The freedom I felt when she said this was immeasurable: So, it's okay that I'm rubbish at cooking because my home is tidy? Hallelujah, waffles for dinner! Of course, you don't have to excel at *either* of these things to be a worthy and successful human, but you get the point—it feels good to embrace the things you value most and let go of the rest.

Before we dig in to improving your health, relationships, finances, and other key areas of your life in the chapters ahead, I want to share a process that will help you identify what to focus on right now. While none of the parts of your life should ever be fully neglected, it is only possible to dramatically improve one area at a time. If you attempt to do everything all at once, it will all be watered down, and your results will be disappointing. I know because I've tried. Repeatedly. *Remember, there will always be a few things that matter more than the rest, and, of those, one will matter most of all.*

THE LIFE AUDIT PROCESS

Every year on New Year's Eve, I sit down and rank each area of my life on a scale of 1 to 5, based on level of fulfillment and overall satisfaction. Once I've ranked each area, I'll jot down some quick reflections, and note a thing or two I can do to improve each area for the following year. This exercise only takes me about thirty minutes and always helps me clarify where I want to focus my time, energy, and effort for the coming season, or even the coming year. Overachievers, take note—the objective here is not to get a perfect score of five in each area of your life. In fact, it's the opposite. This process is designed to help you make intentional decisions about which areas can hang out on the back burner, and which areas need your attention most urgently. It's about making

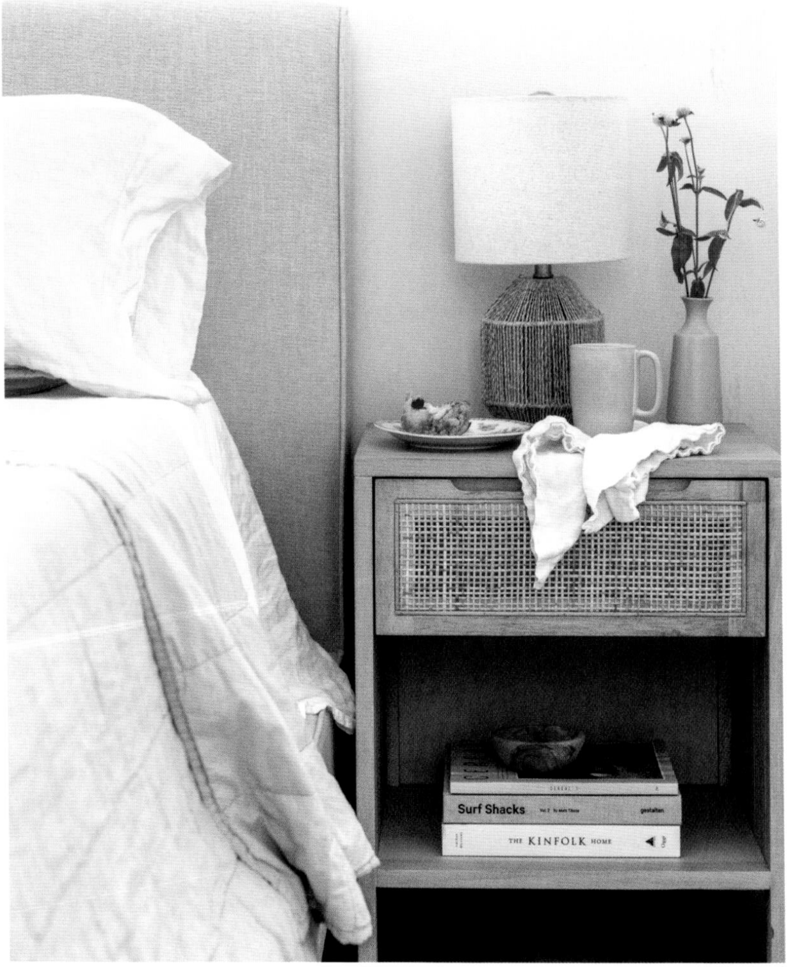
Surf Shacks
THE KINFOLK HOME

thoughtful, clear, and concrete decisions about what you can let go of (for now) instead of trying to do everything, and inevitably failing.

Here's a real-life example of my life audit process in action.

Career and Finance

Score: 4

Notes: Love my career, thriving creatively, need to start adulting with finances.

Priority: Bank account management.

First Little Step: Look at my bank account once a week to review income and expenses.

Leisure and Recreation

Score: 1

Notes: Total rubbish at leisure, always working, no hobbies to speak of! (True story. The first time I took myself through this process, I ranked this category as a big fat 0, and, if I'm being honest, it's still my most neglected area. In a culture that rewards achievement and celebrates being frenetically busy, it can be far too easy to forget to create space to relax and reset. I realized that I need to schedule it to make it happen—to get that big boost in the mental health department and energy for the next big thing I want to cross off my to-do list.)

Priority: Add a relaxing activity.

First Little Step: Read for an hour in bed every Sunday morning before breakfast with the family.

YOUR TURN

Let's do a quick audit of each area of your life to determine what needs the most care and attention right now. Just as a physician can't write a prescription without a clear diagnosis, you must assess how each area in your life is functioning before embarking on a plan toward transformation or change. You can use the broad categories I'll be outlining in the upcoming chapters (health and wellness, home and environment, relationships and community, career and finance, personal development) or create your own. Next, rank each category from 1 to 5, jot down any insights that arise, and take a little time to reflect so you can determine which area you want to invest in improving. To recap:

> Step one: Jot down your broad categories (health, relationships, career, finance, home, personal development, and spirituality).
>
> Step two: Rank each category from 1 to 5, based on satisfaction. These rankings are subjective—be honest with yourself.
>
> Step three: Jot down any notes or insights.
>
> Step four: Pick ONE area to invest in improving right now.
>
> Step five: Write down any first little steps you'd like to take to feel better about that area in your life.

If you feel stuck or unsure, try the following prompts:

- Which area of my life feels the most neglected?
- What is calling out for my attention?
- Which area do I most want to improve?
- What is my deepest need right now?
- What about the lives of others makes me feel the most envious?

The most important thing is to gain clarity about where you want to invest your precious time, energy, and resources *on purpose*. You can approach the following chapters as a choose-your-own-adventure program: If you need to invest in your health, start with the Health and Wellness chapter. If you are craving an environmental shift, hop over to the Home and Environment chapter. Craving a relationship reboot? Head to the Relationships chapter.

My hope is you'll be able to bounce around and find what you need, and then return to this book again and again through transitional moments in each season of your life. You've learned the tool kit; now it's time to put the tools into practice. Off we go!

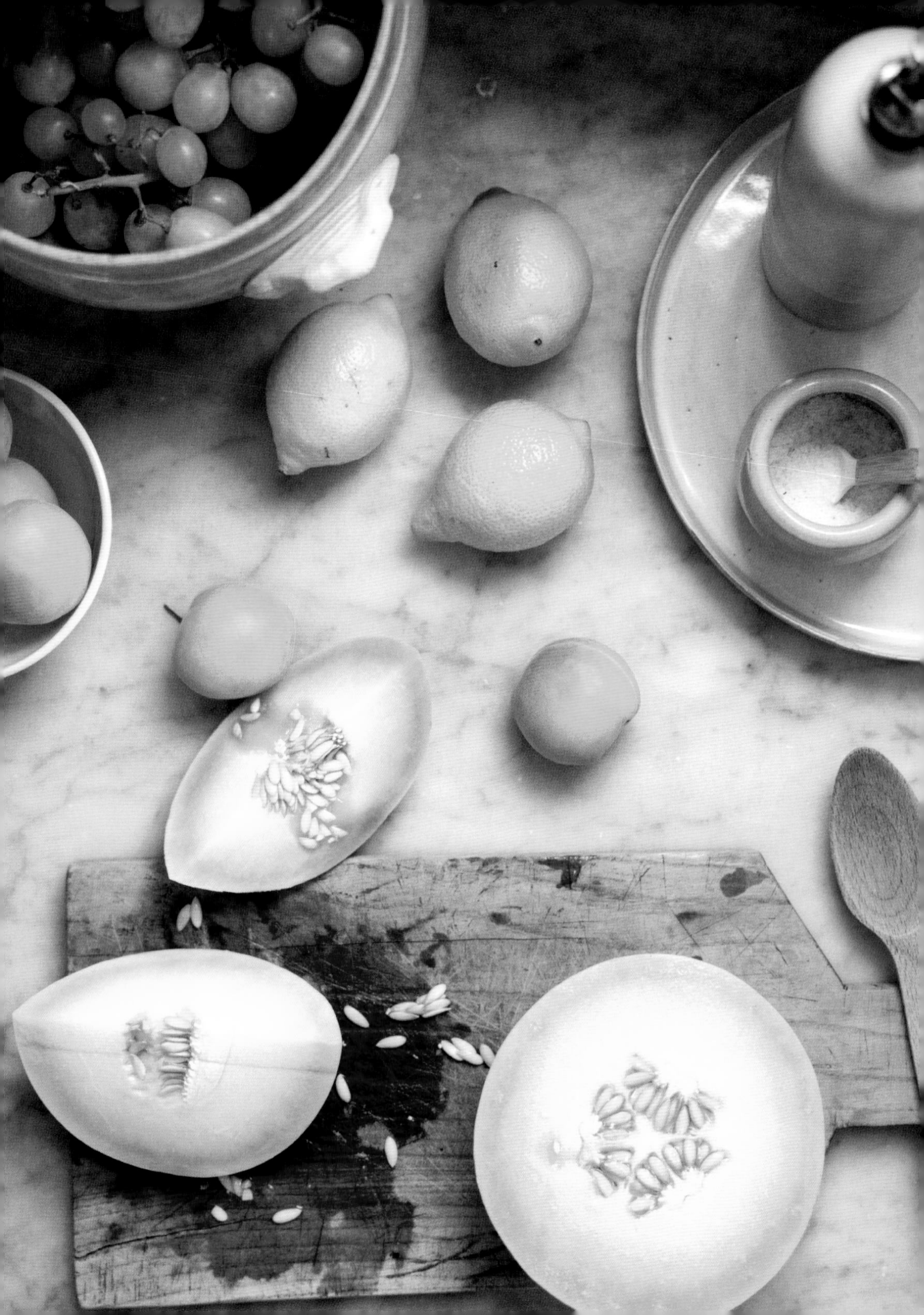

Health and Wellness

As my grandmother used to say, "Without your health, nothing else matters." If you're facing a big diagnosis or health challenge; recovering from childbirth or surgery; or dealing with chronic stress, anxiety, or burnout, you may need to prioritize your physical or mental health above all else. No matter what your current circumstances are, when your physical and mental health are optimized, you'll feel better and have more energy and vitality for the people and things you care about most deeply. In this chapter I'll break down everything I've learned about how to create and implement small, smart, healthy habits that will yield big, powerful results.

ADJUSTING VOLUME:
HEALTH AND WELLNESS EDITION

In the health and wellness industry, there are so many messages focused on dieting and restriction—avoid alcohol and caffeine, say no to gluten, toss the sugar, curb screen time before bed. Cue the sad trombone. I feel myself contract when told what *not* to do, but I can happily lean in to incorporating new healthy habits into my life–things that promote feeling good and staying grounded, strong, and well–both physically and mentally. Below are five straightforward strategies that will help take you from *meh* to *wheeeeee*! Get ready to turn up the volume on good health.

Health Helper One: Identify Your Fuel Foods

I love and find a lot of joy in food, and the philosophy that food is just fuel is not one that I connect with. But the truth is that some foods make me feel like I'm sleeping standing up and some rev my engine. For example, I have a very special relationship with sourdough baguette slathered in Brie, but this combo always makes me feel terrible–headachy, bloated, and fatigued. Many people swear that a handful of nuts can energize them, but salted nuts just make me irritable and thirsty. *"I NEED AN ACTUAL MEAL!"* I have been known to shout at the nut people. My point is that we're all different. When you're eating, pay attention to how different foods make your body feel. Be curious and experiment so you can find the "fuel foods" that provide you with sustained energy and feel good in your body.

TRY IT

Identify a handful of easy-to-prepare fuel foods you can reach for when you are short on time but don't want to end up scarfing down a bag of cheese puffs out of desperation. Jot them down and post them on your refrigerator. Mine include a fruit smoothie with a handful of spinach; raw veggies with hummus; rice cakes with almond butter; and sharp cheddar with a sliced apple. What are yours?

Health Helper Two: Eat Your Veggies

One of the only things that all wellness experts agree on is this: Vegetables are good for you–like *really* good. They're high in fiber, packed with vitamins and minerals, anti-inflammatory, and even capable of

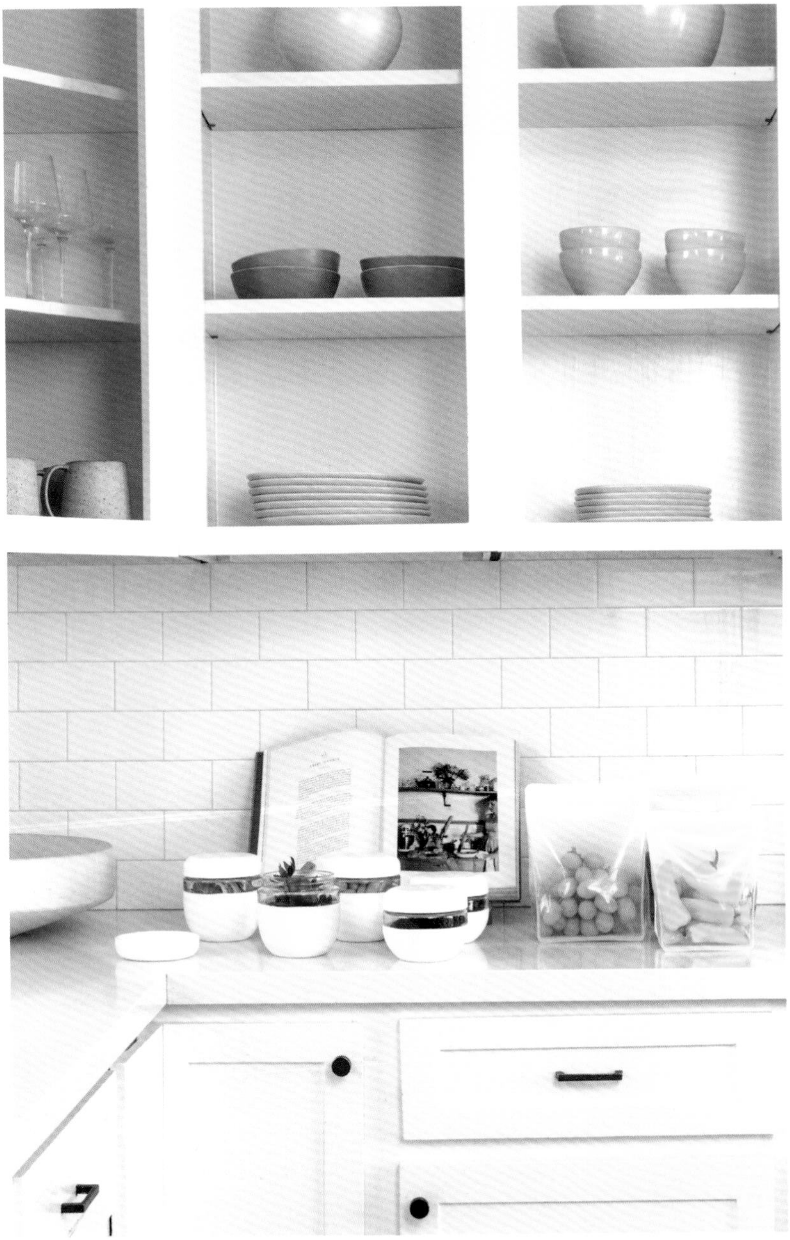

preventing disease. Basically, they're little magic health bullets grow-ing from the ground. If you're not a fan I suggest roasting them on high heat with olive oil, herbs, and really good flaky sea salt. Just don't cook them within an inch of their life or bye-bye nutrients. You can't really overeat veggies, so pick your favorites and knock yourself out. If each plate of food you eat is composed of at least 50 percent vegetables, you're winning. Farmers' markets are great for a lot of reasons, but one of the best is that most of the stands have samples precut or will cut up a sample for you (and for your kids, if you have them), so not only can you find which veggies work for you, but you can see which are in sea-son. You can also ask the person at the stand for tips on how to prepare your new favorite veggies.

TRY IT

Experiment with filling your plate with 50 percent veggies for each meal. I'm feeling healthier already.

Health Helper Three: Hydrate Like Crazy

Remember that movie *My Big Fat Greek Wedding*, where the father suggested that a spritz of Windex housecleaner was the remedy for everything under the sun? That's how I feel about water. My kids will tell you that it's my go-to solution for everything from crankiness and fatigue, to breakouts, to fighting a head cold or congestion (drink up, kiddos!). Not only do we need water to *literally survive*, hydrating also helps us flush toxins from the body and optimize physical per-formance, boosts energy levels and brain function, aids in digestion, improves your skin, and helps you maintain a healthy weight. What are you waiting for? Grab your favorite water bottle and start chugging! Water a little boring for you? I get it. Switch it up by adding different fruits, herbs, and veggies to create your own bougie spa water. Water-melon and mint? Lemon and thyme? Grapefruit and rosemary (I don't know, maybe)? Play around and find your own favorite combos that will keep you drinking all day.

THE BATTLE OF THE BRAIN

Here's what we know about the primitive human brain: It's wired to seek plea-sure, avoid pain, and preserve energy. Its intentions are good (to keep us safe from harm), but those intentions may be undermined when we're trying to gain traction in our lives. Let me explain. Wrapping yourself in a weighted blanket and binge-watching Netflix while scarfing down chocolate chip bonbons checks your brain's feel-good box, but when you wake up a sleep-deprived wreck and have to spend time scrubbing chocolate off your sweatpants (whoops!), you might regret your choices. This may seem rich coming from the queen of ice cream, but we're all working on ourselves here, me included. Here's the thing: Pleasure is typically fleeting and temporary, whereas true happiness is deeper and longer-lasting. Superficial pleasurable activities like shopping, scrolling, and snacking provide a dopamine hit that feels great to your brain (wheee, fun!), but only temporarily. These quick-fix activities typically lead to feelings of regret and possibly a heap of unwanted credit card debt or a sugar crash. Instead of sacrificing long-term happiness and fulfillment for short-term super-ficial pleasure, focus on what you want *most* instead of what you want right *now*. Indulging in feel-good but fleeting distractions is often an indication of deeper issues, like feeling bored, sad, or stressed out (spoiler alert: I never eat a full sack of potato chips with Lipton onion dip when things are incredible). Since we know this tendency is human nature, it's our job to identify the root cause of our feelings so we can focus on making our lives less stressful and more deeply fulfilling. When in doubt, try this trick I learned from my colleague Jamie Green-wood: Ask if your behavior or activity is *numbing* or *nourishing*. This is a great way to clarify whether you like your reasons for making any choice, whether it's eating, drinking, shopping, or scrolling. All of these activities are morally neutral. They can feel good, and even energizing, or they can feel depleting, draining, or hollow. The goal is to focus on building true and lasting content-ment instead of compiling a stack of cheap thrills.

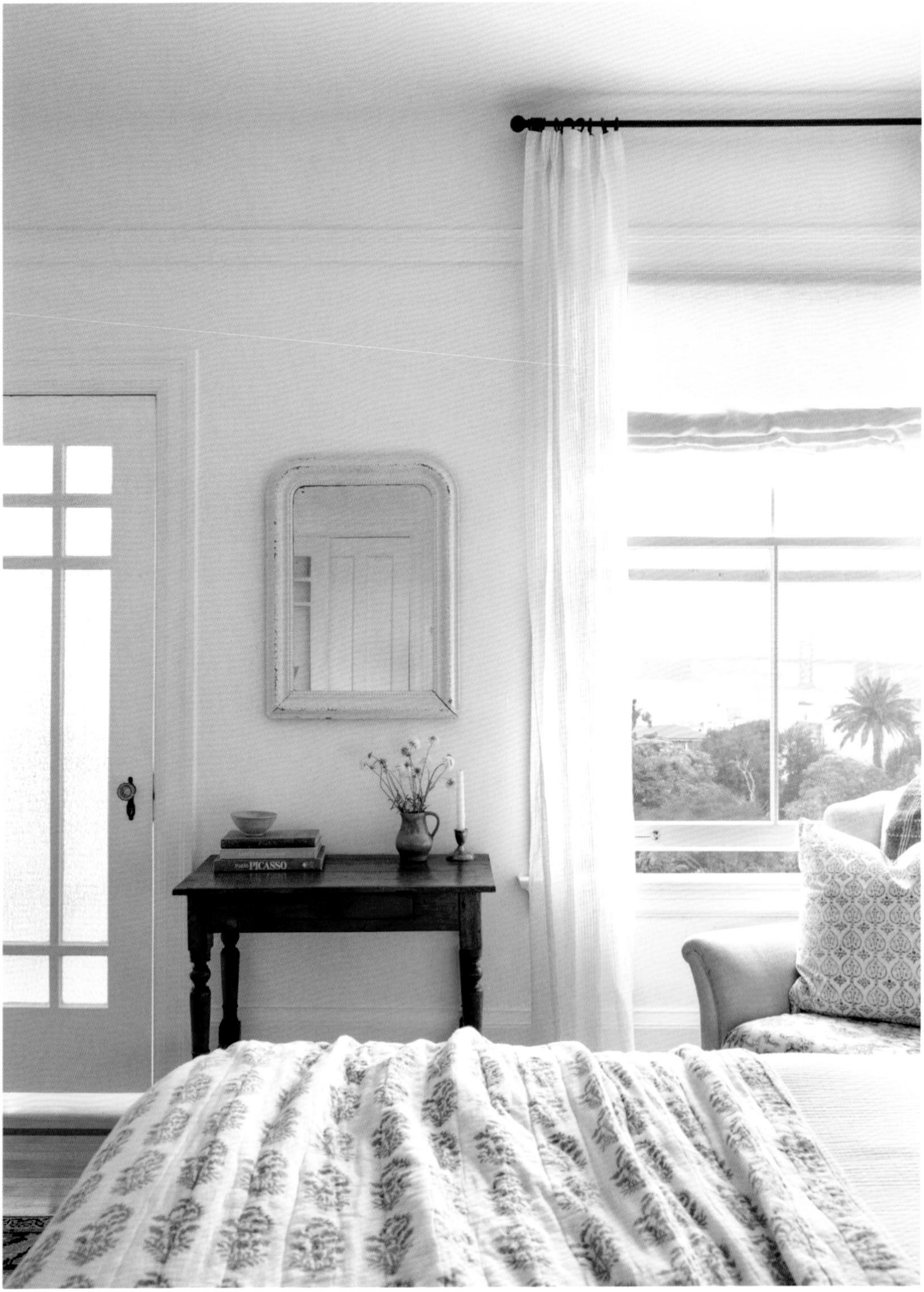
PICASSO

Health Helper Four: Move Your Body

Regular physical activity will boost your mood and trigger feel-good endorphins, improve your sleep, enhance your skin, your brain health, and your memory. It reduces anxiety and depression, and it even decreases risk factors for chronic disease and illness. Translation—it's a MUST. And here's the best news: It doesn't take much movement to make a big difference in your health. Yes, cardio and strength training are key for improving longevity and bone health, but it is always better to do something than nothing. Take the stairs instead of the elevator. Walk to the store and carry your groceries home. Dance in your living room. Take a hike with a friend instead of meeting for drinks. Google FREE WORKOUT VIDEOS and find someone you like on YouTube. Figure out what feels easy (maybe even fun?) and commit to a minimum baseline of daily movement even if it's literally a five-minute stroll to get some fresh air before work. Commit to moving every single day, as if it's your job.

Health Helper Five: Prioritize Sleep

I prioritize sleep like my life depends on it (and it kind of does). Getting a minimum of eight hours of sleep means I can be wildly creative, productive, and friendly during my waking hours instead of depleted, distracted, and cranky. To maintain my hard-core sleep schedule, I occasionally say no to fun events and parties (or leave early). I don't drink coffee and I rarely drink alcohol, so those sleep stealers aren't obstacles for me. However, I have to completely banish phones and computers from my bedroom because I lack any self-control in that department. When I was a new mom, I napped whenever I could, and even set up babysitting swaps with other sleep-deprived moms to catch up on some extra rest. Remember, you don't have to *earn* your right to rest. Rest helps you recharge and function at your highest level. Rest is your responsibility. If you do nothing else in this chapter, figure out your optimum sleep number (in hours) and then get creative (and ruthless) and sort out how you can get the sleep you need. Next up, I'll share my favorite strategies to boost your mood and your mindset.

Mental Health Booster One: Get Outside, Stat!

There are few things that can be as impactful, exhilarating, or good for the soul as simply getting out into nature. I'm a city-mouse to my very core, but I have found that some fresh air, and even a brief exposure to the natural world, can restore my spirits and boost my mood like nothing else. For a surefire perspective shift, step outside and let your senses engage with nature in whatever ways feel the most nourishing. Listen to the wind and water and birds. Look up at the stars. Take a walk by the beach. Gaze at the mountains. Allow yourself to feel tiny in the best way.

Mental Health Booster Two: Feel Your Feelings

I find it oddly comforting to know that none of us are immune from heartache, loss, or suffering. It's simply part of being alive on planet Earth. It's hard being a human, and sometimes numbing the pain with your preferred vice can feel like the best solution, but fleeing from our emotions never actually gets us very far from them. I used to do my very best to avoid negative feelings, but they would always find me, sneaky little buzzards. However, I found I could make the negative feelings more tolerable simply by choosing to feel them on purpose. Now, when facing a difficult emotion like deep sadness or grief, I practice fully surrendering by naming it: *This is just sadness. I'm feeling grief.* I write. I cry. I talk it out. The faster I can lean in to the emotion and actually *experience it*, the sooner it lifts, like a cloud.

Mental Health Booster Three: Don't Take Anything Personally

Fact: If you're looking to find fulfillment and purpose from other people's opinions, you'll never find it. Even before I had a career where perfect strangers could comment publicly on my life on the internet, I used to land in the fetal position anytime someone didn't approve of my actions. I've come to realize that what other people think about you is more a reflection of them than anything else. Generalized people-pleasing is not only exhausting, it takes you away from living a brave, authentic life. Now I focus on staying in my own lane, putting out the best work I can, acting with kindness and integrity, and making sure *I* approve of *my own* actions. Of course, I deeply value the opinions of my inner circle of close friends and family, but I no longer let myself spend a minute obsessing over what Becky227 on Instagram thinks about me or my lifestyle. Not wasting time or mental energy on the haters, critics, and naysayers is so liberating that it makes me want to break out into a happy dance. Starting today, identify whose opinion truly matters to you, and then turn *down* the volume on other people's judgments and turn *up* the volume on being the best, most authentic version of yourself yet.

Mental Health Booster Four: Take Care of Number One (Psst: That's You!)

We've all been told that you can't pour from an empty cup, you must secure your own oxygen mask before you help others, yadda yadda yadda. But because it can feel tricky (sometimes nearly impossible) to prioritize our own mental and physical health, it's worth driving the point home again. Even though it can seem scary or awkward to turn down plans or let people down, I know that I am a useless human when I don't properly take care of myself. Conversely, I am a better wife, mother, daughter, colleague, and friend when I am well-rested, sufficiently fed and hydrated, move my body, and claim a little alone time when no other humans are talking to me. A huge pillar of mental health is identifying what you need to feel grounded, centered, and calm, and prioritizing doing those things above all else. *Repeat after me: Self-care is not selfish and you are not a monster for taking care of yourself.* Anyone who tells you otherwise does not have your best interest in mind.

TRY IT

Jot down two or three self-care strategies that you can call on when you feel depleted or low. How do you recharge your batteries? Identifying a few small actions to take care of yourself in advance will make it easier to shift gears when you feel yourself mentally depleted, sinking, or struggling.

Mental Health Booster Five: Learn How to Be Alone

Feeling the occasional pang of loneliness is not abnormal; it's part of the human condition. Instead of fearing and avoiding loneliness at all costs, learn how to embrace and even enjoy spending time in solitude. Growing up as an only child of divorce, with no other family in the vicinity, I developed this skill by necessity. Oh, how I longed for a big, loud family with raucous holidays and gatherings (pass the eggnog!), but that was not my fate. So, I had to create strategies to entertain myself. I learned how to lean in to my own interests and passions like reading, writing, going on solo city adventures, and even just daydreaming, and now I feel grateful for solo time instead of fearing it.

TRY IT

Pay attention to the things that fuel you. Take yourself on a solo date. Plan an adventure or excursion just for you. Do something you love—party of one edition.

Mental Health Booster Six: Try Stillness

I'm writing this as someone who is admittedly terrible at this, but I know it's true: Any form of regular mindfulness or meditation you can practice will have a positive impact on your overall mental health. Even slowing down to breathe for a single minute will lower your stress and leave you feeling calmer and more grounded. Build it in however you can. Try an app, set a timer, spend a few minutes just being still and quiet before you get out of bed and start your day. Inhale, exhale. I'll practice with you!

Mental Health Booster Seven: Use the "Good" China

It seems to be part of human nature to save our best stuff for some elusive someday, but I promise that you will never regret wearing your favorite dress to the party. Stop waiting for the perfect time and enjoy the good stuff now: Light the fancy candle, sport your finest threads

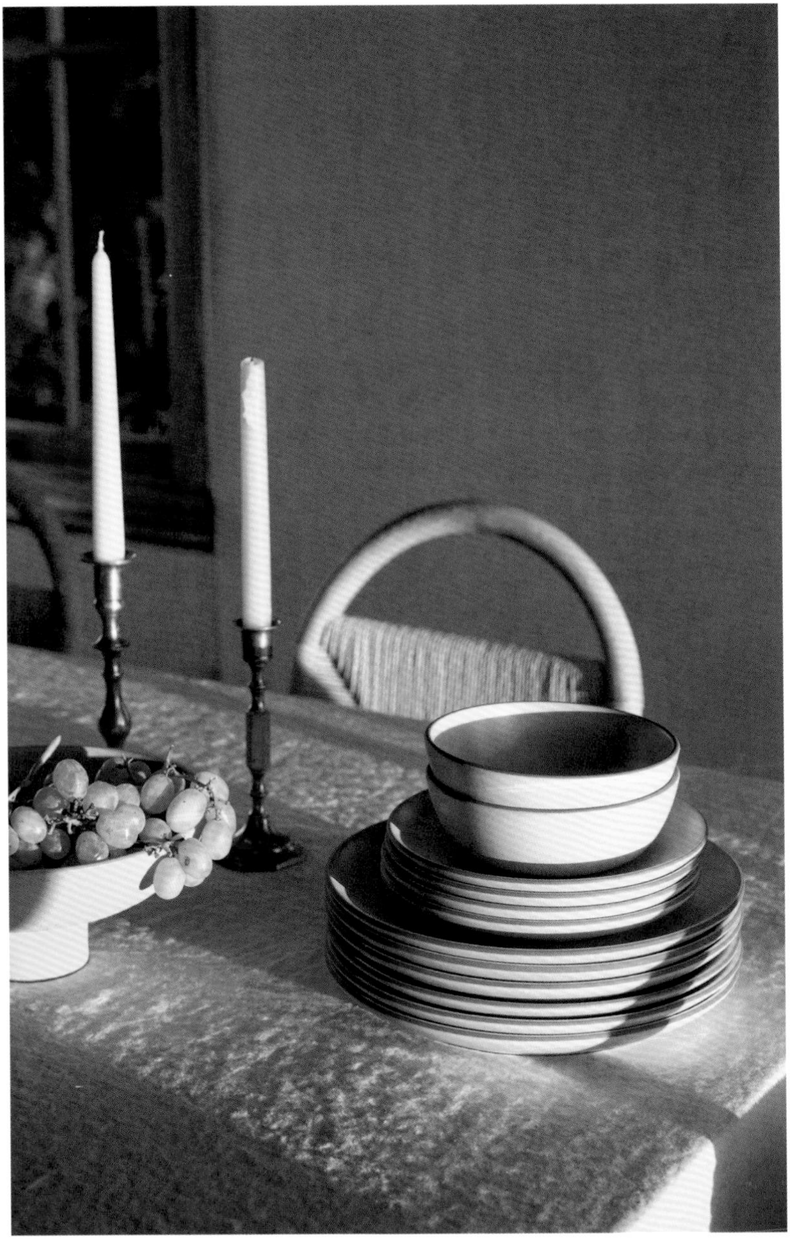

and nicest handbag when you go to the grocery store, break out the best plates, fancy glassware, and cloth napkins even if you're just heating up a frozen pizza. Crack open that really good bottle. Your life is the occasion. Cheers!

Mental Health Booster Eight: Seek Support

There is absolutely no shame in seeking support from highly trained experts, including skilled therapists, psychiatrists, coaches, nutritionists, and healers. I feel especially strongly about this since so many people in my close circle have struggled with mental health challenges, and stigmas around therapy and medication have added an additional layer of unnecessary shame and a double arrow of suffering. Connecting with a skilled mental health professional can be preventive, restorative, and even lifesaving, especially if you are struggling with any form of addiction, depression, anxiety, or mood disorder. Seeking help is a sign of resilience and strength, not weakness. If you need some support, and don't know where to begin, tap into your local community resources, search for a specialist online, or ask your primary care physician for a referral. Let's agree to destigmatize being proactive about our mental health and encourage others to do the same. Deal?

TRY IT

Time to curate your own personal support team. Whether you decide to join a support group, hire an expert, or identify a few people you can rely on within your inner circle, make sure you have a few trusted people you can turn to during particularly challenging times.

Mental Health Booster Nine: Reach Out and Touch Someone

Not in a creepy way. But intimacy and physical touch have been linked to a whole host of mental health benefits. Not to get all science-y, but physical touch increases levels of dopamine and serotonin, two neurotransmitters, which are like little chemical messengers in your brain that help us regulate mood and relieve stress and anxiety. Who doesn't need that? If you live alone or aren't in a partnership, not to worry—a hug from a friend, a cuddle with your dog, a massage, and even wrapping yourself in a soft blanket can go a long way toward improving your mental health.

CREATING SYSTEMS: HEALTH AND WELLNESS EDITION

Okay, so we've talked about how to turn *up* the volume on imperatives like sleep, hydration, fuel foods, fresh air, and movement, and turn *down* the volume on chasing cheap joy, other people's judgments, negative belief systems, and stigmas about seeking support. Investing in your health is one of those things that has zero downside and infinite reward but is so wildly difficult for most of us to commit to. For this reason, we need to lower the bar and take baby steps that will compound to create big change over time. Ready? Small, smart systems to the rescue.

Make Standing Wellness Appointments

It's so easy for checkups and screenings to get lost in the shuffle. Case in point: I've had a colon cancer screening kit sitting untouched in my entryway for weeks and yet I've found time to watch a Netflix show called *Is It Cake?* Fear can lead us to avoid the most important health precautions. Most of us are not dying to get a mammogram or have our teeth scraped with sharp tools, but preventive medicine is one of the most powerful tools we've got to optimize our health and longevity. Get out your little black book and schedule your annual screenings and seasonal appointments in advance. Jot down any health concerns or screening questions in the notes section of each appointment, so you won't forget to ask about them when the time comes. In addition to your traditional doctor's appointments, you may want to invest in other types of wellness treatments or support, like a therapist, coach, nutritionist, chiropractor, masseuse, acupuncturist, or homeopath. I've found that monthly acupuncture treatments have greatly improved my immune system, so I book out appointments as far out as my amazing practitioner will allow me to schedule. My client Roberta, who deals with chronic stress, automates monthly massages in addition to her regular health screenings, and my mother-in-law swears by monthly adjustments from a chiropractor to prevent further back injury. Be proactive, invest in your health, and book your preventive care in advance, automating repeat appointments as you are able.

Create a Low-Bar Morning Routine

The way you approach your morning will not only impact the rest of your day, but possibly your entire life. A strong, consistent morning routine has been linked to heightened productivity, and sustained energy and focus. You don't have to do kundalini yoga or use a copper tongue scraper to have an effective morning routine. Pick a few small, smart habits you'd like to integrate into your morning regimen each day, and wake up a bit earlier if you must. My morning routine is wildly simple, which is why I've been able to maintain it: I jot down any morning thoughts in my journal, drink a massive glass of water, and take a forty-five-minute morning walk before showering and starting my workday. When my kids were younger, I just made my bed and stretched for five minutes because something is always better than nothing. Prioritizing healthy habits first thing in the morning means you can spend the rest of your day basking in the glow of your accomplishments.

TRY IT

Choose *one* tiny habit to integrate into your morning routine (movement, hydration, journaling) and do it at the same time each day, if possible. Once you've successfully integrated one new habit, you can habit-stack to build out a customized morning routine.

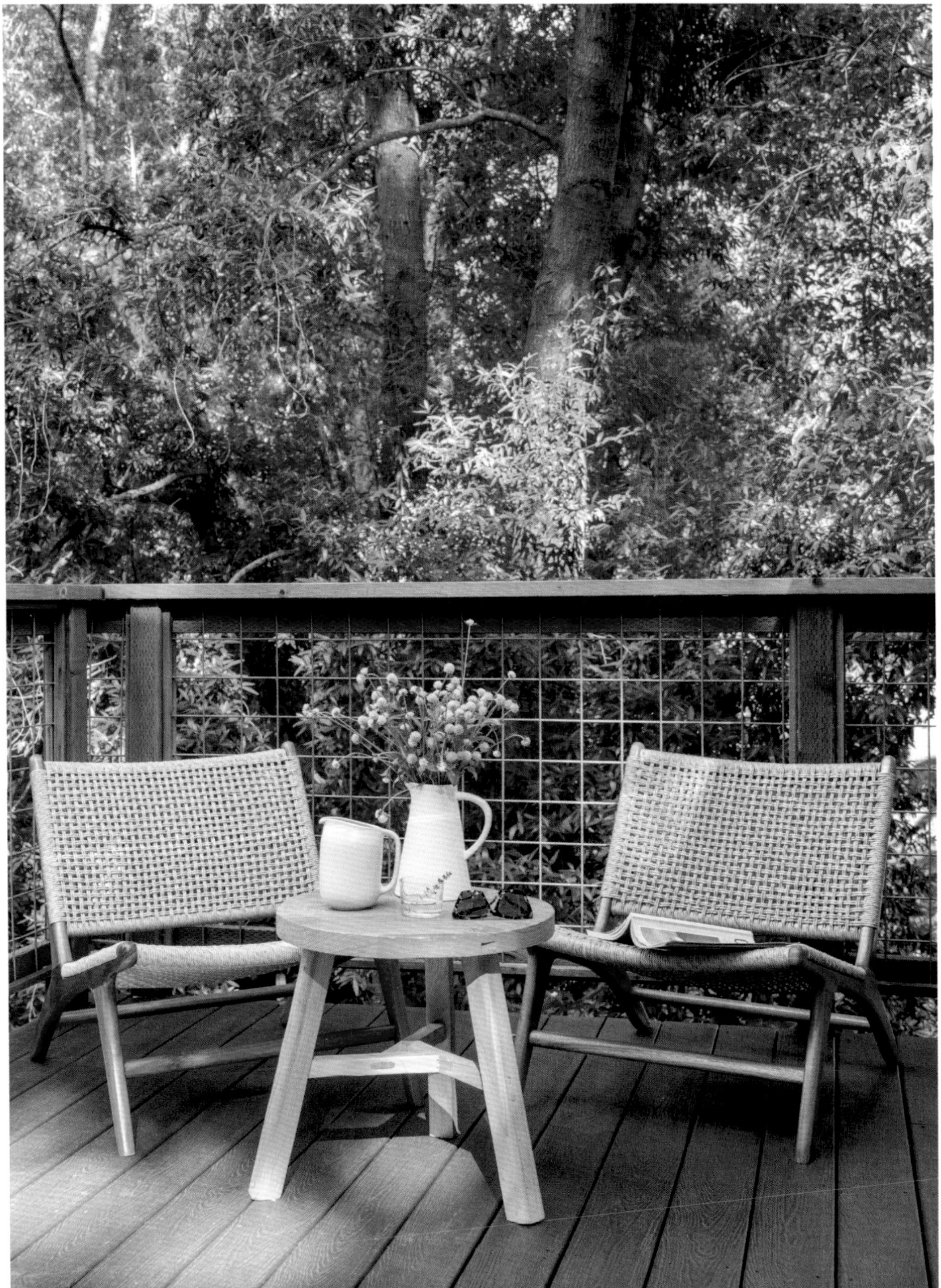

BREAK THE SHAME SPIRAL AND MAKE YOURSELF PROUD

The strategies listed in this chapter are not groundbreaking and probably don't come as much of a surprise. The truth is that most of us know the exact right things we need to do to become a healthier version of ourselves. The issue is building the momentum and discipline to follow through on said things. It's hard. Like *really* hard. Our brain is designed to seek pleasure and avoid discomfort, so pushing through resistance doesn't come easily. And here's the rub: Typically, when we feel resistance, we immediately stop or quit, procrastinate or distract ourselves—*Will somebody please pass the remote and chocolate-covered pretzels?!* Most of us use resistance as a signal or excuse to *stop* taking action, but we need to do the opposite. We must *anticipate and plan for* the resistance and discomfort that will inevitably crop up when we attempt to do brave new things. We need to acknowledge our resistance and then tell it who's boss: *Oh, hey there, resistance, nice to see you again. I'm going to feel you, and then I'm going to get back to taking action so I can make my life better and crush my goals. Later!*

But, more than that, to truly make significant changes in our lives we must not only recognize that there might be discomfort, we must lean toward the discomfort. No one ever made a change by standing still. Once you make an affirmative decision to change and grow, and you acknowledge that a part of that decision is discomfort, you can anticipate and prepare for the inevitable moment when things feel hard and be mentally ready to push through. Practice this thought: *I am a person who is capable of pushing through discomfort.* When you are able to reliably encounter resistance and move forward anyway, you will develop a new level of trust with yourself—a trust that will enable you to take more risks, reach for bigger goals, and accomplish anything you put your mind to.

Food Is Medicine—Like, Really

Humans are inherently lazy and most of us will snack on whatever is closest and easiest. For this reason we need to make it as *easy* as possible to eat healthful, energizing fuel foods, like colorful vegetables. Here's how:

1. Decide *ahead of time* what fuel foods sound good to you.
2. Stock up on those specific foods once a week.
3. Prep your fuel foods so they are highly visible and ready to consume.

Planning one big restock each week means you can eat more intentionally and spend less time on the dreaded "What's for dinner" question. As silly as it sounds, I know I'll munch on whatever is easiest and most convenient whether that's a doughnut or a bowl of sliced melon. By prepping healthy grab-and-go snacks each week, like cut veggies and hummus or apple slices and almond butter, I've dramatically improved my health. Now pass the rainbow carrots!

TRY IT

Peek in your fridge and pantry so you can see what you already have, and then hit the shops or place an online order for what you need for the week. My easy hack is to stock up on five proteins, five veggies, and five bases (rice, tortillas, pasta) that can be mixed and matched for creative dinners all week—hold the meal planning nightmare. You can also subscribe to a weekly CSA box to support your local farmers and add a little seasonal variety into the mix. Always stocked at our home are these cooking essentials: cracked black pepper, flaky sea salt, fresh herbs, basic spices, eggs, milk, butter, lemons, and olive oil. When those are running low, we replenish during our weekly shopping trip. Extra credit: Wipe down your fridge shelves, decant snacks and staples into airtight jars, and prep meals and snacks for the busy week ahead.

Hack Your Hydration

The easiest ways to start drinking more water:

1. Stop buying all other beverages. (Bonus: You'll save a boatload of money and waste going into landfills.)
2. Treat yourself to a water bottle you love (preferably one that's well-insulated and portable, and fits in your cupholder).
3. Add fresh fruit or herbs and pretend you're a Fancy Nancy at the spa (cucumber-lime, strawberry-lemon-basil, and grapefruit-mint are all super delish).
4. Use an app or a timer to alert you to start sipping if you tend to forget.

Bottoms up!

Move It, Shake It

After struggling for years to integrate cardio workouts into my life, I finally gave up and decided to just walk for fifteen minutes every day when I woke up. Something is better than nothing, right? The surprising part is that those fifteen minutes quickly turned into a very enjoyable forty-five-minute loop, and I've now been walking daily for three years. Pick *one* small form of movement you enjoy and *schedule it on your calendar*, ideally at the same time every day. For example, you can send yourself a calendar invite that says, "Walk instead of drive to get the kids from school at 4 p.m." Or "Stretch while you watch *The Real Housewives of New York* reruns at 8 p.m." Make it tiny, easy, and sustainable. Little by little it will add up to a lot.

Schedule Your Rest

Ever notice how most of us schedule things like work meetings and dentist appointments but rarely schedule and prioritize rest? Whether we like it or not, it's imperative to carve out time to rest. You don't have to earn your right to rest, and working around the clock like a zombie

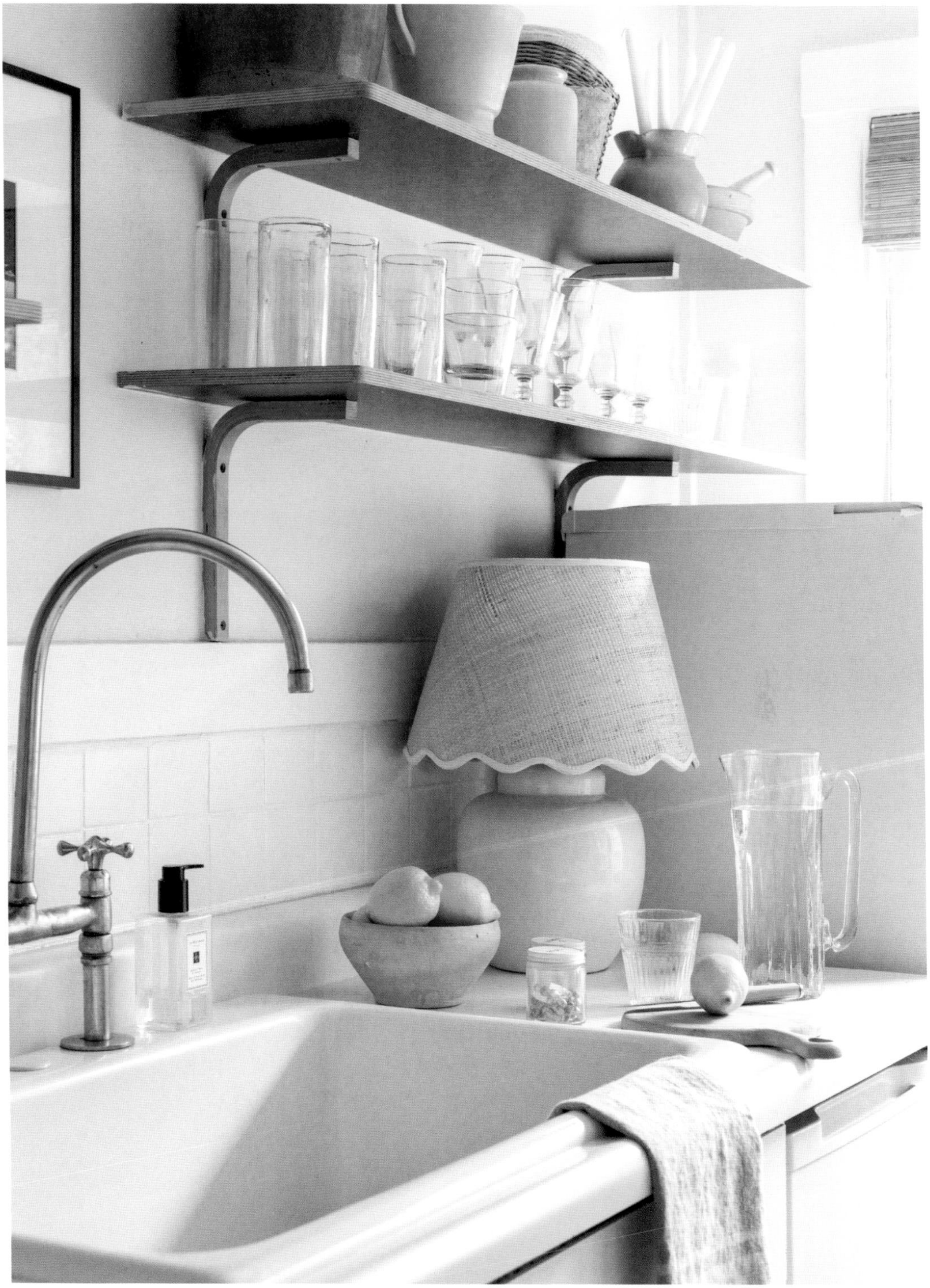

won't make you more efficient, productive, or creative; it will likely do the opposite. We make our worst decisions and poorest choices when we're depleted and exhausted. If you're resistant to rest (my hand is up), remind yourself that rest is where growth, renewal, and recovery happen. Even short bursts of rest will reenergize your body and mind and help propel positive results. As someone who prefers to be wildly busy and productive, I've learned to include time on my calendar that literally says, "TAKE A BREAK NOW" or "COMPUTER DOWN!" in all caps so I can't miss it.

TRY IT

Define what rest looks like for you (a quick snooze, a walk, a reading break) and schedule consistent blocks of dedicated rest time on your calendar. Even if it's just a fifteen-minute break to take some deep breaths, make it all bold, or highlight it in a bright color, so you can honor that time in your calendar. P.S.: Admittedly, I hate sleeping during the day (Jordan calls me a "nap shamer"), but for some a quick nap can be wildly restorative. You do you.

You, Unplugged

It's far too easy to be plugged into screens 24/7, and the programming and apps are built to keep us logged on, so it's up to us to decide *ahead of time* when we will stow our devices away and take a breather. Our family has a rule that there are no devices or computers out during mealtimes so we can be present and fully engage with each other. I also make sure to put my computer and phone in my office by 10 p.m. each night so I don't have blinking lights or texts distracting me or disrupting my sleep. Occasionally I'll commit to a full twenty-four-hour digital detox to fully reset and recharge. Make sure to establish clear boundaries for yourself about when you will unplug, and faithfully honor the commitment you make to yourself—and your family.

If you're looking to improve your tech-life balance, experiment with the following systems and strategies and see what works for you:

- Set daily screen-time limits using an app or timer for added accountability.
- Reduce apps on your devices, silence all notifications, and leave your home screen and desktop blank to minimize distraction.
- Unsubscribe from sales and marketing emails, and mute distracting or annoying social media accounts.
- Identify healthy and enjoyable substitutes for scrolling and screen time so you can get back to simple pleasures like reading, cooking, gardening, making art, or hiking.
- Create tech-free zones in your home or create friction by charging all devices in a concealed station (like inside a drawer or cabinet), away from your bedroom.
- Schedule a weekly or monthly full-blown digital detox to give your brain a break from the buzzing. Integrate back slowly to increase awareness of which apps improve your life and which merely serve as distraction.

Make Space to Treat Yourself

A manicure can make me feel like I'm winning at life, and a crisp white blouse can pull me out of a slump when I've been submitting to the sweatsuit life for days. Do you have pampering practices that make you feel great? My client Amanda lives for an eyebrow tint, while my best friend Hedy breaks for a facial. Automate and schedule these treats for yourself, so you don't have to go months without a little boost. No need to break the bank to treat yourself—my friend Liz has mastered the perfect at-home brow tint, and Jordan recently bought himself a $25 back massager, which he claims has changed his life forever. It's the little things!

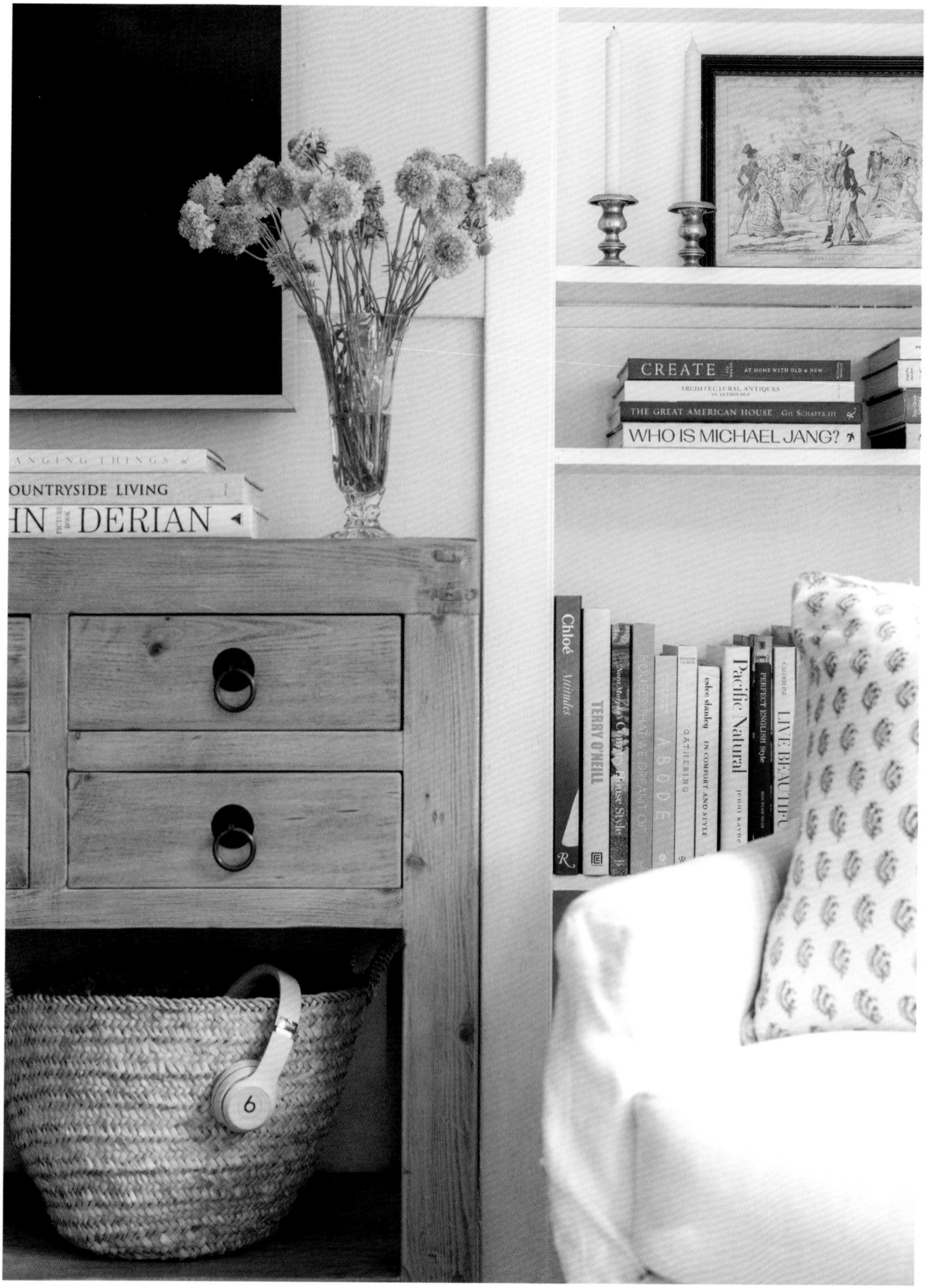
OUNTRYSIDE LIVING
HN DERIAN
PICTURE BOOK
CREATE
AT HOME WITH OLD & NEW
ARCHITECTURAL ANTIQUES
AN ANTHOLOGY
THE GREAT AMERICAN HOUSE
GIL SCHAFER III
WHO IS MICHAEL JANG?
Chloé
Attitudes
TERRY O'NEILL
ABODE
eslee shanley
GATHERING
IN COMFORT AND STYLE
Pacific Natural
jenni kayne
PERFECT ENGLISH Style
LIVE BEAUTIFU

Curate Your Feel-Good Tool Kit

Meditation and bubble baths are not my jam, even though I know the masses support them. When my father died, I signed up for therapy, got a life coach, and joined three different suicide loss support groups. My brother, Max, took a solo trip around the world for a year. We all grieve differently, we all process emotion differently, and it's up to us to find the stress solutions that work best for us. I have experienced a fair number of traumatic events and loss in my life, and I am not one of those cool-in-a-crisis people, so I've had to curate my own tough-times survival kit that I can call on during the hardest of times. My stress management strategies include:

- Walking, spin classes, power yoga, dance classes, or anything that gets my heart rate up and my endorphins flowing.
- Confiding in a friend, therapy, coaching, support groups—anything where I can talk it out in a safe, supportive space.
- Crying it out or having a good primal scream (typically in the privacy of my car so my kids don't get concerned).
- Decluttering my home and buying myself flowers. Creating order and beauty when things feel chaotic or stressful.
- Unplugging and getting out into nature. Staring at the ocean can make me feel very small (in a good way) and give me a sense of calm and perspective even in the midst of grief or heartbreak.

TRY IT

Make a list of your own stress-reducing strategies that you can call on anytime life feels especially challenging or difficult. What provides you with comfort and soothes your soul when the going gets tough? Keep this resource list in a safe place and draw on it when you need it.

IMPLEMENTING HABITS: HEALTH AND WELLNESS EDITION

Attention, please! There are two major factors in determining how you look and feel right now:

- Your genetics
- Your habits

Your predetermined genetics will dictate inherited illnesses or health outcomes, like asthma or allergies, while your habits are actions that are fully within your control, like what time you get into bed and which foods you eat. *Want to improve your health? Improve your habits.*

Health and Habit Loops

Remember all successful habits consist of a *cue*, a *routine*, and a *reward*.

Cues are prompts that remind you to take action and might include:

- When you wake up
- After you brush your teeth
- During your lunch break
- When you finish work
- Right after dinner

Routines might include:

- Drinking a full glass of water as soon as you wake up
- Doing fifty sit-ups after you brush your teeth
- Taking a fifteen-minute walk during your lunch break
- Listening to a meditation app every night right after finishing the dishes

Brains LOVE rewards, and this critical step is guaranteed to help reinforce your new health habit.

Rewards might include:

- After you drink a full glass of water, you can enjoy a cappuccino.
- After completing fifty sit-ups, you'll mark it off on your fitness tracker.
- Whenever you take a walk, you'll get to catch up on your favorite podcast.
- After you meditate, you can watch anything you want on TV.

Make sure you've identified a specific cue, routine, and reward for each new habit you establish so you can supersize your success.

Think Before You Act

Our habits are typically so unconscious that we need to step back and identify them before we make intentional change. For example, I had no idea how much sugar I was consuming until a nutritionist asked me to jot down exactly what I ate in a typical week. Friends, I was shocked. My client Kathleen had no sense of how overpacked her schedule was until we took a closer look and noticed that most of her scheduling was physically impossible–how could she attend a board meeting in Florida when she was scheduled to be at a wedding in New York at the same time? Although it seems minor, just by improving your *awareness* of your current habits you will be moving toward positive change.

TRY IT

Pay attention! Start noticing your daily habits beginning today. Do you frequently forget to eat or hydrate? Are you active or sedentary during the day? Have you scheduled time for rest? Do you tend to overbook your calendar or spend too much time in solitude? Do you commit to being in bed at a certain time or totally lose track of time? Get curious, and jot down your observations.

Now, Act (but Start Small!)

If you want to shift or improve your habits in a sustainable way, you must focus on building or breaking just ONE habit at a time. Minimalism strikes again! I have years of evidence to prove that when people try to integrate too many habits at once they will probably fail and feel shame and possibly give up on their desired habits altogether. Don't let this be you. Instead, commit to ONE new health habit to try out for the next few months and really nail it. Become Helen-the-Queen-of-Hydration or Maggie-the-Magnificent-Meal-Planner or Rhonda-the-Regular-Runner.

> **TRY IT**
>
> Pick ONE health habit you'll commit to starting *today*. This very day. Write it down. Tell your people if you need accountability. Make it your job to do this one thing consistently each day or week. Remember to make your new habit as specific, simple, and repeatable as possible. Some examples:
>
> - Jen decided to walk her kids to school and run home each morning instead of driving and dealing with traffic and parking.
> - Aya decided to invest in a healthy lunch delivery service Monday through Friday so she could avoid relying on greasy fast food, which made her feel terrible.
> - Betsy set up a thirty-minute check-in with her best friend each Friday so she knew she would have a place to vent and process emotions she often kept cooped up.
>
> Identify your small, good-for-you habit, and then create conditions that will make success inevitable. You can make yourself proud starting today. I'm cheering for you!

HEALTHY HABITS FOR YOUR DAY, WEEK, SEASON, AND YEAR

DAILY PRACTICES

- Eating your fuel foods and ditching the foods that make you feel bloated or tired
- Adding fresh vegetables to each meal
- Drinking half your body weight in ounces of water
- Moving your body for at least thirty minutes
- Taking any prescribed meds, vitamins, and supplements
- Making time to recharge (meditate, take mini breaks, stretch, read, journal, nap)
- Unplugging and prioritizing sleep–ideally at least eight hours per night

WEEKLY SCHEDULING

- Gym, cardio classes, strength training, or any form of feel-good movement
- Therapy, counseling, coaching, or mental health support
- Specialists, such as acupuncturists, herbalists, or nutritionists

SEASONAL SCHEDULING

- Dental cleanings and checkups
- Physical therapy, massages, chiropractic care, or other preventive treatments

ANNUAL SCHEDULING

- Annual screenings, vaccines, and wellness checkups

THE BOTTOM LINE

Our physical and mental health affect every single aspect of our lives, and it's up to us to cultivate positive habits to optimize our physical and mental wellness. Instead of focusing on restriction or rigid rules, concentrate on adding in the good stuff, like fuel foods, hydration, movement, rest, and mental health boosters, like unplugging from technology, getting fresh air, and connecting with others. Automation will make your desired habits more easily repeatable, and by challenging yourself to implement just *one* new health habit at a time you will boost your success rate and make yourself proud.

YOUR PROMPTS

Ready to integrate healthy habits into your daily life? Answer the prompts below to get going on your good-health journey. Remember, the more specific, the better!

- Is prioritizing your health a want or a need right now?
- On a scale of 1 to 5, how satisfied do you feel with your overall mental health?
- On a scale of 1 to 5, how satisfied do you feel with your overall physical health?
- How will you make sure you get enough rest, hydration, fuel foods? What systems and habits will you implement?
- What tiny adjustments could make a big impact on your overall health (what you consume, what time you go to bed, getting support from a professional)?
- What daily or weekly or seasonal automations can you create to optimize your physical and mental health?
- What can you do less of that will impact your health for the better?
- Which habits can you add or integrate to improve your health?
- What are your stress triggers? Emotional eating triggers? What do you want to do instead?
- What is one small but critical habit shift you will commit to making to support your well-being and improve your health?

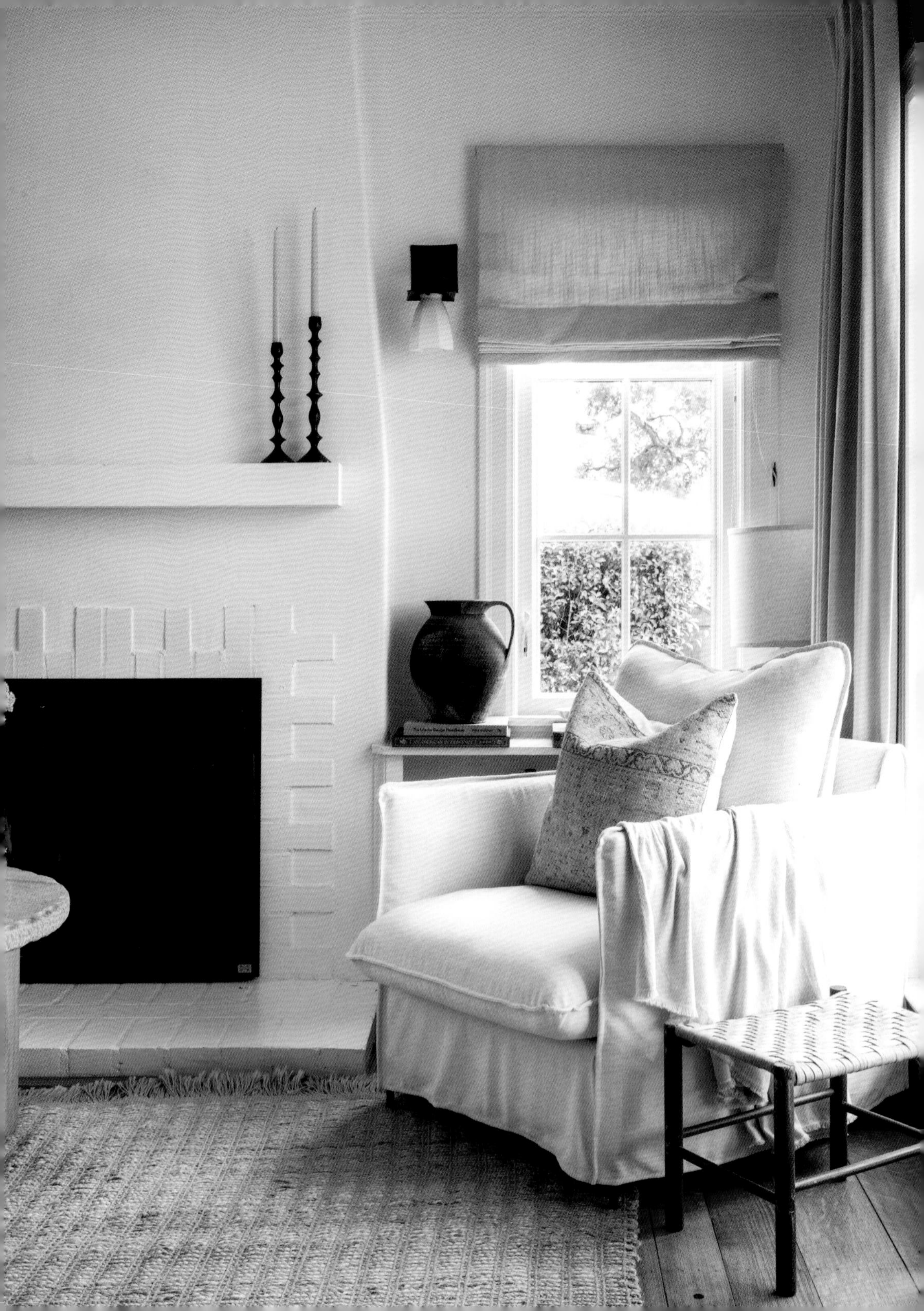

Home and Environment

Is your physical environment currently supporting the vision you have for your best life or is it creating additional barriers, overwhelm, or stress? In this chapter, I'll teach you how to use the volume-system-habits framework to improve your surroundings, boost your mood, and move you closer to your big goals. For better or worse, our surroundings shape our habits, behavior, and results. Want to change your life for the better? Improve your environment. It works. Off we go!

ADJUSTING VOLUME: HOME AND ENVIRONMENT EDITION

My biggest takeaway from organizing hundreds of homes is this: As a society we have a serious volume problem. Overconsumption (particularly in the United States) has become so rampant that we've had to invent a brand-new profession (!) to help people *unstuff* their homes and lives. And don't even get me started on off-site storage. The field of home organization is predicated on a culture that has acquired more than it can keep up with. Our collective excess has led to a whole host of problems, including consumer debt, overstuffed homes, physical and mental stress, and a landfill crisis—one of my clients recently accused his partner of being an *Amazon criminal* because of the volume of packages barricading their front door. But here is the good news! It is never too late to shift our level of consumption and pare down the things that surround us, so our homes feel less suffocating and more manageable. Here's how.

Say No to New

The less stuff you own, the less stuff you'll have to manage. It's simple math. Want more money in your wallet, more spaciousness in your home, and more time to spend doing whatever it is you really want to be doing? Take a break from buying new non-essential things and watch your life improve.

Make It Easy to Donate

From my years in the field, I've noticed that there are plenty of people who genuinely want to donate things they don't need, use, or love, but they don't know where or how. If you've been driving around with a trunk full of donations for the past three months or staring at a pile of overstuffed bags by your front door, you are not alone. Here's what you can do right now to make it easier moving forward.

Identify the following resources in your local community:

1. A convenient spot to drop off clothes, housewares, kid stuff, and furniture. You can always list these items online in your neighborhood, parenting, or community groups, or offer them to places that are already part of your weekly route like your local library, school, nonprofit, community center, theater, church, or temple.

2. A recycling or reuse center that accepts items like old textiles, e-waste, and batteries. Simply look up RECYCLING / REUSE CENTER NEAR ME to find your most convenient drop-off option.

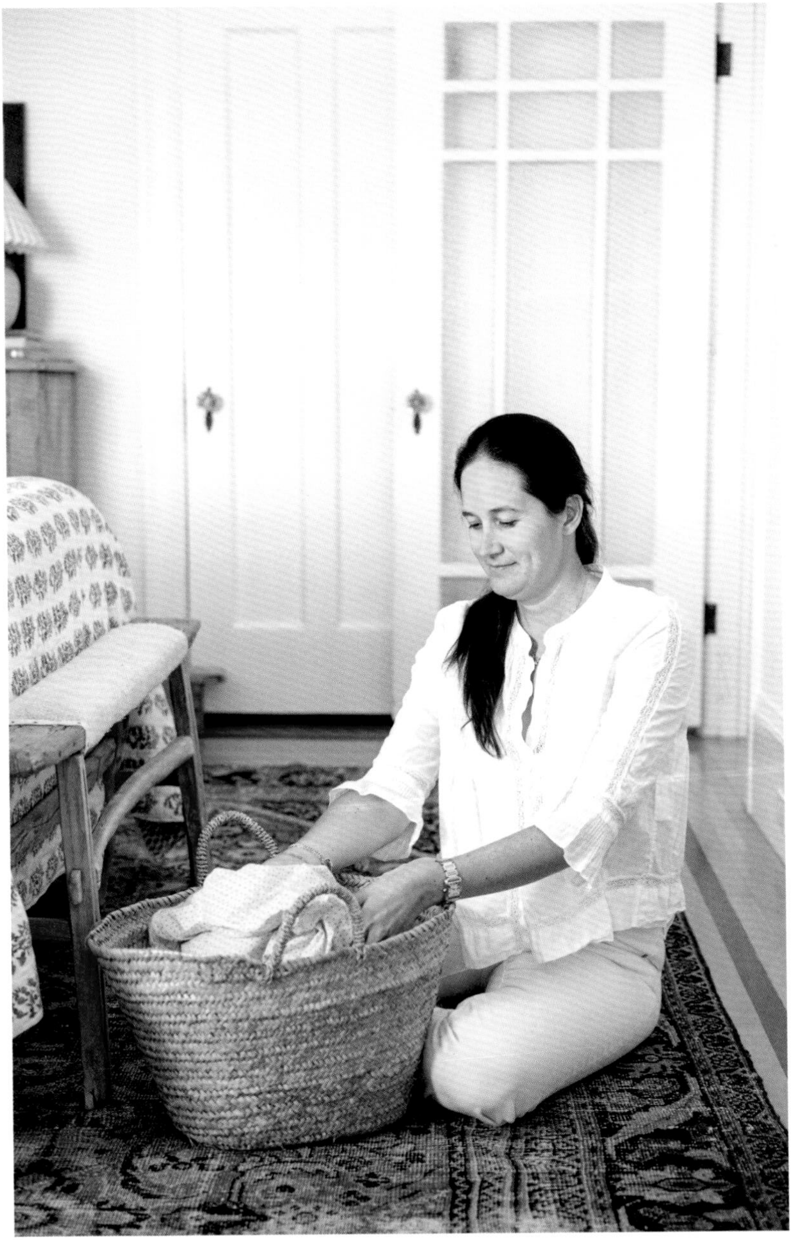

3. A hazardous waste center that can help you safely offload items that are toxic, flammable, or dangerous, like paint, aerosol cans, or gasoline. Simply look up HAZARDOUS WASTE DISPOSAL NEAR ME to find your most convenient drop-off option.

Trust me, I know it seems like a big pain to sort this stuff out and it's just the kind of adulting that gives me a major headache, but do this research just *once* and you will be set for years, or even a lifetime. It feels good to know that you're offloading in a responsible and eco-friendly way, and you may even become a frequent donator and form fun new relationships in your community. (Hi, Frank!)

Take the Shame Out of Your Game

Please take this in: Even if your home reeks of neglect or is teeming with *literal garbage*, I want to assure you that a messy, even chronically disorganized home is not an indictment of your character or inherent value. Dirty dishes, stacks of paper, and heaps of laundry don't mean anything about you as a human being or how worthy you are. They could just mean that you've been busy, tired, distracted, struggling, or overwhelmed. Or maybe you just own more than a person can realistically keep up with and manage. Whatever the reason, let's agree to stop beating ourselves up and put that energy toward creating a home that feels good to you—starting today. Deal?

Start with the Simple Stuff

Editing your home can feel overwhelming, even paralyzing, so here's what I want you to do: Start super small. Nope—even smaller than that. Here are some quick wins that will pack a major punch.

TAKE OUT THE TRASH

Grab a garbage bag and do a quick sweep of your home. You're not trashy if you have trash in your home (you're just human), but who wants to wake up and look at old bills or gum wrappers or the useless plastic nonsense your kids bring home from birthday parties or even the dentist's office. No one, that's who. Do a little trash-pick-up-two-step (kids of any age can help with this) and then promptly take out the trash and recycling. Bravo!

DO THE RELOCATION SHUFFLE

Another quick win. Set a timer for fifteen minutes, walk around your house looking for things that aren't where they belong, and simply put them away. Dump the dirty clothes in your clothes hamper or, better yet, directly in the laundry. Put the stray dishes and coffee mugs in the sink or dishwasher. Tell your kids and other family members to claim their goods from the common living spaces. If they snooze, they lose. Am I really advocating throwing away your family's things? Not directly, but things go missing all the time. . . . Anyhoo, the goal is just to get things back in the rooms they should be living in so they will be easier to find when they are needed.

GET THOSE RETURNS OUT THE DOOR

Round up your borrowed items, library books, and shop returns and get them going, going, gone! It feels like such a big weight to have unfinished business staring you down all the time, which is why it will feel so good to get things moving. I like batching these tasks into a single "get it done day" whenever possible. If you have kids, you can play chauffeur and have them be the "runners," dropping books in the library return slot, leaving borrowed items on your neighbors' stoops, and so on.

EDIT YOUR FACE OFF

Here's what I know for sure: *Reducing volume is the single most impactful thing you can do to instantly improve the look, feel, and function of your home.* Period. End of story. Full stop. Less stuff translates directly into more time, money, energy, freedom, and spaciousness. Since deciding to live with radically less stuff on purpose, I spend so much less time cleaning and organizing. Our home feels more spacious, tidy, and comfortable, and we're always ready for guests to pop over (no frantically

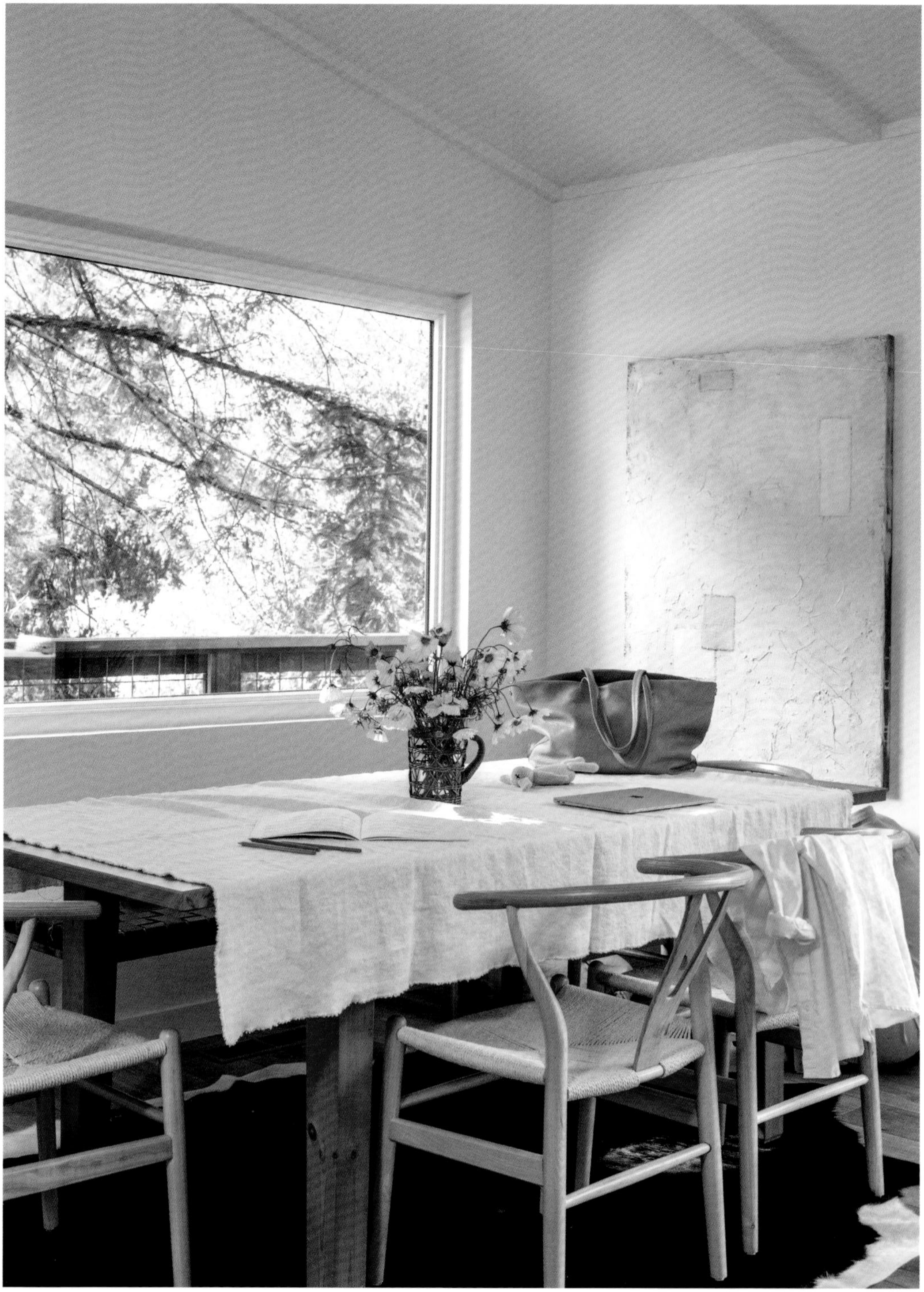

tidying surfaces or shoving things in the closet). Here's the best part: Decluttering your home is totally free and always available. You can shift your relationship with your space and your stuff today just by passing on the things you don't use, need, or love. More good news: It feels really good to be a giver. It's counterintuitive, but one of the quickest ways to feel more abundant is to give generously. You might even make someone's day. I promise you will not regret parting with that dusty old snowboard or that food dehydrator you ordered from an infomercial in the middle of the night ten years ago (and, if you do, you can always rent or borrow one). I also encourage you to let go of things you don't use or need that were expensive and are still in great shape. Being openhearted with your resources reinforces the idea that you have more than enough, and the more you give, the more abundant you will feel. Thank you for coming to my TED Talk. Now, grab your donation bag and start filling it up!

Fifteen-Minute Decluttering Wins

Here is a roundup of quick decluttering projects designed to be completed in fifteen minutes or less. Do not worry about organizing or styling these spaces. Just focus on removing clutter and *decreasing volume*. Roll up your sleeves and do as my friend Elsa from *Frozen* wisely instructed, "Let it go, let it gooooo . . ."

- Edit your makeup and cosmetics.
- Minimize your bathroom products.
- Clean out your medicine cabinet.
- Clear off your nightstand.
- Thin out your sock drawer.
- Pare down your cleaning supplies.
- Transform your junk drawer.
- Declutter your linen closet.
- Edit your coffee mugs.
- Curate your desk or work surface.

If you can commit to a single fifteen-minute win each day (or even each week), your quick wins will stack and compound to create big, transformative results over time.

EDIT, THEN ELEVATE

In my own home, I crave comfort, spaciousness, and beauty. I want to *minimize* the things I have to manage, clean, organize, and maintain, while *maximizing* aesthetics and functionality. By paring down to the essentials, we can simplify our lives. By adding items of beauty or significance, we can make our homes feel aligned, authentic, and personal. When it comes to adjusting volume in your home, I'm quite partial to reduction, but it's also worth considering how you can consciously, intentionally *add* elements of beauty and personal expression—I call this *elevating the space*. While beauty is often dismissed as superficial, the value and impact of creating beauty in your home should not be underestimated. Aesthetic pleasure has a profound impact on our emotions, creativity, and well-being, lifting our spirits, reducing stress, and promoting feelings of overall contentment. Here are some low-effort ways you can add in these moments of beauty and joy throughout your space.

Highlight Personal Objects

Add art, photography, or objects that feel special, personal, and meaningful. One of my clients had little jars of sand displayed on her mantel, representing all the beaches she had traveled to since childhood. I framed and displayed a heavily annotated recipe for mac and cheese my father used to make for me when I was little. My friend Leila loves to decorate her home with found items from her travels—a smooth rock from Tel Aviv, a feather from Costa Rica. Consider putting these meaningful items in unexpected places, like your closet or propped up on a kitchen shelf.

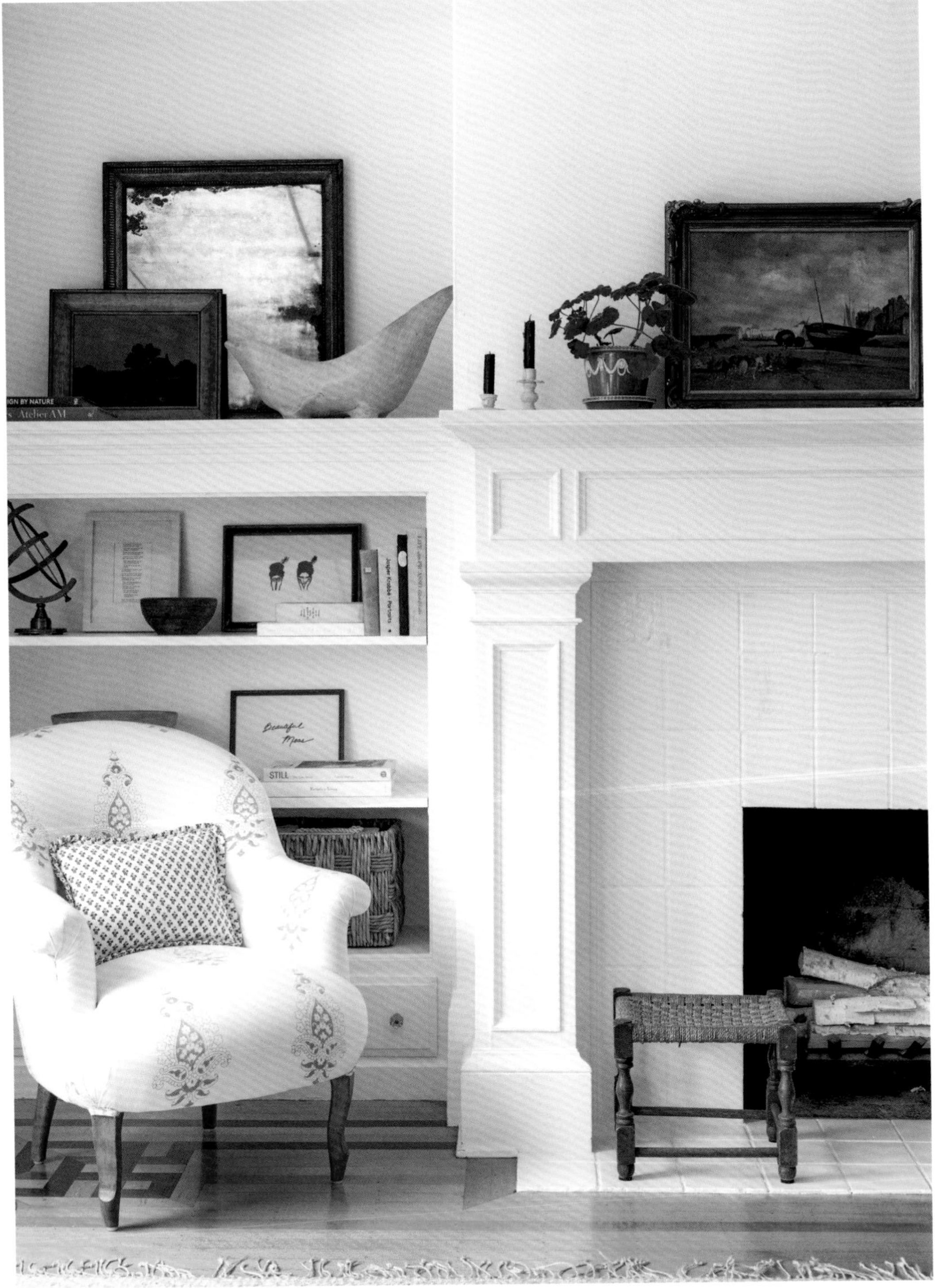
Atelier AM
Jasper Krabbé · Portraits
STILL

THE MINIMALIST HOME–
A CUSTOMIZABLE CHECKLIST

If you're looking to downsize, right-size, or just experiment with a minimalist lifestyle, start by making a comprehensive list of the things you *need* and then a list of the things you *want*. Creating a thoughtful inventory will enable you to start fresh and be more intentional about the things you own and bring into your home. Here are some examples of items I've chosen to live with purposefully–a combination of my wants and needs.

Furniture and Home Decor

Beds and Bedding (need)

Area Rugs (want)

Candles (want)

Books and Art

Dining Table and Chairs (need)

Couch (need)

Kitchen Essentials

Stove / Oven (need)

Refrigerator (need)

Toaster Oven (want)

Ice Cream Maker (want, but also need)

Ice Cream Scoops (need, need, need!)

Dining Essentials

Napkins (need)

Placemats (want)

Serving Bowls and Platters (need)

Vases, Candles, and Seasonal Decor (want)

Household Essentials

All-Purpose Cleaner (need)

Laundry Detergent (need)

Paper Towels (want)

First Aid Kit and Medications (need)

Emergency Kit and Flashlights (need)

Personal Care Products

Shampoo and Conditioner (need)

Body Wash and Face Soap (need)

Toothbrush, Toothpaste, and Floss (need)

Face Cream (want)

Nail Polish and Face Masks (want)

Wardrobe

Daily Uniform: Jeans, Blouses / Sweaters (need)

Shoes (need)

Socks, Underwear (need)

Jewelry and Other Accessories (want)

Light Jackets and Coat (need)

Storage Essentials

Memorabilia (want)

Letters (want)

Tax Documents (need)

House Documents (need)

House Paint (need)

TRY IT

Make your own list. Start with your needs. What do you require to eat, sleep, live, and work? Then add in your wants, or nice-to-haves. What are the things that elevate your home and enhance your quality of life? What do you want to add or keep on purpose? Making this intentional and customized list can help illuminate how little you really *need* and (bonus!) help you be much more intentional about what you acquire moving forward.

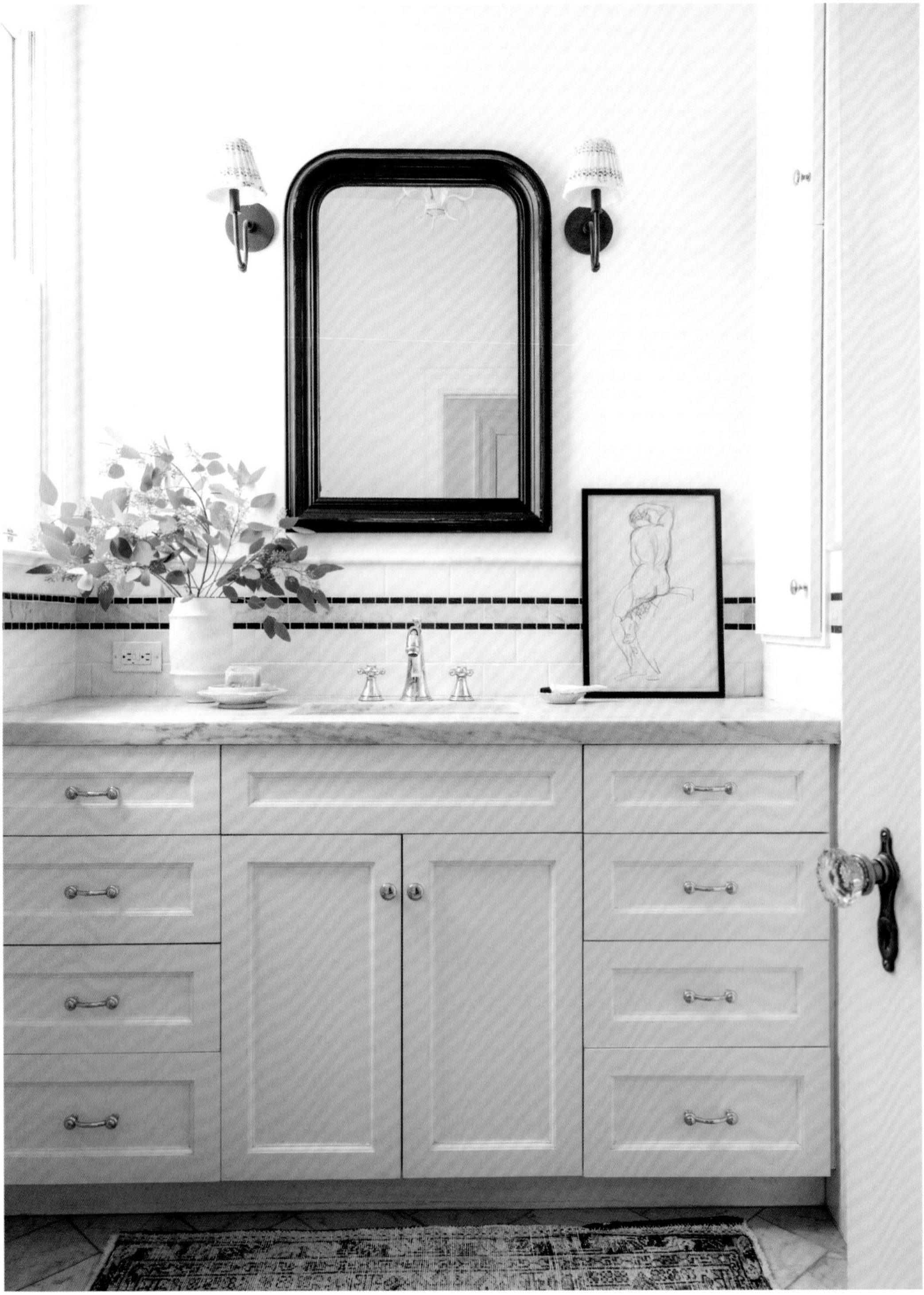

Let There Be Life

Add some potted plants to your living spaces. Display some garden clippings or branches in your favorite vase. Treat yourself to a beautiful floral arrangement for your nightstand. It's shocking how much bringing the outdoors in can do to refresh and beautify your space.

Invest in Fewer, Better Things

I can't stress enough how impactful it can be to upgrade the items you engage with every single day. Invest in one set of high-quality sheets and towels that you love. Treat yourself to hand, dish, and body soap in pretty glass bottles with pumps. Toss your kitchen sponge and replace it with a stylish and sustainable wooden dish brush. These thoughtful upgrades will improve your space and might even boost your mood.

Make It Uniform

A little home-organizing hack: When investing in storage vessels, opt for a singular style and color to create a calming aesthetic that's also nice to look at. Try matching wooden hangers in the entry, a row of identical bins in the pantry, a stack of uniform storage boxes in your home office. Environmental uniformity means less visual information for your brain to process and more energy for your mind to spend on other pursuits.

Add a Fresh Coat of Paint

Want to refresh your space without breaking the bank? Just add paint. A fresh coat of paint will make your pantry, or closet, feel brand-new. You can also use the magic of paint to transform a bench, side table, or other furniture. My colleague Devin (founder of the Modern Minimalist) even spray-paints the doorknobs, light fixtures, and cabinet hardware in her rental apartment for a more customized and cohesive aesthetic.

Spruce It Up

My friend Naomi, a busy ER doctor with three children, sets the table each night with a beautiful linen tablecloth, a pitcher of water with lemon, and a few beeswax candles. Despite a grueling work schedule and kids who need her attention, she takes this moment each evening to create a little calm amid the chaos. Elevating your surroundings doesn't have to take a lot of effort. Light a candle. Turn on some music. Use the good china. Add lemon wedges to your pitcher of water. Put some garden clippings in a mason jar. Surround yourself with beauty whenever possible.

Make It Easy on the Eyes

While I am all for elevating the utilitarian items in your home (I see you, stylish scissors and cute tape dispenser.), most of us also own practical items, such as chew toys for your pup or that training potty for your toddler, that aren't exactly lovely to look at. Here's what to do: *Conceal* all of your unsightly (but necessary) items behind closed doors and *display* only the items you love to look at. My very stylish friend Fiona who lives in a space-challenged home in San Francisco installed white, slim IKEA cabinets all over her home to tuck away housewares like her tool kit, gift wrap, batteries, light bulbs, and house paint. The cabinets disappear into her white walls, resulting in a streamlined aesthetic that's both clean and functional.

Do the "Stuff versus Space" Calculus

When it comes to arriving at the right volume for you, you'll just need to clarify which you value more—stuff or space. Ask yourself, "Am I more attached to my physical possessions or the opportunity to have more open space in my home?" A combination of editing and elevating will help you arrive at the perfect amount for you. There is truly no right or wrong here. It's about making decisions that support the life you want to live in the environment that feels best to you.

Creating Systems: Home and Environment Edition

The goal of a system is to solve a problem or create a specific outcome or result. Before you start setting up systems in your home, it's worthwhile to step back and consider how you want your home and environment to look, feel, and function. Do you want to create a quiet retreat? A family homestead? An artistic abode? What specific activities do you want to facilitate? Gathering? Eating? Working? Relaxing? Creating? Once you have a clear vision, you can start to set up specific systems that support the life you want to live.

Example 1. In my own home, we have a party bin we keep stocked with non-perishable treats, cocktail napkins, votive candles, wine openers, and basic decor. This system makes it easy to welcome guests and host at a moment's notice.

Example 2. My client Amanda wanted to make it easier to work out at home since she was struggling to get to the gym with three young kids and a full-time job. We set up a workout bin in her living room, stocked with weights, resistance bands, and a yoga mat. This simple system enabled her to get a little movement in even when she was just watching TV or hanging out with her toddlers.

Example 3. My client Nora lives and works out of a small garden apartment in Brooklyn, New York. She wanted to create a clear boundary between her career and her personal life but was tight on space. The solution was simple: We set up a rolling cart where she could store her work supplies, including her laptop and portable printer, and tuck the cart into her closet when she was done with work each day. Out of sight and out of mind!

Consider: What problems do you want to solve in your own home? Which activities or habits do you want to facilitate?

TEN GAME-CHANGING SYSTEMS
FOR YOUR HOME

Below is a roundup of the ten simple systems that I set up in nearly every single home, regardless of style, size, or budget. Try them, keep the ones that resonate, and create your own that make sense for you.

The Entry Station

This one is super simple but can be truly transformative. Every home needs a place to drop bags, coats, shoes, mail, dog leashes, baby carriers, and all the other things that come and go each day. Take a quick inventory of what typically gets dropped by the front door (or dumped elsewhere), and create simple systems to contain them in your entry area. I suggest sturdy hooks for coats, bags, and hats, a basket or tray for mail, and cubbies or just a simple basket for shoes. If space allows, set up a durable tray, basket, or tiered shelf to drop rain or hiking boots, soccer cleats (there will be no more turf pellets in my home), and other messy business. If you have specific items you like to stow by the front door like AirPods, gloves, sunscreen, or hand sanitizer, you can corral them in a bin, basket, or tray for easy access. Note: Most entryways have a major volume problem. If you're struggling to set up systems because you can't sort out how to contain thirty-two pairs of shoes, and a mountain of coats, start by editing down to the essentials and relocating items that are out of season.

The Inbox

Probably the simplest but most effective system in my entire home. We have a single basket that sits on a credenza in our entryway and serves as our family inbox. The inbox contains incoming mail, bills, and invitations, as well as school forms the kids need us to sign—basically anything that requires action or attention. I do my best to sit down, review, and process the contents of the inbox once a week so the pile never turns into a paper mountain. I swear this simple system is one of the most impactful things you can do to feel more in control and on top of your life.

Set up *one* centralized place in your home to corral all mail, bills, forms, invites, and paper documents that require your attention. A tray, bin, basket, or wall-mounted pocket will do the trick. Your new mantra will be: "Farewell random piles of paper strewn all over my home. I've got an inbox!" Also, please don't panic if your pile is less of a molehill and more of a Mount Everest situation at first. That's totally normal, and if you chip away at it fifteen minutes a day you'll be feeling sweet relief in no time.

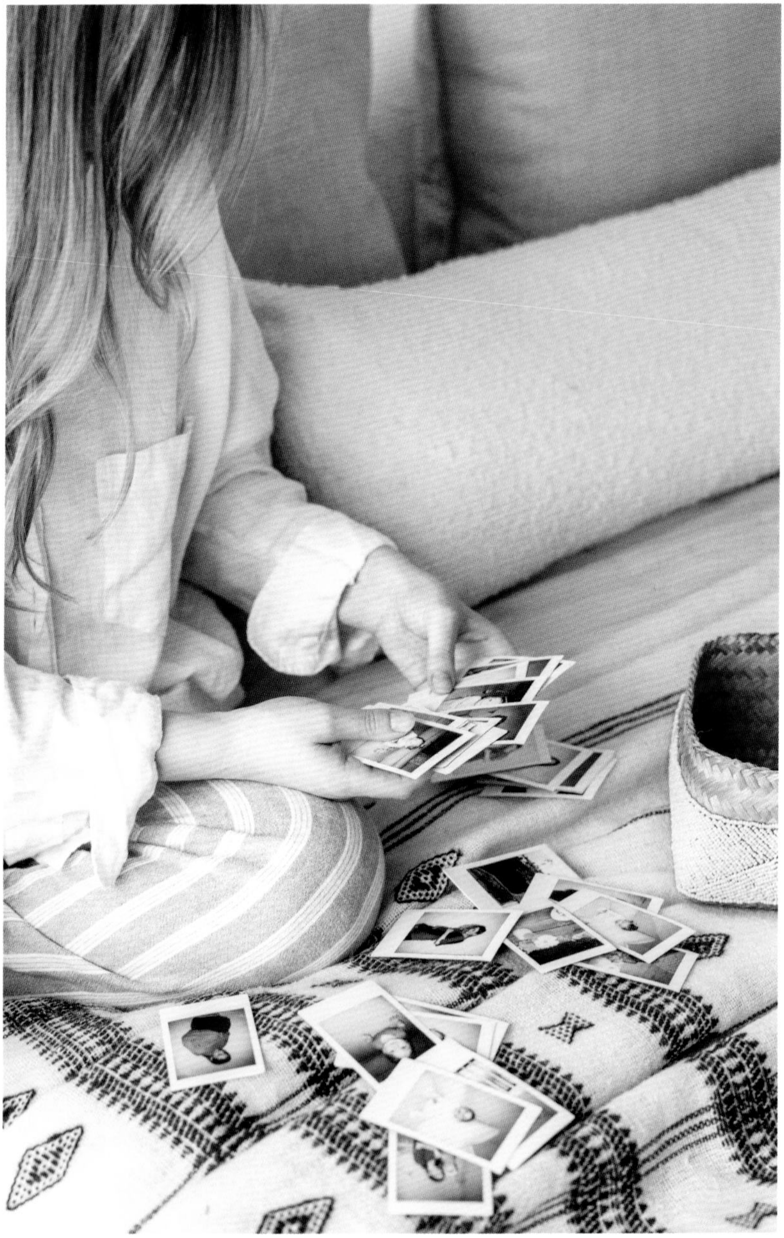

The Memento Bin

One of the most common questions I get from clients is "What do I do with this card / note / art / letter / photograph / memento?" I like to keep things simple so I always suggest a single box for each member of the family that can serve as a catchall for anything that's deeply sentimental. Slap a label on it, store it in a convenient place (closet shelf, desk drawer, or bookshelf) and be discerning with what you fill it with.

The Out-the-Door Basket

An out-the-door basket is a simple hack you can use to cut the clutter by the front door and corral the items you frequently need as you head out the door. Since we don't have a proper entryway, I hang an oversized French market tote on a hook by the front door, and it functions as a catchall for everything from my daughter's bike helmet to the dog's leash, harness, and balls. The beauty is we can dump these unsightly (but necessary) items in the basket and easily grab what we need as we head out the door. If you find yourself without a place to centralize shop returns, library books, or the roasting pan you borrowed from your neighbor, an oversized hanging tote or basket placed near the front door will do the trick.

The No-Stress Paper Storage Solution

Friends, there is no need to overcomplicate paper processing and storage—life is simply too short. As far as I'm concerned paperwork always fits into one of three categories and can be easily systematized:

Action Items: Anything that needs your eyes or attention. Pop in your inbox and commit to reviewing and processing everything in that inbox at least once a week.

Reference Materials: Items you need to keep but only reference occasionally, like insurance info, home-related documents, wills and trusts, or receipts. Store in broad categories in file folders in a file box, cabinet, or even standing files. Add labels to make it easy to find what you need.

Archival Items: The boring stuff you have to keep, but never touch, like past tax records or original house plans (make sure to consult your CPA or tax professional if you need to clarify which documents you need to hold on to). Store these items in airtight, weatherproof, labeled bins in a cool, dry place.

No need to color-code, alphabetize, or overcomplicate this. When it comes to paper, it pays to make things as simple as possible.

The Activity Tote

Not sure how to store your gear and accessories for specific activities? Enter the activity tote. Most of us already own a whole collection of tote bags, so let's put them to good use. Take the gear, uniforms, and accessories you use for sports, hobbies, and outings, and centralize these items in their own tote bags. My daughter Chloe has a bag with her ice skates, warm hat, and gloves that she can grab right before ice-skating lessons each week. My daughter Emilie has a soccer tote stocked with cleats, shin guards, sunscreen, and headbands that she brings to practice each day. Jordan keeps a small duffel ready for the gym that contains sneakers, workout gear, deodorant, and extra headphones. I avoid all sports but do keep a tote in my trunk with picnic gear (competitive picnicking?), so I'm ready for summertime outings with friends and family.

The Art Gallery

If your kids are prolific artists (like mine, yay—but also, oy!), enter the "art gallery." In our house it's a strip of sheet metal (bought from a hardware store on the cheap), mounted with screws onto our kitchen wall that uses magnets to display the current favorites. As the kids produce more and more art, they get to decide which items stay displayed, and which get rotated out (either recycled or moved into the single bin each kid has to store their most treasured creations). Art is meant to be seen and enjoyed, not shoved in dusty bins in the basement, and this simple system ensures that the art they create is celebrated. Hooray! If you're not interested in drilling sheet metal into your wall (understandable), you can use an oversized corkboard, a long ribbon with clothespins, or the good old-fashioned magnet-on-refrigerator method. Display away!

The Tech Hub

Modern life seems to come with a whole bunch of pesky charging cords, doesn't it (holds head in hands)? While my general rule is to ditch as much as possible, we always end up with a small collection of headphones, cords, and cables that my family claim are totally necessary. Fine. But in order not to have them floating aimlessly around our home, I have set up a bin labeled Tech Hub, so it is all out of sight. Our bin is tucked away in our media cabinet in the living room, and whenever anyone is frantically looking for anything tech-related, they can predict my response: "Check the tech hub." If it's not there, it's not anywhere. Thank you, and good night. Bonus: You can use cord labels to jot down which cord belongs to which device, and put an end to the game of what-does-this-belong-to-and-do-I-even-need-it?

The Three Sheets to the... Bin

For those of you rare unicorns who have mastered the art of folding the fitted sheet in a perfect compact little bundle, I bow down to you. For the rest of us, allow me to introduce you to the concept of the "Bedding Bin." After spending far too many waking hours watching sheet folding tutorials, I've made peace with the fact that expert folding is just not my zone of genius. Instead of staring at a linen closet packed full of very sad-looking, balled-up sheet bundles to remind me of this truth, I pop each backup set of bedding (we keep one extra set per bed) in a labeled linen bin that beautifully conceals my poor folding. The bins create a cohesive aesthetic in our linen closet that's both pleasing to look at and functional to house our sheets and pillowcases together in organized harmony. Yes, please!

The Stray Sock Solution

If you've had it with trying to track down stray socks (seriously, where do they migrate to?) to pair up long-lost mates, I've got an easy hack for you: Invest in *one* style and color of sock. That's it. That's the whole hack.

IMPLEMENTING HABITS: HOME AND ENVIRONMENT EDITION

Even the most brilliant systems will be rendered useless if we fail to practice and uphold consistent habits. When it comes to your home, ask yourself: What is the result I want to create? Which habits will help me get there? In our house, we've implemented a handful of consistent habits that result in a tidy, easy-to-manage home.

DAILY

- Make the beds.
- Put away sleepwear.
- After breakfast: Place dishes in sink and do a quick wipe-down of counters and dining table (my home office!).
- After school / work: Drop shoes, jackets, backpacks, and mail in our entry station.
- Bring water bottles and lunch boxes to the sink.
- After dinner: Clear the table and wipe down all surfaces.
- Wash, dry, and put away the dishes.
- Make school lunches and prep water bottles.

WEEKLY

- Review inbox and process mail, bills, school forms, and invitations.
- Do a quick fridge cleanout and wipe-down.
- Grocery-shop for the week and restock fridge and pantry.
- Do laundry every Sunday.

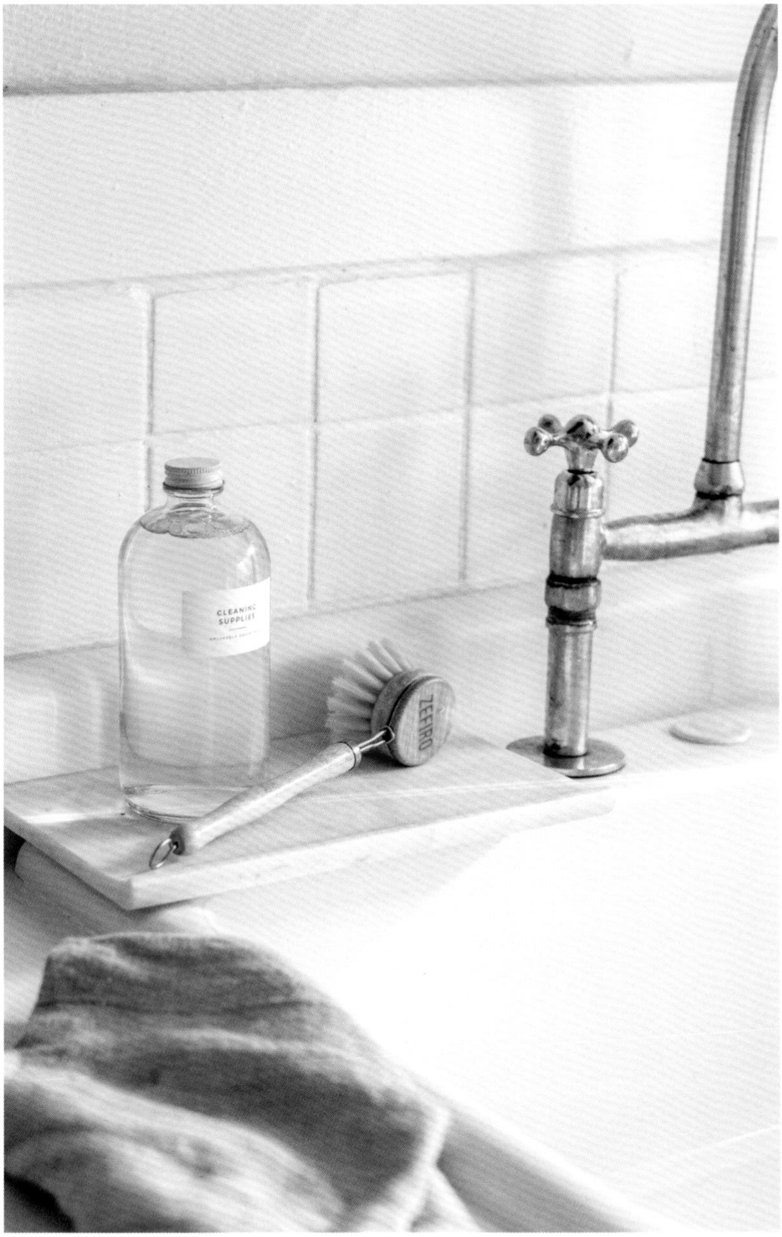
CLEANING
SUPPLIES
ZEFIRO

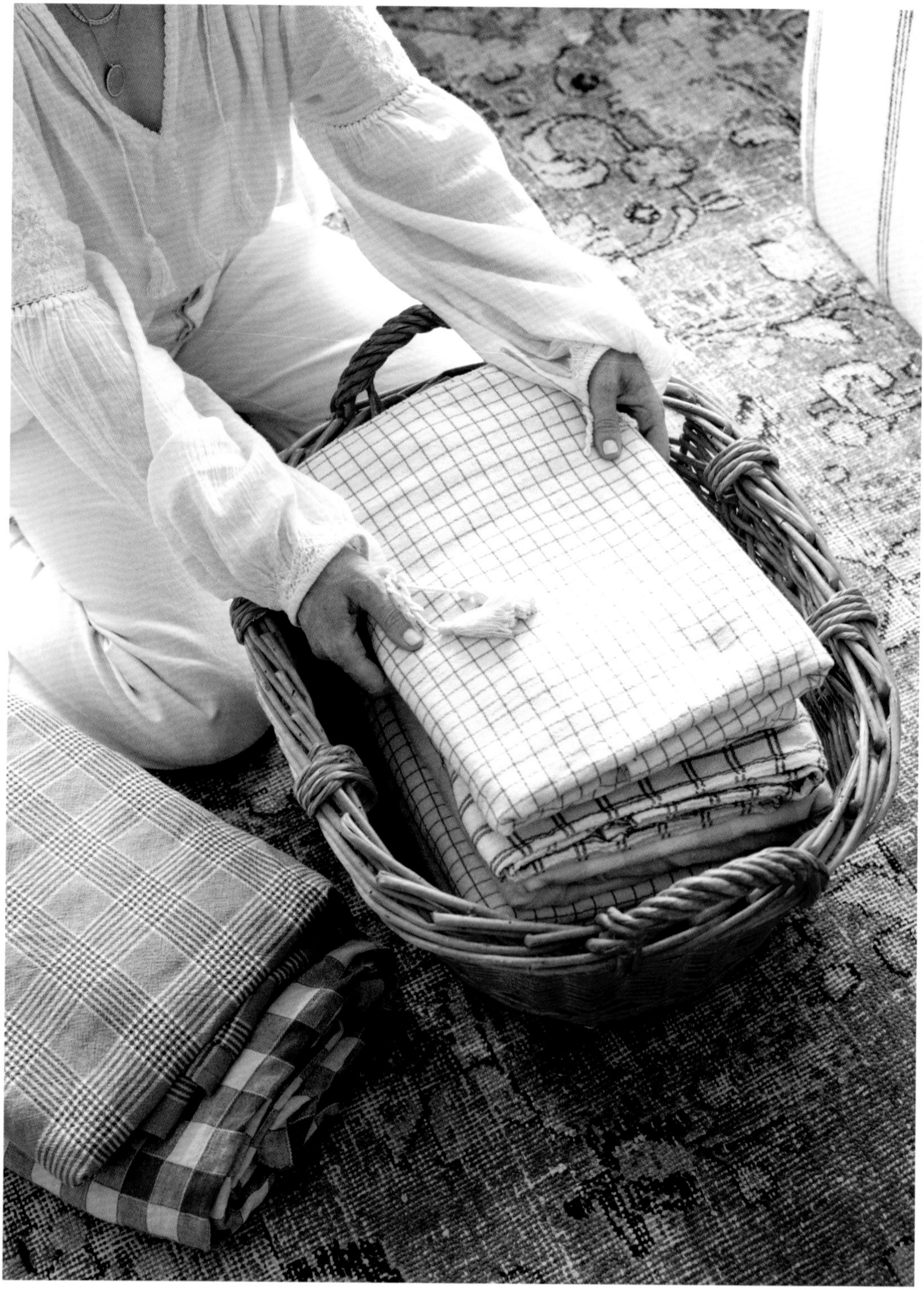

SEASONALLY

- Lightly edit clothing, housewares, books, and games (typically before birthdays and holidays when new items will be coming in).
- Swap seasonal items like heavy coats and boots for summer hats and sunscreen by the front door.

ANNUALLY

- Declutter files and paperwork.
- File taxes and add records labeled by year to our tax box, stored in our basement.
- Clean out closets.
- Refresh pillow and mattress covers that are past their prime.
- Do a deep house clean (eek—those baseboards and vents get so dusty).

TRY IT

Which daily habits will you start implementing to get you closer to your #housegoals? I suggest starting with one small new habit and integrating more only once you've mastered the first one. Since the biggest pain points for people tend to be dishes, laundry, and paperwork, I suggest starting with one of the following:

- Implement a regular laundry schedule so your laundry doesn't pile up, or even consider outsourcing your laundry to a local wash-and-fold service (my friend Laura says this has changed her life!).
- Designate one day a week to review and process paperwork (we love Sunday evenings for this dreaded task and always add treats or snacks).
- Implement a consistent dishwashing routine at the end of each day. I've tasked my teenagers with knocking out the dishes each night after dinner and it only takes them fifteen minutes to wash, dry, and put away (no drying rack or dishwasher necessary).

THE BOTTOM LINE

The most impactful thing you can do to make your home easier to manage is to reduce the volume of things you own and stop buying new things recklessly, without clarity or intentionality. Setting up simple systems to corral the things you use and love into intuitive categories will make it easier for you to find what you need with ease. Consistent habit implementation will reinforce your desired systems and help them stick.

YOUR PROMPTS

Want to take the first step to get the home and environment you've always wanted? These prompts will get you started:

- Rank how satisfied you are with your physical environment on a scale of 1 to 5.

- Jot down a few tiny changes that would instantly improve the state of your home; e.g., clearing a cluttered surface, organizing a drawer, dropping off the donation bags piled by the front door.

- Identify one small thing you can subtract to improve your home.

- Clarify one small thing you can add to improve your home.

- Sort out how you can optimize and systematize your physical environment to improve your desired results in terms of intimacy, relaxation, creativity, and quality family time. Consider what you would you need to add / subtract.

- Commit to one small but critical new habit you will implement to improve the form or function of your space.

THREE WAYS TO MAKE YOUR HOME HABITS STICK

1. Bring in the Troops!

Why do we always think we have to do everything alone? I suggest looking for every possible opportunity to employ help and support when it comes to home maintenance (and really everything else in life). As my old summer camp director used to say, "Shared space is shared responsibility!" Consider how can you delegate or share in tasks, chores, and home upkeep with your partner, housemates, or children. Even *toddlers* can put toys back where they belong and help with small tasks like taking in the mail or breaking down cardboard boxes for recycling. I had a wild idea one night when I was exhausted: that my preteen daughters were perfectly capable of washing and putting away the dishes. My suggestion was met with minimal resistance (I'm shocked, too!) and their consistent help with this task has been a game changer for our busy family.

2. Create Habit Loops

Habit loops typically consist of a *cue* (something that triggers us to take action), a *routine* (a series of actions), and a *reward* (a feel-good result). The habits that have been the most consistently upheld in my home consist of all three components.

Example 1. The Entry Loop

Cue: The girls arrive home after school.

Routine: They immediately remove their shoes and place them in the basket by the door, hang their backpacks on the hooks in the entry, and bring their lunch boxes and water bottles to the sink.

Reward: They have free time to relax and eat really good snacks.

This habit loop has been reinforced for so long it's become second nature.

Example 2. The Post-Dinner Loop

Cue: We make a point of eating dinner as a family most weeknights. Jordan cooks–bless that man!

Routine: Immediately following dinner, we clear all the dishes and I wipe down all of the surfaces and wrap up leftovers while the girls wash and dry the dishes and then prep their school lunches for the next day.

Reward: Once completed, we have a clean kitchen and free time for relaxing, watching a family show, or a mini excursion to get a post-dinner treat.

This habit loop has been going strong for nearly five years now and only takes about twenty minutes in total.

Example 3. Get Your Trash Out of My Car

Cue: Parking the car.

Routine: I remind my children that my vehicle is not a trash receptacle and they remove all of their belongings, including trash and recycling from the back seat.

Reward: They get to get out of the car and move on with their lives!

Hot tip: The reward is the most important part of forming new habit loops because the brain is wired to seek pleasure. Make sure that every time you complete your new habit you remember to treat yourself. High five!

3. Reframe the Game

Mindset is everything. If you're struggling to cultivate a new home habit because it feels annoying and unpleasant, try on an attitude of gratitude and abundance. When I *really* don't want to do the laundry or dishes, I remind myself that I am one of the lucky ones who has a warm, cozy home filled with creature comforts like nice clothing and housewares. By saying "I get to" instead of "I have to," I can instantly shift my perspective. Note: This is not about toxic positivity, but rather, an opportunity to flip the script on how we think about our habits. Saying, "I'm doing the dishes because I want to have a clean and tidy kitchen when I wake up" instead of "Ugh, I have to do the dishes" makes a world of difference in how we approach the task and feel while we're completing it.

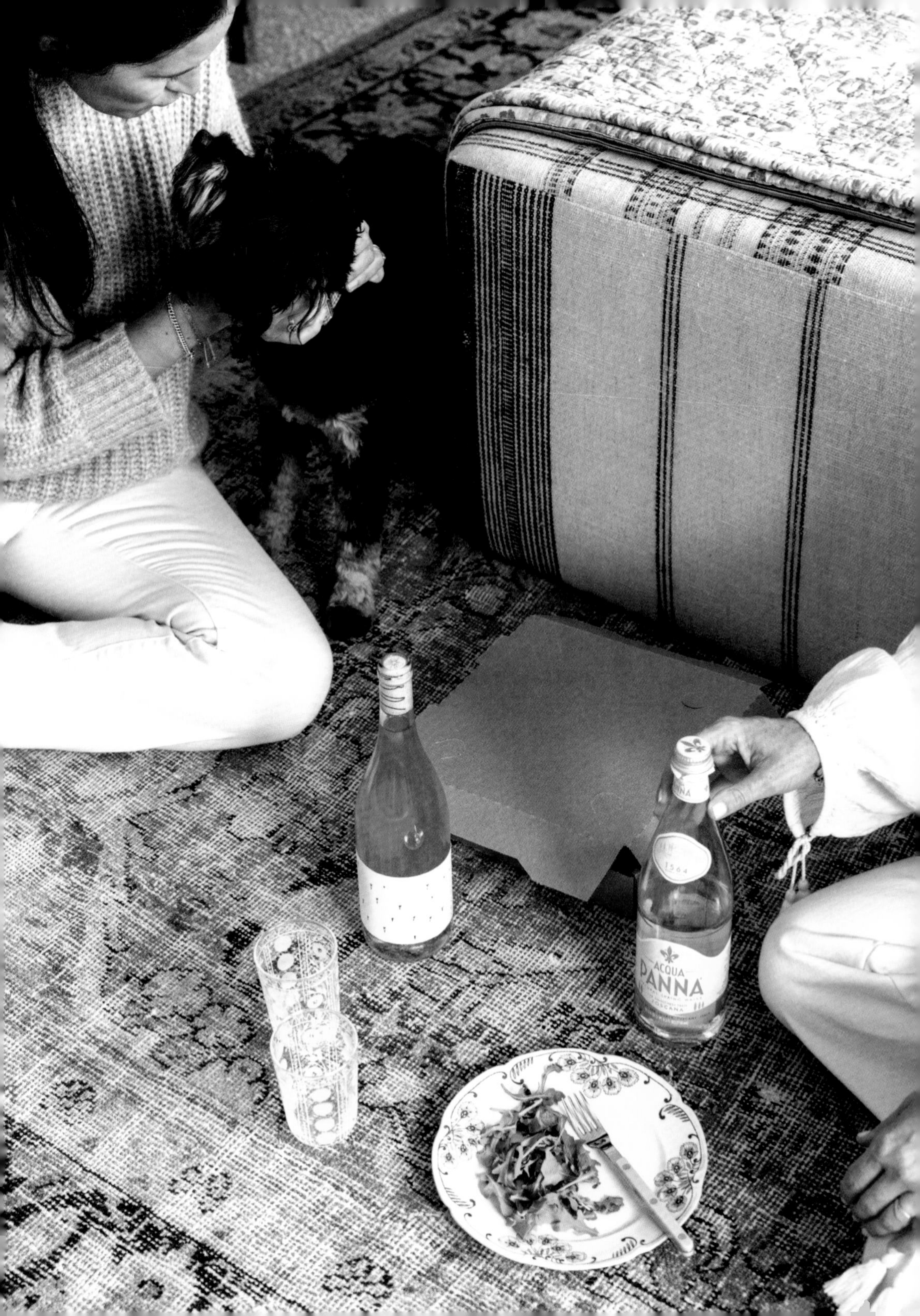
1564
ACQUA
PANNA

Relationships
and Community

Much has been said about the power and importance of maintaining a strong sense of community, yet the many pressures of modern life, combined with the proliferation of technological tools geared toward convenience and efficiency, can leave us feeling isolated, disconnected, and lonely. If you're feeling adrift when it comes to the relationships in your life, you're not alone (see what I did there?). By getting clear on what's lacking, or where you're spread too thin, you can start to edit and improve the personal relationships in your life.

ADJUSTING VOLUME:
RELATIONSHIPS AND COMMUNITY EDITION

Whether you feel bogged down by too many relationships to successfully juggle, or find yourself craving more intimacy in your life, the volume tool can help you recalibrate and improve this critical part of your life. Get ready to turn up the volume on fulfilling and meaningful connections and dial it down on draining relationships and social plans.

Start with Yourself

Perhaps the most important relationship we will ever establish is the one with ourselves. This is difficult but critical work. I believe that all of us are 100 percent complete, whole, and worthy all on our own, even though messages in the media might tell us otherwise. Forming a strong relationship with yourself will boost your self-confidence, resilience, independence, and freedom—and, ironically, greatly improve your relationship with others. Here are some ways to get started:

- Disconnect to reconnect: Try unplugging and taking yourself on a solo date. You could take a book to a café, go on a hike in nature, treat yourself to dinner and a movie—whatever sounds appealing and helps you get comfortable being out in the world as a party of one.

- Lean in to your personal preferences: Identify how you most enjoy spending time and cultivate your own interests and passions. Stop putting energy into things you don't care about.

- Make peace with the whole package: Instead of beating yourself up for perceived weaknesses or failures, treat yourself with empathy, kindness, and acceptance, the way you would treat a child, or a puppy, or your BFF. Decide which parts of your personality you want to lean in to and embrace, and which things you want to shift or work on.

- Start a writing practice: Writing is a great way to tap into your unconscious and get to know parts of yourself that may not be at the forefront. Try jotting down a stream of consciousness first thing when you wake up or try writing a letter to your future self about your greatest hopes and aspirations. Be curious and pay attention to what emerges.

- Celebrate your successes: Most of us are very good at celebrating others but quickly dismiss our own victories and even deny ourselves the feeling of pride altogether. The next time you accomplish something, *anything*, make sure to properly acknowledge it. Tell yourself, "Good job, I'm proud of you. Well done, you!" as often as possible.

Developing a strong relationship with yourself is essential for personal growth, overall well-being, and the ability to foster healthier connections with others. Be open to exploring new methods and commit to prioritizing self-discovery and appreciation. Three cheers for you—from you!

Curate Your Ideal Connection Cadence

My husband is so extroverted that he literally strolls around our neighborhood greeting strangers and hoping he runs into someone (anyone!) he can strike up conversation with. On the other hand, I love the people, but I also become a hollow shell of myself when I don't have enough alone time. After a few hours of solid socializing, my body and brain completely shut down and I need to flee the scene to recharge. I used to reject this sensitive part of myself, but the older I get, the more I lean in to it. I've been known to put end times on party invites and unapologetically duck out of late-night events by 10 p.m. to go to bed. Put a fork in me, I'm done. The point is, we all need to strike the right balance between meaningful connection with others and a strong relationship with ourselves. What is your ideal connection cadence? Start by identifying where you're longing for more or less connection. Consider your relationship with:

- Yourself
- Your friends
- Your partner, spouse, close friend, or dating life
- Your larger community

If you're feeling maxed out by an overstuffed social calendar, you might consider editing your plans and declining future invitations until you can catch your breath. If you're feeling hungry for more intimacy or connection with others, you'll need to invest more in cultivating new or more meaningful relationships. Consider how often you would ideally want to:

- Meet up with friends
- Go out on dates
- Be intimate with a partner
- Connect with a greater community

How many social plans would you like to have in a week? How many bigger events or parties would you like to attend per season or year? How frequently would you like to engage with your neighborhood or community? If the answer is exactly zero, that's okay. Just make sure to get as specific as possible about your unique needs and clearly define your ideal connection cadence.

Cut the Relationship Clutter

Anyone ever feel super lonely, even though they *seem* wildly social and busy from the outside? I'll go first. I did. All the time. Or at least I used to when I was friends with everyone and no one at the same time. Introverted tendencies aside, I am a very social person, but I have often fallen into the trap of having a ton of friends and acquaintances I see in random bits and bursts when all I really wanted was a few very tight, consistent relationships. Fewer, better friendships? Sign me up. Over the past several years I've leaned in to prioritizing a handful of very close friendships and cutting back on the superficial or draining connections that just didn't feel valuable or fulfilling. My new relationship motto is *all killer, no filler.*

TRY IT

How can you build your relationship dream team? Start by identifying which current connections you'd like to cultivate or invest in more, and which relationships drain or distract you. Make sure you're prioritizing the relationships that sustain you and divesting from the ones that don't feel worth your while— even if that's hard or awkward to do.

Clarify Your Relationship Deal Breakers

What are your values with regard to friendships and partnerships? We all have different standards and boundaries when it comes to what we will and won't tolerate. Here are my relationship deal breakers:

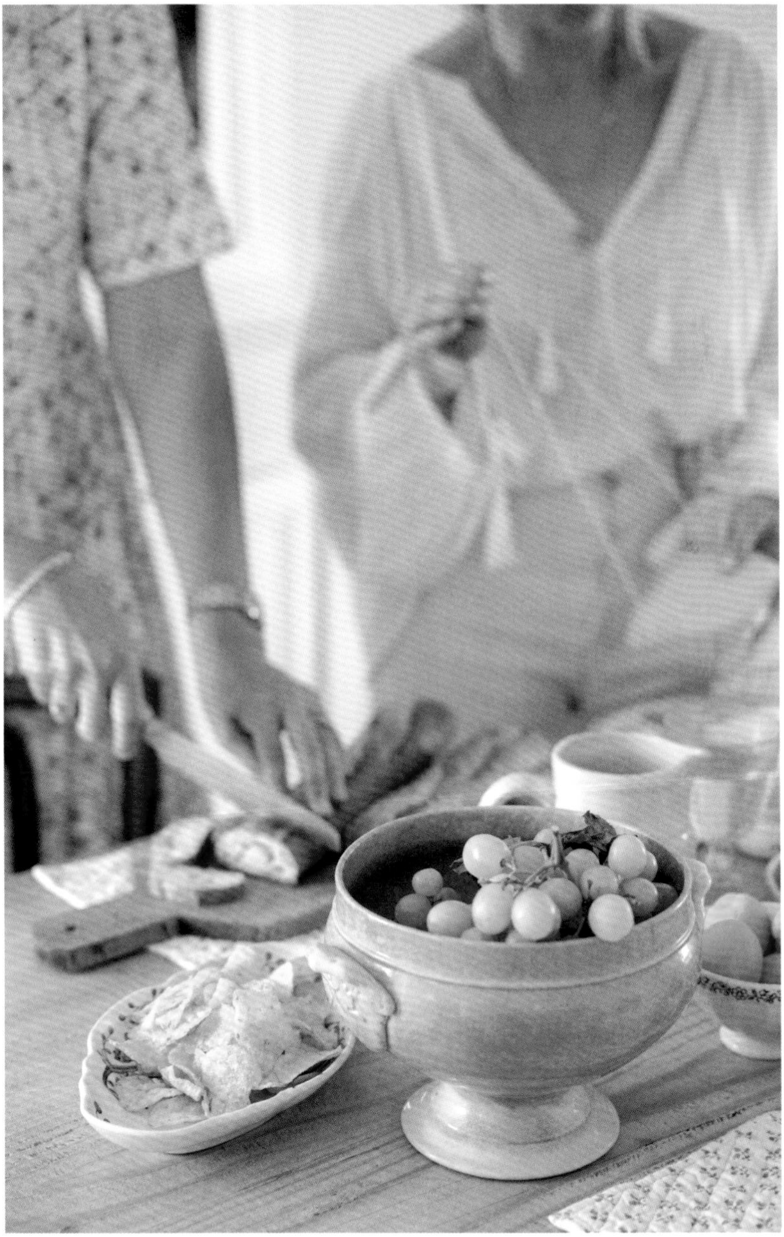

- Any form of racism, bigotry, or discrimination toward others. A total non-starter for me.
- Any expression of emotional or physical abuse. Bye.
- Lying, betrayal, manipulation, or dishonesty. Nope.
- People who are consistently unsupportive, critical, or negative. Hard pass.
- Those who are unable to show up when the going gets tough. The job description includes good and bad times.
- Those who are chronically flaky or late to plans. I know it's not personal, but it just doesn't work for me.
- Those who are always creating unnecessary drama. Check you later, Agents of Chaos!

TRY IT

Jot down your personal relationship deal breakers. What will you never tolerate or put up with? Make decisions ahead of time and be clear and firm with your communication toward others if they violate your deal breakers. If you have current relationships that leave you feeling consistently depleted, exhausted, or frustrated, come up with an exit strategy. Remember to be sensitive with timing and approach the conversation with empathy and kindness. It can feel hard and painful and clumsy, but ultimately worth it to honor your personal values. If you need a script, you can try something like this: "I've really valued our relationship, but need to take a little break now. I'm sorry if this feels hurtful. I care about you deeply and wish you nothing but the best." Remember, we all have limited, precious time on planet Earth. Surround yourself with people who are able to show up for you, are enjoyable to be with, and add value to your life.

STOP TRYING TO CHANGE OTHER PEOPLE

If I had a magic formula for how to get other people to act exactly the way we wanted them to, I would scream it from the rooftops (and also probably be a billionaire). But here's the thing: Trying to change other people (even when totally justifiable) simply doesn't work. Even if you ask very politely. Even if you could win an award for your brilliant communication style. Even if your requests are totally reasonable and valid. Here's the deal: Other people only change *if they really want to change.* And we have zero control over that. Seriously zero. But before you slam this book shut, here is the great news: It only takes *one* person to change a relationship. And that person is you! You get to determine how *you* show up, what you say or don't say, how you act or don't act, how much time you spend with that other person, what boundaries you set, and a million other things. And if you make even the tiniest shifts in how *you* show up, even the most challenging relationships can't help but change. And, of course, you always get to decide if and when it's time to exit stage left. Sometimes taking a break or even breaking up is the most loving thing you can do.

Mini Life Lesson: Don't Take Anything Personally

It has taken me my entire life to fully comprehend that other people's thoughts, feelings, and actions are a result of their own backgrounds and belief systems and have absolutely nothing to do with me. Like, zero. When we choose to take things personally, we can become easily triggered, hurt, angry, or defensive. When we instead ask ourselves, *Why might this person be acting this way, and how do I want to feel about it?* we can feel empowered, curious, and creative. For example, if someone is chronically late to meet you for plans, you could assume they don't respect your time or value the relationship, or you could consider that maybe they just struggle with time management. Of course, you get to set boundaries about what you will and won't tolerate in any relationship, but when you release the burden of taking things personally, you will spare yourself from so much unnecessary suffering.

Diversify Your Relationships

No one person can be all things to us. We are sold a false narrative that it's possible to find a single partner who will provide us with everything we've ever wanted for all of eternity (thanks, Hollywood). Not only is this is unrealistic, but it can also be deeply damaging. Instead of expecting a single partner to fulfill your every need, try cultivating deep connections with a variety of people you enjoy spending time with who can cumulatively fulfill your different needs and interests. This will not only take the pressure off your relationship, but it will also feel deeply empowering. A personal example: I've been with my husband Jordan for more than twenty years. While we share similar values and love spending time together, we also have *zero* shared interests. Zero! When I talk about entrepreneurship and personal development, his eyes glaze over, and as much as I've tried to stomach the ins and outs of politics or care about professional basketball (Go, Warriors?) I just really . . . can't. Jordan prefers the familiar and requires a predictable, laid-back routine, while I'm an adventure seeker who can't sit still. Still, we've managed to remain wildly compatible after more than twenty years, an achievement that I attribute to our mutual acceptance that we are each responsible for fulfilling our own needs (augmented with a large dose of humor, when necessary). Case in point: A few years ago, Jordan joined a men's basketball league, and found people he could talk to for hours on end about both sports and politics. BINGO. I've joined several women's groups that focus on entrepreneurship and personal development, and scratch some of my travel itch with my brother, who shares my wanderlust. It's more likely that your partner or spouse *can't* provide you with all the things you're looking for than that they *won't*, and what I am saying is that they shouldn't. There are tons of creative ways of filling those gaps if you think outside the box and take responsibility for meeting your own needs. Having positive, enriching outlets outside of your primary relationship will create a more well-rounded life and take stress off both of you.

Make a list of things you are longing for in your own life. Then consider how you can fulfill these needs on your own or by connecting with a friend, colleague, or group who shares your goals and interests. Your goal here is many eggs in many baskets.

A Quick Word About Love Languages

A few years ago, I read about the five love languages, developed by Gary Chapman. It's basically a breakdown of the most common ways people give and experience love. I immediately identified myself as a "quality time" and "acts of service person," and Jordan instantly resonated with "words of affirmation" and "physical touch." I got a little prickly (and judgy, if I'm being honest) about the whole enterprise once I realized that we had completely different and seemingly opposing love languages. I'm a total sucker for a voluntary ride to the airport while Jordan just wants me to put my hand on his leg and tell him he's doing a good job. I don't lead with hugs or compliments, just as Jordan doesn't long for long nighttime chats about the possibility of life on other planets. The love language topic made both of us a little bit cranky, but also a little more aware of what the other person longed for to feel loved. The other day Jordan bought and replaced our old toilet seat without being prompted, and I'm still beaming.

How to Find Your People

Cultivating new friends or breaking into or creating a new community as an adult can feel nearly impossible. I had no problem making friends as a kid, but as a solo entrepreneur living in a city where everyone seems to be busy or working *all the time*, I've honestly found it very challenging. While I have daydreamed about moving to a small town where I would surely be greeted by kind neighbors with freshly baked pies, I'm a big city person to the core, so I've had to get creative and resourceful to forge new relationships and build community (minus the pie). Here's what's worked for me.

EMBRACE VULNERABILITY

A few years ago, I confessed to a few friends that my social life was sorely lacking, and they were shocked. Their assumption was that I was wildly busy and had no time for socializing or new friendships. After my confession, these friends started reaching out more to invite me to social gatherings and urged me to do the same. A few told me that making advance plans was out of their comfort zone, but if I pinged them spontaneously, they would always want to meet up. Who knew? Opening up about what you're missing or lacking feels terribly vulnerable but will almost always lead to deeper friendships and connection.

CHOOSE YOUR OWN FRIENDSHIP ADVENTURE

For whatever reason (every movie and TV show!), I always imagined that the moment I had a baby I would instantly, almost magically, find other cool, fun moms who had babies the same ages as my kids, and we and our babies would all become best friends and live happily ever after. THIS DID NOT HAPPEN FOR ME. Despite joining not one, not two, but three new moms groups, I just did not find *my people*. I also did not find them at toddler playdates, or music classes, or at jungle gyms or parks. Mainly, I just got reminded time and time again that I hate making small talk at parks and really don't like sand in my shoes.

But, once I gave up on the notion that my new BFF had to be a fellow mom with a kid my kid's age, things started happening. I made friends with people who had no children by choice (so much easier to make plans with!) as well as my sister-in-law, who happens to be more than a decade younger than me (Love you, Sile!). I also became super close with my much younger brother, with whom I share a father and many of my father's best attributes, and who has become my all-time favorite travel companion. If you're limiting yourself when it comes to new connections because of some silly preconceived notion of what friendship should look like–like age, gender identity, or other factors, open your mind to brand-new possibilities and let the new friendships begin.

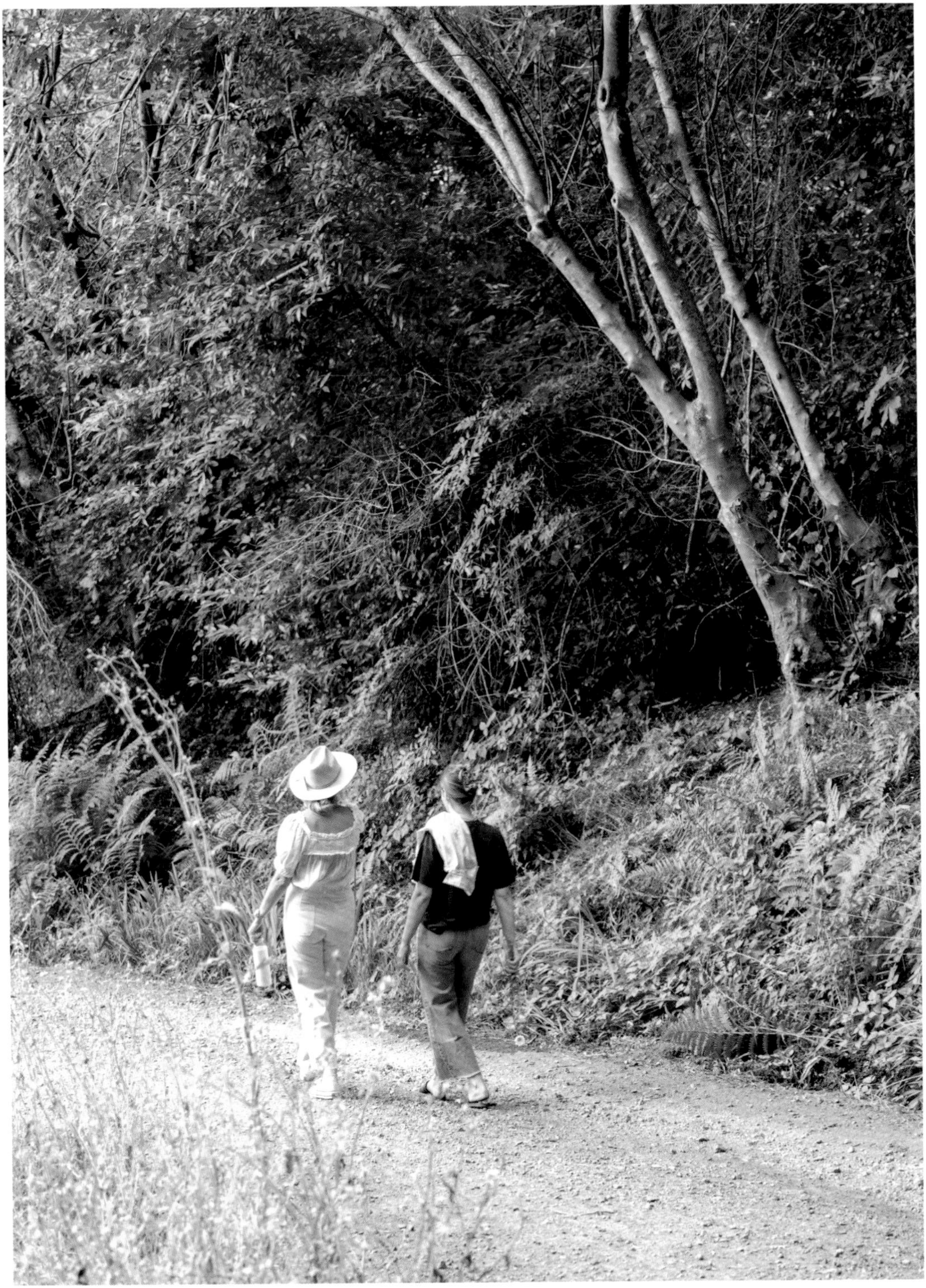

BECOME A JOINER

I found it very easy to make friends as a kid because I was part of a theater company from the age of eight on. Joining the theater community connected me to a sea of people who valued creative expression and loved playing "freeze" and "pass the imaginary energy ball." Theater kids, represent! I see you! My daughter, Emilie, joined a competitive soccer league and quickly bonded with her teammates who share a love of kicking black and white balls, high-fiving, and competing for trophies on grassy fields. Pickleball people are really excited to talk about pickleball. My point is that a structured group activity is often the most direct route to finding your people.

Nearly all the friends I've made as an adult have been made through entrepreneurial groups. When I was new to running my own business, I started a small meetup for other female founders and we met for a drink once a month and formed friendships that lasted for years. Later, during my life coach training, I was introduced to a wide range of women from all over the country. We instantly bonded over our shared passion for personal development, reflection, and growth. I'm currently part of a collective of solo entrepreneurs I could talk to all day. Realizing that I connect easily with passionate, ambitious entrepreneurs, I now have a place to focus my friendship-making efforts.

TRY IT

Identify a few activities, hobbies, or interests that float your boat, and sign up for a group that meets regularly, like a book club, a cooking class, or a team sport or hiking club. You might also consider signing up for a retreat or a group travel opportunity that focuses on personal growth, wellness, or adventure. These experiences often involve spending several days together in close quarters, à la summer camp, allowing you to connect and bond with others on a deeper level while exploring shared interests and experiences. I cannot promise you insta-friends but I can assure you that if you stick around, you'll find at least a few new people to connect with and opportunities for genuine friendships to develop.

TRY A CO-WORKING SPACE

If you work from home, you may want to consider joining a collaborative project or co-working space where you can meet and engage with other professionals. Getting out of your house and working at a shared space even once a week can help you meet and connect with new people. I've found that I especially love working alone while surrounded by the busy hum of people and conversations even if (especially when) I'm not part of them.

GET A DOG

No one is as shocked as I am that I spent practically a lifetime avoiding dogs (the wild tongues! the shrill barking!), until my kids presented me with a very persuasive essay, and my husband put the ball in my court. Basically, it was three against one and I gave in because I was outnumbered. Now I spend my days cupping our mini–Australian shepherd's face in my hands while locking eyes and stage-whispering "I LOVE YOU SO MUCH." It's utterly mind-blowing how much I love this dog. Aside from the loyalty and deep swells of unconditional love, having a dog means that in addition to all my neighbors, I have now met a sea of friendly strangers who love talking to and about dogs. Dogs are the ultimate icebreaker, and one of the most surefire ways of connecting with new people in your neighborhood and community. Dogs bring joy, connection, and, shockingly, even community. When we went out of town and entrusted my brother with our pup's daily walks, he had to put on headphones and sunglasses to avoid the onslaught of questions and comments from kind strangers who wanted to talk to him as they passed by. There are neighbors who never said a word to us before Patches appeared in our lives. *We have dog friends now. We go on dog playdates with people we never knew before.* The takeaway? Get a dog, make new friends.

GET ACTIVE IN YOUR NEIGHBORHOOD

Even if you live in an urban area, as I do, there are plenty of ways to tap into your local community. Join your local neighborhood group or

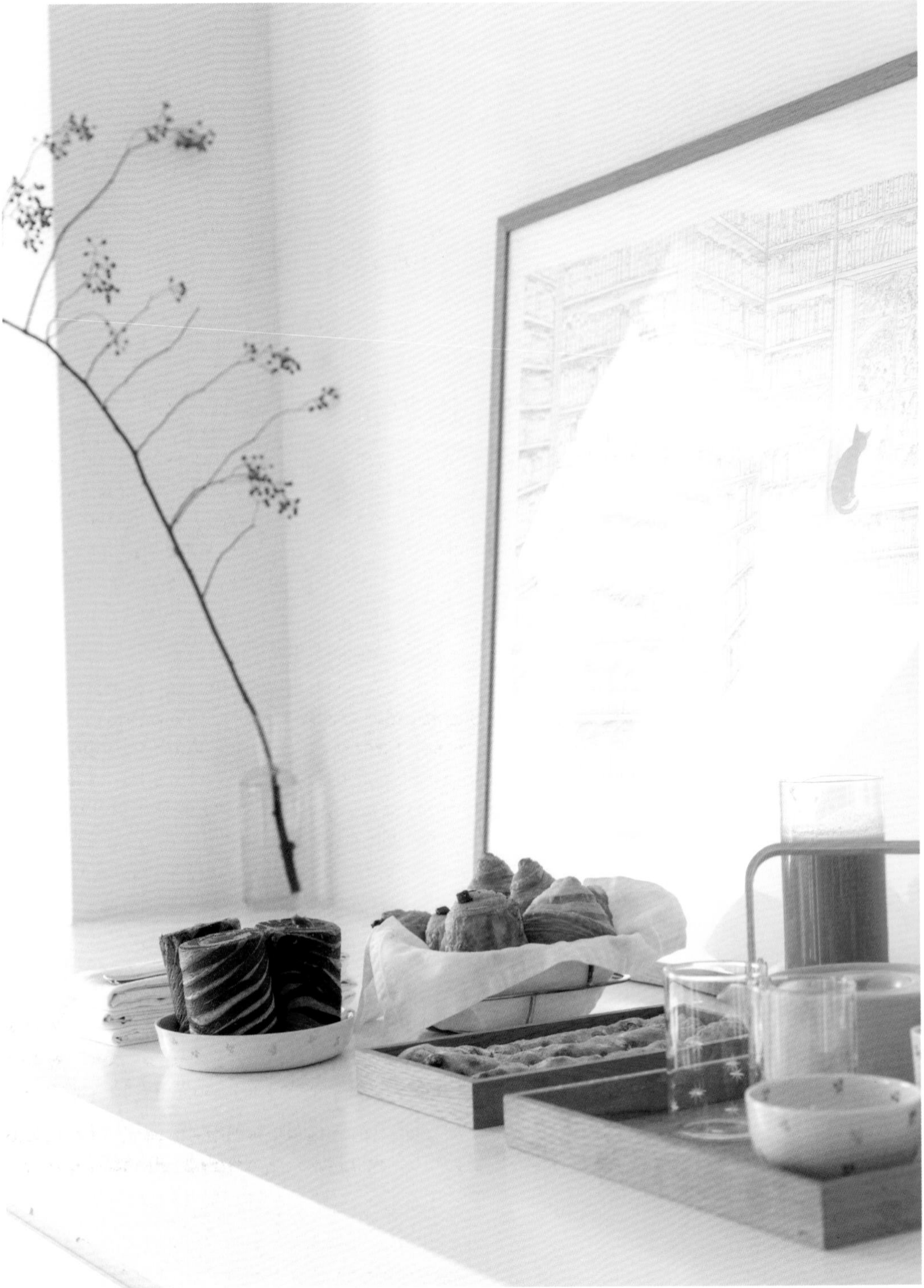

committee. Start a community garden project and pull together some neighbors who want to plant flowers or contribute to a mural. Pick up litter and help maintain the public spaces in your neighborhood. I make it a point to pick up trash in our neighborhood once a week (yes, I do own one of those robot arm grabber things) and have met a handful of friendly, similarly minded neighbors who have been eager to grab a trash bag and pitch in.

RAISE A HAND AND VOLUNTEER

Volunteerism is underrated! Helping in your community will create a sense of purpose, boost your happiness, and connect you with like-minded individuals who are committed to similar causes. Whether you decide to volunteer at your kid's school, help at your local soup kitchen or homeless shelter, or participate in a community effort like a beach cleanup day, working toward a shared cause is a breeding ground for connection. Now go do some good!

PLAN YOUR OWN PARTY

A few years ago, my friend Kate realized that she wanted to take control of how she celebrated her birthday so she decided to treat all her closest friends to lunch. She planned, hosted, and paid for it herself—and the whole thing clearly brought her great joy. The celebration was generous and lovely, and, most important, Kate didn't spend a second waiting around hoping someone remembered her birthday. She created the exact birthday she wanted. The moral: Don't wait for the party. Plan the party.

TRY IT

Want to activate your social life? Take initiative and plan something—or a lot of somethings. Invite a group over for a low-key meal. Set up a regular hiking date with a friend. Plan a party just because.

Remember, building new connections and lasting friendships takes time and effort. Be patient, open-minded, and authentic in your interactions and don't be discouraged by initial setbacks or attempts that don't pan out. Cultivating meaningful connections requires being willing to step outside of your comfort zone and take some social risks. While this can feel awkward (or even wildly uncomfortable), investing effort now can plant the seeds for new connections that ultimately develop into rewarding new friendships with people who share your passions, values, and interests. So worth it.

CREATING SYSTEMS: RELATIONSHIPS AND COMMUNITY EDITION

Remember, the key to successful life design is making intentional decisions about how you'd like to spend your time so you can create a schedule that's reflective of your values. Guess what? Maintaining and prioritizing meaningful relationships is no different. Refer back to your ideal connection cadence so you can map out the week, month, and season ahead and utilize your limited time in a way that supports your goals and prioritizes the relationships and social (or solo) plans you value most.

Plan and automate the following.

Solo Time

How often do you want/need to be alone? Consider blocking out regular (daily? weekly?) solo time that you can use to reflect and refuel. When I was raising a baby and a toddler who both seemed inclined toward diving back into my body, Jordan and I agreed that he would take both kids from 9 a.m. to noon every Saturday so I could claim some much-needed solo time. Sometimes I would meet a friend or take a yoga class. Other times I would literally just hang out alone in our bedroom, staring at the ceiling and savoring the silence. Since I was the primary caregiver during those first years, that planned time gave Jordan a chance to bond with the kids and allowed me to recharge in peace. A win-win if there ever was one.

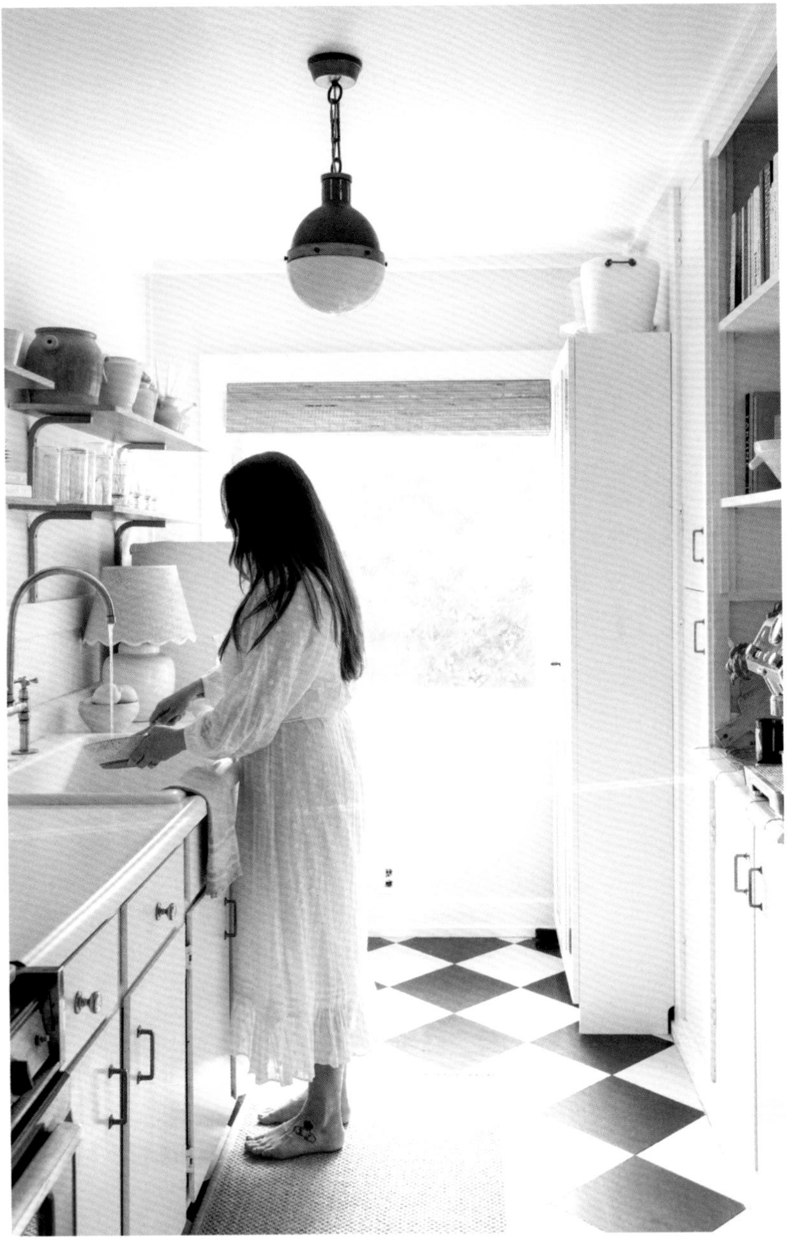

How often do you want or need some solo time? Claim and schedule this time as a regular date on your calendar. Even if other things come up that sound interesting, protect the time once you've scheduled it, and reschedule it within the same day or week if something comes up that you simply can't pass on. I helped one of my clients, Liv, block out three hours each Friday when her family was occupied, and another client, June, decided to treat her kids to a home movie each Saturday morning so she could sleep in and start the day slowly. Consider if you need to line up childcare, arrange for a babysitting swap, or request a break from your partner, spouse, roommates, or kids.

Go on Friend Dates

Every Tuesday at 7 p.m., rain or shine, I meet my friends Laura and Caitlin for dinner. We order takeout so it's easy on everyone and then fill each other in on the details of our lives. Caitlin hosts, and Laura and I bring wine and fancy chocolate. We've been doing this for years now, and it's one of my very favorite rituals. No more text volleys trying to coordinate dates, times, and locations–having a weekly plan is a simple, automated way to prioritize our friendships and ensure that we see each other consistently without any of the headaches of dealing with planning or logistics. Another example: My friend Tiffany and I live a bridge apart, so we meet once a month for lunch. We both travel a lot, so she suggested that we just check our calendars and schedule our next date at the end of lunch before we say goodbye. It takes about two minutes and spares us from the draining emails back and forth. My client Rupa stations herself at her favorite café each Friday morning and lets all the people in her life know they are welcome to drop by for coffee and a chat. She is delighted by new guests each week and doesn't have to plan a thing. My friend Greta makes pasta and garlic bread each weekend and lets her friends know they're always welcome for Spaghetti Sundays. My colleague Satsuko schedules her annual holiday party on the same date each year (the first Saturday in December) so she never has to think about it, and her inner circle can save the date well in advance.

TRY IT

Who do you want to see more of? Consider how you can automate and simplify your meetups and social plans with friends. Try scheduling a weekly or monthly or seasonal date with your best buddies so you can skip the scheduling nightmare.

Get in Quality Time with Your Partner or Spouse

Oof, this one definitely tends to get lost in the shuffle (sorry, Jordan!). Between the endless juggle of work, kids, and other responsibilities, romantic relationships can easily be relegated to back-burner status (if they're even on the stove at all). If your partnership has become more of a logistics and roommate situation (Who's getting the kids from soccer tomorrow? Did you fix the drain yet? Did you eat my apple?), it's best to start getting deliberate about mapping out some quality time together. While Jordan and I have tried the Saturday night date night thing, we've personally had better luck with daytime dates when we're more . . . awake. A long, leisurely lunch when the kids are set up with plans goes a long way, and we've also enjoyed city walks, hikes, or a social activity like miniature golf or bowling–which, unfortunately, Jordan is much better at than me.

TRY IT

Whether you opt for a daily check-in, a weekly date night, or a seasonal mini getaway, make sure to plan and prioritize some consistent and enjoyable quality time with your partner or spouse. Don't forget to stow the screens to help minimize distraction and maximize connection.

Prioritize Family Fun

Our family is very busy and independent, but we make a point of eating dinner together almost every night at 6 p.m. Jordan typically cooks, I set a nice table, and we each share a few highlights and lowlights from our day. Dinner often culminates in warm cookies and milk, or an outing to our favorite neighborhood ice cream spot for a scoop. This simple evening ritual ensures that we remain connected and in the loop on each other's lives. In addition, I do my best to take each of my girls out for solo dates, and even occasionally a mother-daughter trip, which engenders a different kind of quality time and connection.

> **TRY IT**
>
> When it comes to family time and connection, what are you craving? How frequently or infrequently do you want to spend time with close and extended family? Identify a minimum baseline for how often you will host or participate in family meals, get-togethers, holidays, and events, and coordinate standing repeatable dates. The work you put in to coordinate plans and outings now will spare you from the seemingly endless text or email thread trying to line up schedules later.

Tap in to Your Community

Connecting with your local community can offer endless advantages, including extending and diversifying your social circle, cultivating a deeper sense of belonging and purpose, and reducing loneliness through regular social interaction and support. Community-oriented groups and organizations are incredibly welcoming to newcomers, so dip a toe in, and be open-minded. At varying times I've joined childcare co-ops, taken part in neighborhood meal swaps, attended local fundraisers, and volunteered to pick up trash or work at a soup kitchen. While I haven't always met my forever friends at these events, I continually find these community-focused events engaging, inspiring, and uplifting.

THE LIFE-CHANGING MAGIC OF BABYSITTING CO-OPS

When our girls were six and four, we found out some great news: We had won the childcare lottery. You see, we live in a neighborhood that happens to include one of the oldest (and possibly the most organized) babysitting cooperatives in the country. A few months after joining the waiting list, we got the good news: We were officially in! We were initiated with forty "cards" (old computer punch cards from the UC Berkeley computer science department) and given the full breakdown on how the co-op was structured:

- Each card could be redeemed for thirty minutes of childcare, regardless of how many kids you had in your family.

- The thirty co-op families took turns hosting each Friday and Saturday night, all year round, between the hours of 5 p.m. and midnight, and were tasked with providing a simple art activity, dinner and dessert, and a movie for the kids who were dropped off by other co-op families.

- Host families were reimbursed in cards by the families who dropped off their kids, at the same rate—one card per family for thirty minutes of care.

The kids in the co-op ranged from two to eleven years old, and while our girls were initially skeptical, after one night of finger painting, mac and cheese, movies, and brownie sundaes they begged us to go on more date nights.

We also found that we loved hosting the merry band of kids who ran around our home as if it was their own. The co-op changed our lives: Our girls got to play with different neighborhood kids of all ages each weekend, we became more connected and engaged with our local community, and anytime we wanted to we could get out of the house and spend time as a couple without hemorrhaging money to pay for childcare in addition to whatever we did on the date.

TRY IT

Try teaming up with a few neighborhood families you trust and see if you can swap childcare, meals, or anything else that would feel like a relief.

TRY IT

Consider how you'd like to engage with your local or broader community and map out plans for the season or even the year ahead. This effort could be as simple as volunteering for a few hours each holiday season at a local food bank, taking turns making a low-bar weeknight dinner with a few friends or neighbors, or attending a community fund-raising event for a cause you believe in.

IMPLEMENTING HABITS: RELATIONSHIPS AND COMMUNITY EDITION

Consistent and intentional habits can ensure that we create and maintain the relationships that are the most important to us. Habits consist of a regular routine or practice that helps facilitate a desired activity or goal. Consider the following.

Habits to Connect with Yourself

You might experiment with a fresh morning routine, a journaling practice, a solo walk or hike, or a creative outlet like painting, writing, or playing music.

Habits to Improve Your Relationships

How can you leverage habits to ensure that you connect and engage with the people you care about? Identify a few ways you'd like to show up more for the people in your life through small, intentional habit shifts. Lots of ideas coming right up ...

Show Appreciation: I'm not in the words of affirmation love language camp (acts of service and quality time, please!), but it turns out that many people are (hi, Jordan!). Especially if it doesn't come naturally to you (or you don't require it from others), practice expressing the things you love and appreciate about the people in your life. Who doesn't love a thoughtful compliment from time to time?

Be Reliable: Show up on time, return calls and texts, avoid canceling plans at the last minute (so rude!) unless absolutely necessary.

Offer Help (preferably without being asked): Change a light bulb if you've been blessed with the gift of height. Drop off a meal if you love cooking. Run an errand if it's on your way. Offer to pick someone up from the airport. A little effort goes a long way in this department. Fun fact: Rides to and from the airport are my love language!

Be the Cheerleader: Celebrate and acknowledge tiny accomplishments as well as bigger milestones and birthdays. A simple "I see you out there!" goes a long way.

Minimize Distraction: News flash! It's not enjoyable to spend time with people who are always on their phone, taking calls, or multitasking when they're with you (again, sorry, Jordan!). Do your best to stow electronics and minimize distractions when you're with others so you can ensure that your quality time is actually . . . quality.

Banish Gossip: It's SO fun, I know. But it leads to nothing good.

Reach Out and Touch Someone: With consent, obviously! Again, not *my* love language, but, for some, physical touch leads to a much greater sense of connection and intimacy and releases happy hormones like serotonin. Even if it's just a hug or a quick pat on the back, try throwing the touchy-feely people in your life a bone.

Check In: Sometimes we have no idea when even our closest friends are struggling with something or really suffering. A simple "Just thinking about you" message takes exactly three seconds and can make someone's whole day.

Get Curious: Ask how you can be a better friend, partner, parent, or colleague. Sometimes just showing interest can make the other person feel seen and appreciated.

Crowdsource: Some people are less in touch with what they want or need, and when you ask for guidance on what you can do for them or get for them, they are stumped. Asking their siblings, parents, or friends for specific ideas can generate creative and thoughtful ideas, and shows you really care.

THE BOTTOM LINE

Cultivating strong, meaningful relationships is the cornerstone of a well-rounded and thriving life. You can use the volume tool to *increase* the energy and effort you invest in the relationships that nourish you and add value, and *decrease* time spent on connections that feel draining or imbalanced. Not only will diversifying your relationships ease the burden on individual connections (buh-bye codependency), but that will enrich your life through a broader range of experiences, perspectives, and support. Thoughtfully scheduling and automating the right number of social plans, gatherings, and events for *you* will ensure that you prioritize the relationships and connection cadence you crave, while still leaving room for solo time to recharge. Small, smart habit shifts, like being supportive, helpful, and reliable, can improve all aspects of your relationships with others. Take responsibility for creating and maintaining healthy relationships and get real about how you can be a better partner, friend, colleague, or family member.

YOUR PROMPTS

Want a boost in the relationship department? Try these prompts:

- On a scale of 1 to 5, how satisfied do you feel when it comes to your relationships?
- Which relationships do you find deeply satisfying?
- Which specific qualities do you value most in a relationship?
- Which relationships do you find draining or difficult?
- What is one boundary you can assert to reduce relationship stress, pressure, or guilt?
- What is one small thing you can do to cultivate community (join a club, take a class, volunteer, introduce yourself to a neighbor or colleague, etc.)?
- What is one small but critical action you can take to improve your dating life, romantic relationship, or marriage (e.g., set up regular check-ins, dates, or outings)?
- How can you use the less-but-better principle to improve your most important relationships—e.g., a special monthly date with each child or a quarterly weekend away with your partner or spouse.
- Which meetups, gatherings, or events can you automate to ensure frequency and ease of planning?
- What is one small habit shift you can integrate to improve your existing relationships and show the people you love how much you value and appreciate them?

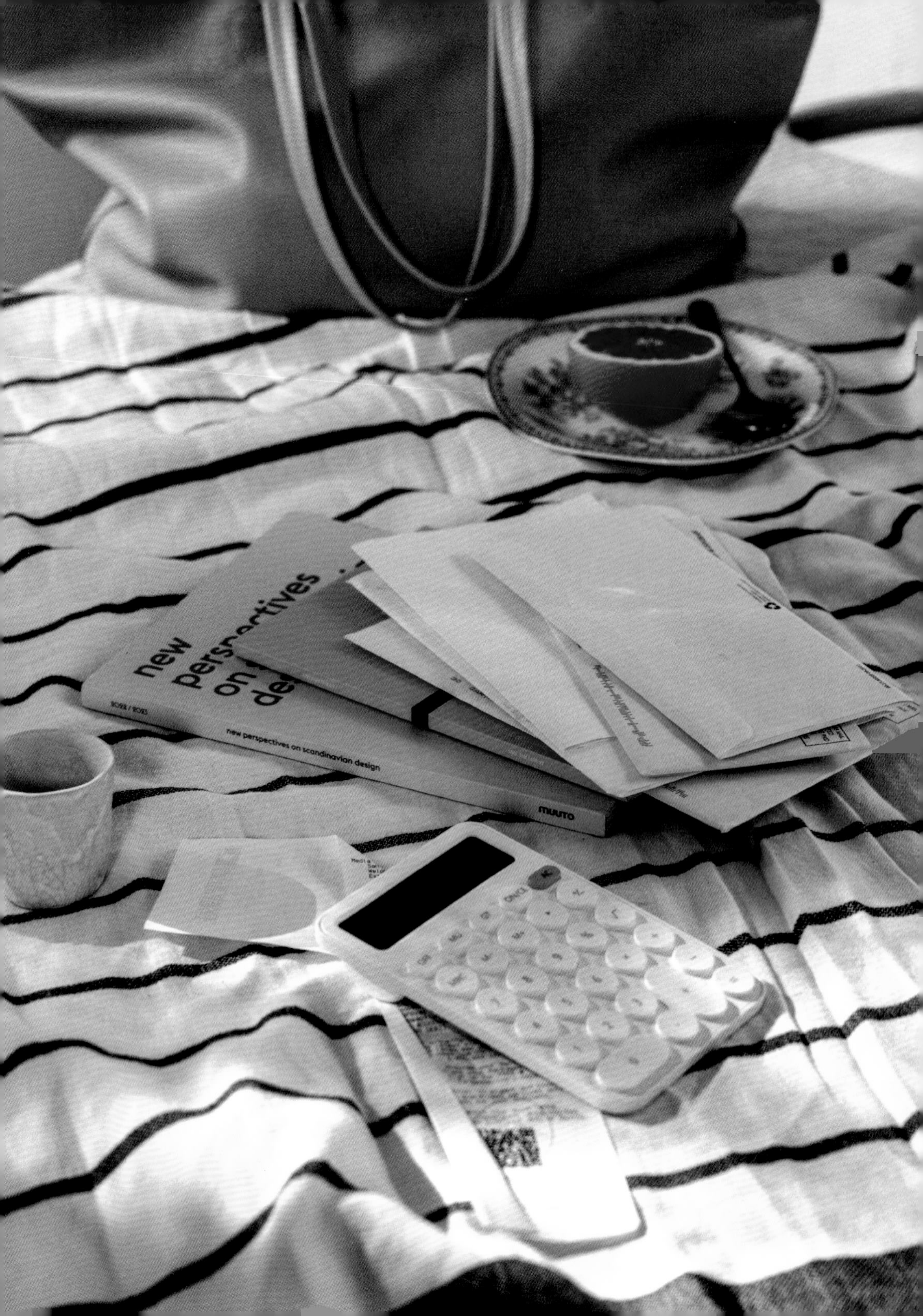
new perspectives on scandinavian design
MUUTO

Career and Finance

A disclaimer of sorts: I'm probably not the best person to be offering financial advice to people. I have always liked earning money, and I've had some form of a job since I was permitted to work at fourteen, but my eyes glaze over when people talk about index funds or diversified investment strategies. Yet, despite my complete and total lack of interest in the financial sector, I have reached all my financial goals by using intentionality as my guide.

- I carry zero consumer debt.
- I have created a thriving business that is able to comfortably support my family.
- I am able to give a portion of my income each year to organizations that I believe in.
- I can also put aside money annually for retirement and for my kids' college funds.

I've done all of this without swearing off pleasure or fun, and without knowing what the Nasdaq is. I don't have a can't-miss get-rich-quick solution to give you (if I did, I would give it to you and use it myself). What I do have are some simple but effective strategies I've used to make sure I am in good financial shape and I can support the life I want to live. Let's get into it.

ADJUSTING VOLUME: CAREER AND FINANCE EDITION

If you're currently feeling out of touch with—or not in control of—your finances, the underlying stress can make it difficult (nearly impossible, really) for the other areas of your life to run smoothly. In this section, we'll reevaluate and improve your relationship with your money, and dig in to some simple mindset shifts that can help you infuse more passion and alignment into your work. Ready to start feeling like you have both hands on the wheel when it comes to your money and work? Right this way.

Redefine Enough

Our Western society is built on competition and consumption, creating a world where *more* is always the answer. Bigger homes. Nicer cars. More stylish clothes. More money in the bank. As a result, many of us find ourselves in an endless rat race—working harder and harder to scale and acquire and impress, leaving us feeling exhausted, depleted, and unfulfilled. Any feeling of contentment achieved through acquiring material assets is fleeting, and so the chase for more and better will always continue—if we let it. If we want to change our own personal experience within this reality, our job is to redefine *enough* and learn to feel peaceful, abundant, and grateful for what we already have.

Want to know a secret? I've had the opportunity to spend time with some of the wealthiest and most successful people in the world and can report that they are no happier than anyone else. In fact, many of them are totally miserable. It turns out that owning properties all over the world, collecting fleets of luxury cars, and keeping closets that look like department stores can't do anything to protect you from illness, human suffering, or heartbreak. Even the most elite among us, those who on paper are killing it and whose sheets have outrageously high thread counts, still struggle with the same challenges, insecurities, and interpersonal dramas the rest of us deal with.

At the end of the day, most of us yearn for the same basic things: a healthy and functioning body, a safe and comfortable home, a loving community with intimate relationships, and a job that pays enough to meet our needs and feels interesting and meaningful. Sure, flying on a private plane sounds like fun, and I'm a sucker for a great pair of shoes, but these are merely bells and whistles—they're not ingredients for lasting fulfillment and provide little more than a fleeting dopamine rush. I know people who have more money and assets than I could ever dream of, who spend their days looking over their fence and trying to keep up with their neighbors. I also know people who live very marginally but embody such a profound state of joyful abundance, generosity, and gratitude, it would make you fall off your chair. How could these two things be true? It turns out that true abundance is not a dollar amount, but a mindset. By aligning our financial goals and behavior with our deepest values and priorities, we can ensure that the money we make, spend, save, and invest feels meaningful and intentional.

TRY IT

Freedom, vitality, and peace will come from clarifying exactly what abundance looks like to you. Take a step back and reflect on your core values. What do you truly care about? How do you define a good life? What does financial freedom look like to you? What amount of money will help facilitate the life you want to lead? How much is *enough*?

Quick Win

It's easy to focus on scarcity, lack, and all of the things we yearn for but don't yet have, but far more productive and satisfying to shift our focus to the abundance that already exists all around us. Jot down ten things that you once really wanted and now have. If you need help, look around your home and write down what you see. As I write this, I see: A warm bed. A nightstand with books I'm excited to read. The breakfast on my plate. The plate my breakfast is on. A mug of hot coffee on the dresser (my husband's, but he's a nightmare before he's had coffee, so I am grateful for it). But, seriously, let's take a minute to appreciate what we already have, from the roofs over our heads to the clothes on our backs. I'm feeling more abundant already.

Vote with Your Dollars

President Joe Biden famously said, "Don't tell me your values. Show me your budget and I'll tell you what you value." This made me nervous because I'd been spending a lot of money on vintage denim at the time. My takeaway was this: *Time to start intentionally aligning my spending with my values.* I shared this philosophical adjustment with my home-editing clients, and it resulted in some meaningful and impactful shifts:

- Sloane, who deeply valued philanthropy, looked around at her closet full of designer handbags and decided to sell all but five of them and donate the proceeds to refugees.

- Nusha pledged that her future purchases would reflect her desire to support BIPOC-owned businesses in her local community. She identified not only shops and boutiques, but BIPOC-owned grocery stores, restaurants, and a historic Black-owned bookstore to support with her dollars.

- Christina, who worked in green energy and sustainability, was mortified by the pile of Amazon boxes in her entryway. She made a commitment to start buying from local secondhand shops and deleted her credit-card information from her Amazon account so she could curb her one-click spending habit.

Most people wouldn't say that they prioritize clothes, shoes, or material items, but take a closer look at what you're spending your money on and where you're spending it, and you might be surprised at what it reveals. If you value philanthropy, are you actively giving at a meaningful level? If you care about your local community, are you supporting small, local shops? If you value sustainability, are you supporting businesses with ethical practices and finding products with minimal packaging?

Quick Win: Let's Get Intentional

Get a piece of paper and make two columns. On one side make a list of things you value that you want to invest in. My list included physical and mental health, travel, and philanthropy.

On the other side make a list of things you don't want to invest in. Mine included nice cars (I still drive a 2013 Toyota with a broken trunk), fine jewelry (I wear the same handful of pieces every day), and electronics (hard pass on standing in line at the Apple Store to get the latest whatever). What's on your list? How can you turn *up* your spending on goods and services you value, and dial *down* your spending on items that just don't line up with your values? Remember, there is nothing wrong with splurging on designer clothes, fancy cars, or anything else as long as you have good reasons for doing so. The goal is to make sure that your spending is fully aligned with your goals, values, and priorities.

Own Your Money Mindset

We all have deeply ingrained beliefs about money, developed through our upbringing and life's experiences, and those beliefs will both determine our relationship with money and our relative feelings about abundance or scarcity. Some of those long-held beliefs may be lousy or unproductive ("I'll never be able to get out of this debt spiral") and some may be inspiring and motivating ("I'm endlessly resourceful and resilient!"). Most of our beliefs are unconscious, so it's our responsibility to uncover them and examine the results they are producing in our lives.

For example, if you believe that money is the root of all evil, chances are good that you won't be inviting more cash into your life anytime soon. If you believe that accumulating consumer debt is inevitable, then BINGO, you've set yourself up for a trip to debt city. As someone who grew up feeling scarcity and believing that wealthy people were selfish and shallow and that creatives were honorable but destined for a life of financial struggle, I've had to do *a lot* of work on my money story. What's yours?

Grab a pen and paper and jot down your answers to the following questions:

- What beliefs did you *inherit* about money?
- What do you currently *believe* about money?
- What do you *want* to believe about money?
- What beliefs about money do you want to *subtract* or let go of?
- What *new* beliefs will you start *adding* or integrating to improve your money mindset?

Make sure the shifts you want to make in your money mindset are small and truly believable for you, or they will just feel pointless and inauthentic. If you don't believe you have the capacity to earn a lot of money, you could practice a belief like, "I can definitely make more money than I am making right now."

Here's the best news: No matter what beliefs you inherited from your family, or picked up from your friends or colleagues, you get to decide what you want to believe about money *today* and moving forward. Like you can change your beliefs starting this very second. *Identifying and replacing your limiting beliefs about money is the single most important step to creating financial freedom and even wealth.* It's your responsibility to take full ownership over your money mindset. Take the time necessary to thoughtfully surface and replace your unproductive beliefs about your capacity to earn, save, spend, and invest.

Quick Win

Try integrating a money mindfulness practice into your day. Even a couple of minutes each day reflecting on the things you *do* have, the money you *have* earned, or visualizing your ideal financial future can help cultivate a more abundant mindset.

Know You Have the Power to Make More Money

A quick story: A few years into my career as a professional organizer I applied to train and get certified as a life coach. I was immediately accepted into the program, but I nearly backed out because the tuition was $12,000. At the time I was grossing $40,000 dollars a year with my business, and I just couldn't wrap my head around the leap of such a large investment. Thankfully, Jordan encouraged me to take the money out of the savings we'd built and to bet on myself. Before I paid for the program, I made a decision: If I was going to spend our hard-earned savings on it, I would go with a specific mission in mind—to earn back our money immediately following the program by learning how to double my income. I was so committed to this mission that on the first day of training I announced my plan to the founder of the school, and all my peers, so they would hold me accountable. I showed up fully. I asked a lot of questions. I found other women who made far more money than me and ate lunch with them so I could ask how they had done it. With the tools and mindset shifts I learned during my training, I was able to double my income that year, and then again the following year, and I've continued increasing my income every year after that doing work I love. Here's how.

STEP ONE: DECIDE THAT YOU WANT TO MAKE MORE MONEY

I know, I know. It sounds so silly, but this may actually be the most important step. I spent the first few years in my business plugging away, feeling grateful that I could spend most of my time raising my two daughters while also supplementing my husband's income doing something I loved. I happily coasted for many years without any specific financial goals or benchmarks other than making enough to help pay our expenses. It was only when I *decided* I wanted to earn more money that the amount of money I earned started changing. Want to make more money? *Decide that you are committed to making more money. Write down exactly how much money you want to make and create a specific timeline for doing so.* You don't have to know the *how*, but you do need to know the *why*. In my case, I wanted to prove to myself that I was capable of supporting our family without any help. I wanted my girls to grow up seeing their mom as a self-sufficient earner so they would believe they could do the same for themselves. This reason lit me up inside and propelled me forward even when I was plagued with doubt.

MY MONEY STORY

I come from a long line of immigrants who fled persecution in Russia and Europe. My grandparents arrived in the United States on boats with next to nothing, and they ingrained in their children that a good education and hard work were their only means of escaping poverty. My father, who was raised in true poverty, took his parents' advice and went on to receive a PhD in psychology, and built a thriving private practice as a forensic psychologist. My mother (whose parents had to drop out of school to beg for food) graduated as valedictorian of her class and went on to earn multiple master's degrees, started a nonprofit, became a published author, and was able to support herself as a single mother after having to financially start over following a difficult divorce.

To me, both were living examples of the ethos their parents preached: They worked hard to earn their own success, saved more than they spent, and far surpassed the conditions in which they were raised.

My parents ended up not having much in common as a couple, but as parents they were both deeply invested in passing on the importance of education, intellect, and the arts, and raised me to focus on cultivating meaningful work rather than material wealth. With their encouragement and support I chose to pursue life as an actor in the theater, convinced that I would be happy living in a shoebox if I got to spend my days engaging in collaborative and creative work onstage. And, for well over a decade, I was. Working as an actor connected me to a dynamic and passionate community of artists, and my time in the theater was rich and deeply fulfilling. But as I approached my thirtieth birthday, living from job to job and paycheck to paycheck began taking a toll. I took a full-time job as an event planner because I liked food and parties, but my role in this new industry didn't pay well or feel particularly meaningful. I just couldn't pretend to care about whether the linen cocktail napkins were *champagne* or *alabaster*. When I was laid off at eight months pregnant with my first child, I was relieved.

Now, here's where the story gets interesting. I had to find a way to bring in income to contribute to our growing family (Jordan made a modest living in the nonprofit sector) and we relied on a dual income to pay the bills. I couldn't think of a single job I was qualified to do that would pay more than the astounding cost of childcare in the San Francisco Bay Area, so we got scrappy. We decided that I would stay home to raise our daughter Chloe during the week while Jordan worked a nine-to-five. Then on weekends I started offering home-organizing and decluttering services to other busy moms while Jordan took over the childcare responsibilities.

Let me be clear: I had never imagined myself to be capable of entrepreneurship. I had no business plan, no mentors, no trust fund or savings to fall back on, and not a clue as to what I was doing. What I did know was that I loved helping people organize their homes and lives, and my friends told me I was really good at it—so I figured it was worth a shot to see if people would pay me to help them. Offering my services to strangers was terribly vulnerable at first, but I built confidence by focusing on service ("How can I help?") instead of ego ("Am I talented enough to do this?"). Nearly fifteen years later, I have built a thriving career as a home-organizing expert, author, and small-business strategist. I could write a whole other book about the lessons I've learned from becoming an entrepreneur (and maybe I will), but the point I want to drive home with my story is this: I created money with my mind. Not in a woo-woo, magical-thinking kind of way, but in an I-need-to-figure-this-out-so-it's-worth-a-shot kind of way. I figured out a way to package and offer something I felt naturally good at in exchange for money. And you know what? You can, too.

> **TRY IT**
>
> Write down how much money you would like to earn in the next year and define your compelling reason for making more money— perhaps something that feels bigger than yourself. Remember, you must decide that you want to create more money *and* also be open to receiving it. This is a good time to unpack any limiting beliefs around your potential to earn or biases against people with money.

STEP TWO: HIRE A COACH

Hiring a coach or a business strategist, or teaming up with a mentor, will ensure that you have built in structure and accountability. Even when I didn't earn a lot in my business, this was always my number one investment as an entrepreneur, and it always paid off in spades.

> **TRY IT**
>
> What kind of support could make a big difference in advancing your career and financial goals? Decide who feels like the right fit for you and set up the support you need. Many coaches offer a limited number of scholarships or sliding-scale spots, so if it feels just out of reach, make sure to ask. If you don't have the resources yet to hire a professional, you can explore a skill share or trade. In my early years as an entrepreneur, I traded my home-organizing services for business strategy and coaching, as well as help with marketing, branding, and photography.

STEP THREE: IDENTIFY A SPECIFIC PROBLEM YOU CAN SOLVE

If you want more money, you *must* come up with a specific problem that you can solve, which people are willing to pay for. It really is that simple. In my case, I wanted to help people who were overwhelmed (or even paralyzed) by disorganization and clutter. I did this by creating an efficient process to help them systematically edit, organize, and style their homes while addressing common pain points, such as sourcing the

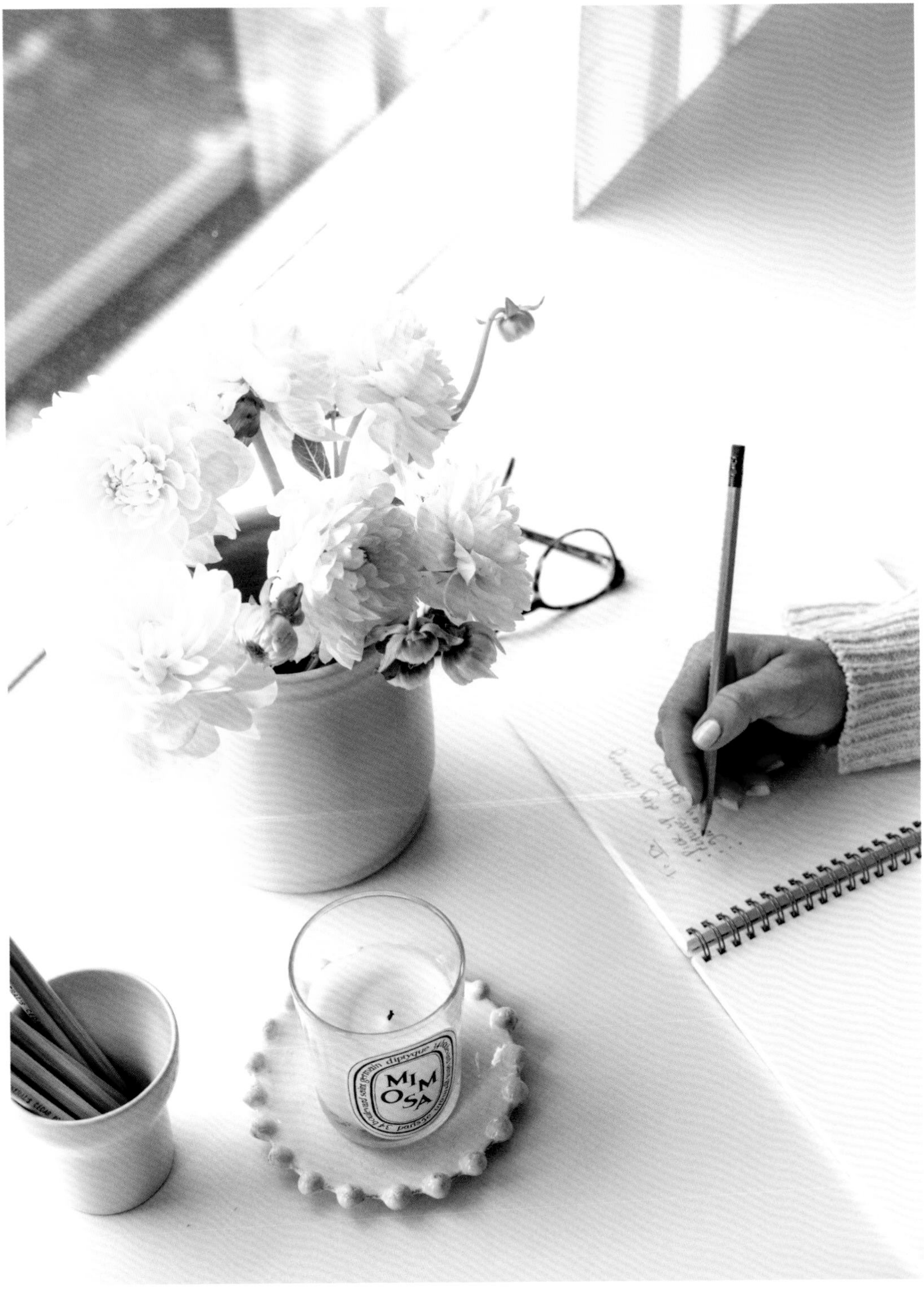
MIM
OSA

right storage solutions and coordinating donation pickups. My clients were delighted to pay for these services because they tackled very real problems that impacted their overall quality of life. Over time, as my experience and reputation grew, I was able to raise my rates accordingly.

> **TRY IT**
>
> Clearly define the specific problem you can solve, and who you want to solve it for.
>
> Examples:
>
> - I want to help busy working moms declutter and organize their homes. (I made a living doing this for more than a decade.)
> - I want to help teams of tech workers connect through play. (My brother-in-law made a career out of this!)
> - I want to demystify menopause for women. (Menopause influencers and educators are a legit career path now.)
> - I want to design beautiful drought-resistant gardens for retirees in Palm Springs. (Why not?)
>
> Get crystal clear about what problems you can solve and for whom. How can you leverage your natural-born talents, education, and interests in order to help others?

STEP FOUR: MAKE AN ACTION PLAN

The first and most important step is to decide that you want to make more money (see step one), but that is not enough on its own (if only it were). Once you make that decision, you must create a specific plan of action. In my case, the plan was simple (but absolutely terrifying). In order to double my income, I doubled my rates. Your plan might involve taking a second job, starting a side hustle, selling a product or service, or adding more value at work and requesting a raise. Make sure your plan is specific, measurable, and actionable.

TRY IT

In addition to obvious methods, like raising your rates or asking for a salary increase, there are so many creative ways to make more money:

- Monetize a favorite hobby by selling goods or services within your community.
- Create and sell digital products, like courses, stock images, or templates.
- Offer a workshop or consulting services, or teach a class.
- Rent out your home, office space, or other assets.
- Offer pet-sitting or dog-walking services.

Make sure your plan is specific and actionable and will help you realize your specific goals.

STEP FIVE: TAKE MASSIVE ACTION

And now for the hard part. Once you've committed to making more money, made an action plan, and set yourself up with support, it's go time. Taking massive action means committing to taking continuous action in pursuit of your goals until you meet them. That means you'll take action even when you feel scared or tired or vulnerable or irritable. It means you'll keep going even if you face rejection or fall on your face. Actually, especially when you fall on your face. This is some of the hardest and most uncomfortable work you will ever do, but if you can push through to the other side, you will feel a sense of pride and accomplishment that you never thought possible. I still remember what it felt like to look at my balance sheet with my coach at the end of that first year and realize that I had surpassed my goal and earned $100,000 with my business in a single year. I told my girls at the dinner table that I had accomplished something that once felt unthinkable, and that they could, too. It remains one of the proudest moments of my life.

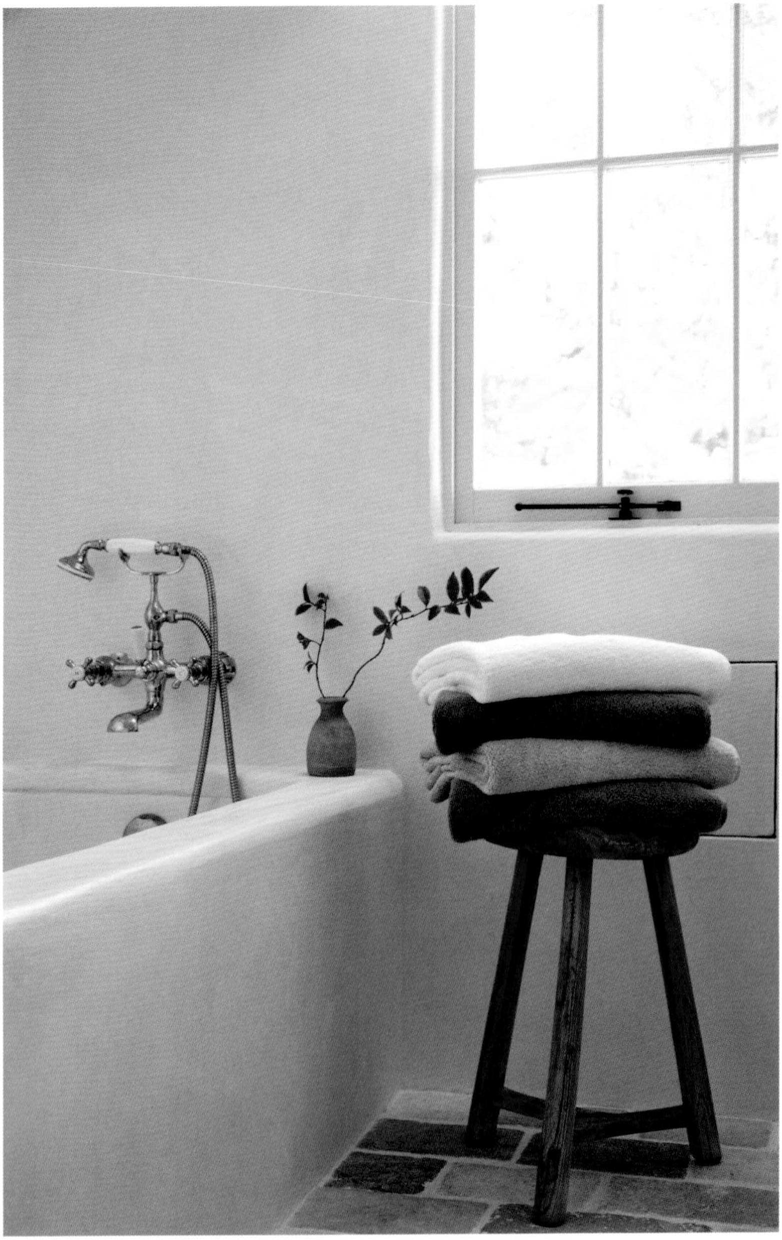

TRY IT

Jot down ten specific actions you will try to get closer to your financial goal. Some examples include:

- Checking in with a past client
- Lining up a meeting with a supervisor to learn about opportunities for growth and salary advancement within your company
- Changing your email signature to include your website with a clear call to action (like booking a free thirty-minute consult)
- Joining or starting a networking group

Commit to trying them (and perhaps/likely many more) until you meet your goal. As one of my mentors used to say, "There is either succeeding or learning—the only failure is the failure to try."

More Joy, Please

For many of us, most of our waking hours are spent at work, meaning our jobs have a huge impact on our overall quality of life. While you may decide you're a work-to-live and not a live-to-work person, there's no downside in making your time at work feel more meaningful and enjoyable. I've had the great pleasure of mentoring over one hundred women who wanted to create more fulfillment in their careers, and I firmly believe that we all have the capacity to find more joy in our work at any phase of life. Because, look, life is hard enough, right? Regardless of how old you are, you can always choose a new career path that feels more aligned with your natural interests and talents.

You don't have to start from scratch or quit your job to infuse more joy into your career. You can start small just by looking for opportunities to do more of what you love.

HOW TO RUN A MINIMALIST BUSINESS

Want to apply minimalist principles to all aspects of your business—from your physical workspace to your hiring practices and everything in between? Here are a few quick tips from my own minimalist business.

Kick-Start Your Productivity with a Minimal Workspace

A cluttered workspace bombards our brains with excessive stimuli and signals to our brains that our work is never done. *Le Sigh.* If you want to boost your productivity and creativity at work, do yourself a favor and clear the surface(s) you work on. It took giving up my home office so my kids could have their own rooms to realize how few things I needed to run my business. I scaled back from having an entire room filled with furniture, electronics, and office supplies to a single bin that holds my laptop computer, headphones, notebook, and pen. Paring down to the absolute essentials has given me the freedom to work from literally anywhere, and (Bonus!) I have next to nothing to clean up at the end of the day.

Say No More

I'm a natural-born people pleaser and often agree to take on projects or events. But real talk: Saying yes too much can get in the way of staying on track with my goals and creating the most high-quality content and value for my clients and my community. It took receiving an actual *crate* of apple cider gummy vitamins that I had agreed to taste and review, to make me realize I had to put some clear parameters on which collaborations, partnerships, and other opportunities I would accept. Now I take the time to evaluate incoming requests more thoughtfully and I only move forward with opportunities that feel completely aligned with my mission, values, and current goals—typically less than 5 percent. As a result, I've been able to increase my impact—and my income.

Curate a Lean Team

The only employee in my company is me. Party of one! Over the course of my career, I've slowly, and intentionally, built my own incredible team of creatives and experts—all independent contractors who set their own rates and hours that work for them. I've hired people to help me with website design and maintenance, graphic design, photography, tech support, communication, bookkeeping, business strategy, and coaching. What I love most about this business model is that I get the *exact* support I need when I need it—all while reducing overall operating costs and supporting a talented group of freelancers. While I occasionally feel envious of my colleagues who run large teams and have built-in lunch buddies, I don't envy the stress of hiring and firing or the pressure of maintaining payroll and insurance during slower months. The decision to keep my business small and simple has created tremendous freedom and flexibility in my life and business.

Streamline Your Offerings

There's a little bakery near me called Bakesale Betty that only sells fried chicken sandwiches, cookies, and strawberry shortcake. The bakery is only open for a few hours each day, and people line up around the block to grab a cookie and a sandwich before they sell out. And they *always* sell out. They've been running a thriving business for years, and I greatly admire the simplicity of their model: Only do a few things . . . but do them really, really well. Although it's tempting to try to be everything for everyone, I have intentionally made my home-organizing and coaching packages as focused as possible. Instead of having multiple tiered packages and price points, I only offer *one* eight-week coaching program and a single-day rate for any and all on-site projects. Having only one online offering and one in-person offering makes accounting and invoicing a breeze and is easy for my clients to understand and set a budget. A total win-win. Running a minimalist business has enabled me to focus on the things I love and do best, kept overhead low, and provided me with the ability to shift or take a break at any time. Freedom!

A few examples from some of the incredible women I have mentored:

- Dany had never been to design school but realized that she loved helping people style their spaces. She started offering home-styling packages to people from work, and her boss took note of her talent and hired her to design the interiors of that boss's new vacation home.
- Aviva loved photography but also had three kids to juggle and very little free time. She started offering family photo-shoot packages each weekend to people at her church as a way of slowly building her dream job.
- Ellen was a radiologist hungry for more creativity in her life. She developed an online program to teach women how to embrace midlife and beyond through movement, mindfulness, and meditation.

TRY IT

Want to find more passion and purpose at work? Answer the following questions:

- What's one thing you are really, really good at?
- What's one thing you do in a flow state—that is, when you lose track of time?
- What's one thing you do that makes you feel joyful and alive?
- What's one skill you're proud of?
- What's one thing you'd be thrilled to do more of at work?
- What's one thing you do to help or contribute in your personal life or in your community?
- What's one way you can infuse more of what you love into your existing career?

There you go. Now, stop settling and start building!

A Quick Story About My Uber Driver

I want to share a story about an Uber driver who changed my life. Let's call him Mike. After a long family trip, Jordan, our girls, and I arrived at the San Francisco International Airport, exhausted. Mike pulled up wearing a pressed suit and greeted us with a huge smile. He took our bags and offered us a tray of piping-hot coffee with cream and sugar. He was ready with bottled water, gum, and granola bars for the kids (who happened to be starving and cranky). I was confused. I had been in many, many rideshare vehicles before, and I'd never experienced anything like this. As we sat down, he presented us with a kit stocked with every imaginable charging cord in case our mobile batteries were low. This guy had thought of everything. Were we on some sort of hidden camera show? I was so curious and impressed that I spent the whole ride home interrogating him. I learned that he picks up a fresh batch of coffee to offer his passengers every hour or so. He has his car professionally cleaned each day and detailed each month. Each day he restocks his car with bottled water, gum, granola bars, and kid snacks. He wears a neatly pressed suit because it makes him feel polished and professional while he works. I learned that he had been a high-paid executive, and that this was a transitional job for him while he looked for the right next thing. "So why do you do all of this?" I asked. "Why put in all of this effort for a temporary job driving people home from the airport?" His response has stayed with me for years: "Anything I do, I give my all to. That's just who I am."

So many of us are biding our time in jobs that feel pointless or unfulfilling, but there is always an opportunity to show up in a different way. Instead of waiting for your job to fulfill you, ask *who you want to be* at work. Mike decided that no matter what he was doing he would operate with absolute commitment and integrity. He would overdeliver for his clients and do his best work each day. Why? Because not only would it have a positive impact on everyone he came into contact with, but it also just made him feel good.

TRY IT

Try taking 100 percent responsibility and ownership over how you show up at work. Yes, even if your boss is the *actual* worst, and Bob in accounting (yes, that one) is a total nightmare. How do you want to think, feel, and act *no matter what*? How can you show up as your best self? Who do you want to *be*? How can you *overdeliver, surprise, and delight*?

CREATING SYSTEMS: CAREER AND FINANCE EDITION

Now that you've learned how to own your money mindset, spend according to your values, and integrate more alignment into your career, it's time to set up some structure to help you stay organized, disciplined, and on track with your financial goals. Being more intentional with how you spend, save, and invest will make you feel more confident and in control—and ensure that you don't end up staring at a heap of shopping bags in your closet, wondering how you got there. Let's talk systems!

Centralize and Organize Your Finances

Do you know where your money is? Time for some real talk. In my experience most people are wildly checked out when it comes to their finances. Despite being an organizing expert, I've had to confront my own blind spots in this department and do some real work to become more engaged and conscious about where my money is. Getting real about your finances can feel overwhelming, vulnerable, or even triggering, especially if you're facing divorce, unemployment, or other financial challenges. Even if you'd rather do anything else, I encourage you to take charge of your finances with the following five steps.

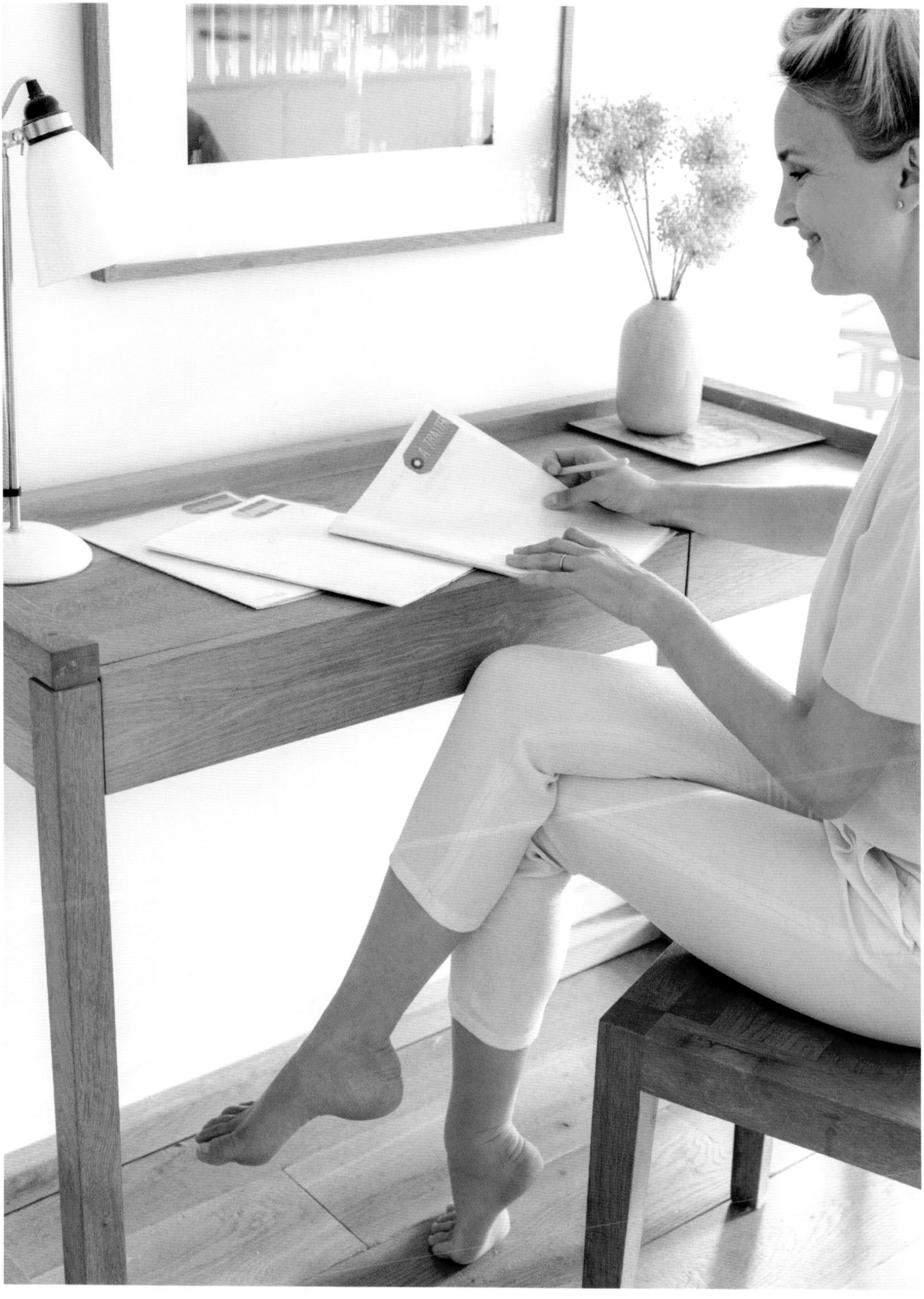

1. Centralize all your login and password information in one secure place. You can use a reputable password manager, such as LastPass or 1Password, or set up your own password-protected document. Boom.

2. Invest in a fireproof and waterproof lockbox or safe to centralize and store all of your important physical documents including:
   - Will and trust documents
   - Property deeds and titles
   - Mortgage or lease agreements
   - Vehicle titles and registration documents
   - Investment records
   - Stock certificates
   - Tax returns
   - Passports, birth certificates, social security cards, marriage license, and other legal documents
   - Health records and immunization records
   - External hard drives with important digital files, photos, and videos

3. Make a list of every credit card you carry, and jot down any outstanding debt for each one.

4. Note all your accounts, including checking, saving, and investment accounts with total balances for each one.

5. Make a list of all your assets, including your home, vehicles, and other items that contribute to your net worth.

Believe me, I know this is not a small ask, but having all your finances in order is essential for your peace of mind and will also be a true gift to family members who may need to resolve your estate after you die. Note: If you're in a marriage or partnership where the other person handles the finances, set up a time to have them give you a tour of your accounts, assets, and liabilities so you can fully understand where your money is going and learn how to access all your accounts and important documents.

Get Yourself a Budget, Stat!

Making a budget can sound like major snooze, but if you think of budgeting as a system of life design, it gets a lot more fun. Budget nerds, unite!

STEP ONE: GET REAL ABOUT YOUR CURRENT SPENDING

A budgeting app can automatically track and categorize your transactions so you can see where all your money is going in real time (I spent *what* on eating out last month!?) and make some thoughtful adjustments (time to stock up on groceries and get creative). High fives all around!

STEP TWO: CREATE A BASELINE BUDGET

We should all have a good sense of how much we need to cover our basic expenses and it doesn't take long to sort out. You can look up BASIC BUDGET TEMPLATE online or use the broad categories listed below to create your own baseline budget.

- Housing (this includes rent or mortgage as well as property tax, and home or rental insurance)
- Transportation (car payment, maintenance, gas, registration and insurance, rideshares, public transportation, parking, and tolls)
- Food (groceries and meals out)
- Utilities (water, gas, electric, garbage pickup, cable, internet, phones)
- Insurance (car, life, health)
- Medical (prescriptions, copays, out-of-pocket expenses)
- Childcare and/or pet care
- Debt (student loans, credit-card payments, personal loans)
- Taxes (although not a *spending category*, it's essential to consider taxes while budgeting–especially if you are self-employed or have any other forms of income that are not automatically taxed)

Get as specific as you can so you can add up these categories and easily see *exactly* how much money you need to cover your basic expenses. Depending on your current circumstances, this exercise can be liberating (Whoa, that's less than I thought!) or stressful (How on earth am I going to sustain these expenses?). Remember, you can always employ creative strategies to shift your lifestyle, location, or earning capacity to make the numbers work. Getting real about how much money you need to have or earn to pay your bills is an essential part of becoming a card-carrying adult.

STEP THREE: CREATE A DREAM BUDGET

Once you have a sense of your actual basic expenses, I encourage you to make a dream budget that includes all the extras that enhance your quality of life. This list might include:

- Home decor
- Clothing and accessories
- Personal-care treatments (massages, haircuts, waxing, facials, manicures)
- Travel
- Restaurants and entertainment (concerts, events, sporting events, movies)
- Mental health services (coaching, therapy, psychiatry)
- Health and fitness (gym membership, group classes, personal trainer, nutritionist, bodywork)
- Professional services (housecleaner, gardener, dog walker, tutor)
- Saving (retirement, college funds, emergency fund)
- Charitable giving

Make sure to customize your nice-to-have list, including only things that truly add value to your life. Estimate how much these things would cost each month and add this sum to your baseline budget total. This number represents how much you need for your ideal lifestyle. Now if you calculate how much you earn (or collectively earn with a partner) each month, you can clearly see what the gap is, if any. Say your ideal budget, added to your baseline budget, comes in at $10K a month and you currently earn $7K a month. You might give yourself the goal of earning an additional $3K per month, or you always have the option of deciding which of the additional items feels the most important and adding them one at a time until you hit your maximum. As a goal-setting junkie, I love having a financial goal rooted in exciting opportunities like traveling to Thailand, hosting a big party, or making a large contribution to an organization I love.

TRY IT

Total up your baseline and dream budget to calculate exactly how much money your ideal lifestyle costs. Take note of the gap between what you currently have or earn and the amount you would need to live your ideal life. This number can become a concrete financial goal to work toward and save for. You deserve it!

Automate Everything

Automating your finances can help you effortlessly contribute to savings, investment funds, college savings accounts, retirement funds, and philanthropy, as well as ensuring that you avoid late fees and penalties by paying your bills on time. It's a win-win-win situation.

Know That Compound Interest Is Your Friend

Here's the basic concept: Compound interest is the concept of earning interest on both the initial amount of money you invest, as well as on the earnings the capital accrues over time, resulting in exponential growth. It's like a snowball effect, where your money keeps growing faster and faster over time. Cha-ching! Here's how to get started:

- Educate yourself (or hire a financial expert) so you can choose the right investment strategy for you, depending on your income, risk tolerance, time horizon, and performance goals.

- Start early: The sooner you start investing, the more time your money has to grow on its own. It's like planting a little money tree and watching it flourish with each passing year. Grow, money tree, grow!
- Make regular contributions: To reap the full benefits of compound interest, make sure to contribute on a regular schedule no matter how seemingly small or insignificant the amount.
- Take advantage of tax-advantaged accounts: Individual retirement accounts (IRAs) or 401(k)s offer tax benefits for retirement savings and can help you grow your money faster by reducing tax burdens.

Did anyone else fall asleep? I know—not the jazziest of sections. I recognize that the strategies I'm suggesting don't exactly fall under "quick win" territory, but organizing your finances, creating an intentional budgeting strategy, and leveraging the power of automation and compound interest will set you up for financial freedom in the long run.

IMPLEMENTING HABITS:
CAREER AND FINANCE EDITION

When it comes to finances it truly is the little things that add up to make a big difference. A roundup of small but mighty habit shifts to optimize your financial wellness coming right up!

Practice:

- Checking your money mindset and tweaking, if necessary.
- Spending according to your values (a spending journal may help increase awareness of your daily spending habits).
- Limiting impulse purchases and shopping with a budget and a plan.
- Reviewing your budget seasonally and making any necessary adjustments.

- Trying a purchase pause for a set period of time so you can save money and increase self-awareness of your shopping triggers.
- Paying bills on time and/or checking that auto-payments went through.
- Automating contributions to investment, retirement, and education accounts.
- Setting up an annual time to update passwords and logins, and clear out and shred any unnecessary documents.
- Implementing a simple gratitude and mindfulness practice to cultivate abundance.

A Quick Word About Debt

The amount of consumer debt amassed by the average household in the United States is staggering. I've been to homes where entire closets are packed with clothes (with tags still on) that have never been worn, and appliances that have never even been unboxed. All those items used to be time and money. Ouch. Luckily, the solution is simple, and you can start today by following these two golden rules:

- Do not spend more than you have.
- Do not buy what you don't need. Period.

If you are already living with consumer debt, you are not alone. Before you can start thinking about saving or adding lots of fun stuff to your budget, make a plan for how you intend to pay off your debt (and not incur any additional debt). Your plan should include the following items:

- Stop spending on your credit cards—use cash or your ATM card to pay for everything so you are only spending money you have.
- Work with a debt counselor to figure out how to consolidate and potentially reduce your outstanding debt.
- If you are unable to consolidate your outstanding debt, create a strategy to pay off accounts with the smallest balances and/or the highest interest rates first.

- Determine the maximum amount you can afford to pay toward your debt each month and set it up as an auto-payment from your bank account.

THE BOTTOM LINE

Money is a tool we can optimize by thoughtfully aligning our values with our earning, spending, and saving. We can start to feel more abundant by redefining *enough* and managing our money mindset, and we can claim control over our finances by setting a budget, automating bills and contributions, and organizing our financials and documents.

YOUR PROMPTS

Ready to give your career and finances a kick in the pants? I got you. Consider these prompts to get you going:

- On a scale of 1 to 5, how satisfied do you feel with your financial circumstances?
- Which do you need to focus on most right now: Earning, saving, or investing?
- Do you know where your money is stored and have login and password info organized for all your financial accounts?
- Do you have a values-based financial goal you want to work toward?
- What's one small but critical change you will commit to making toward improving your finances? (Examples: Gathering logins and passwords, getting real about debt, creating a monthly savings goal, and selling things you don't need.)
- What's one way you can infuse your work with more of your passion and purpose?

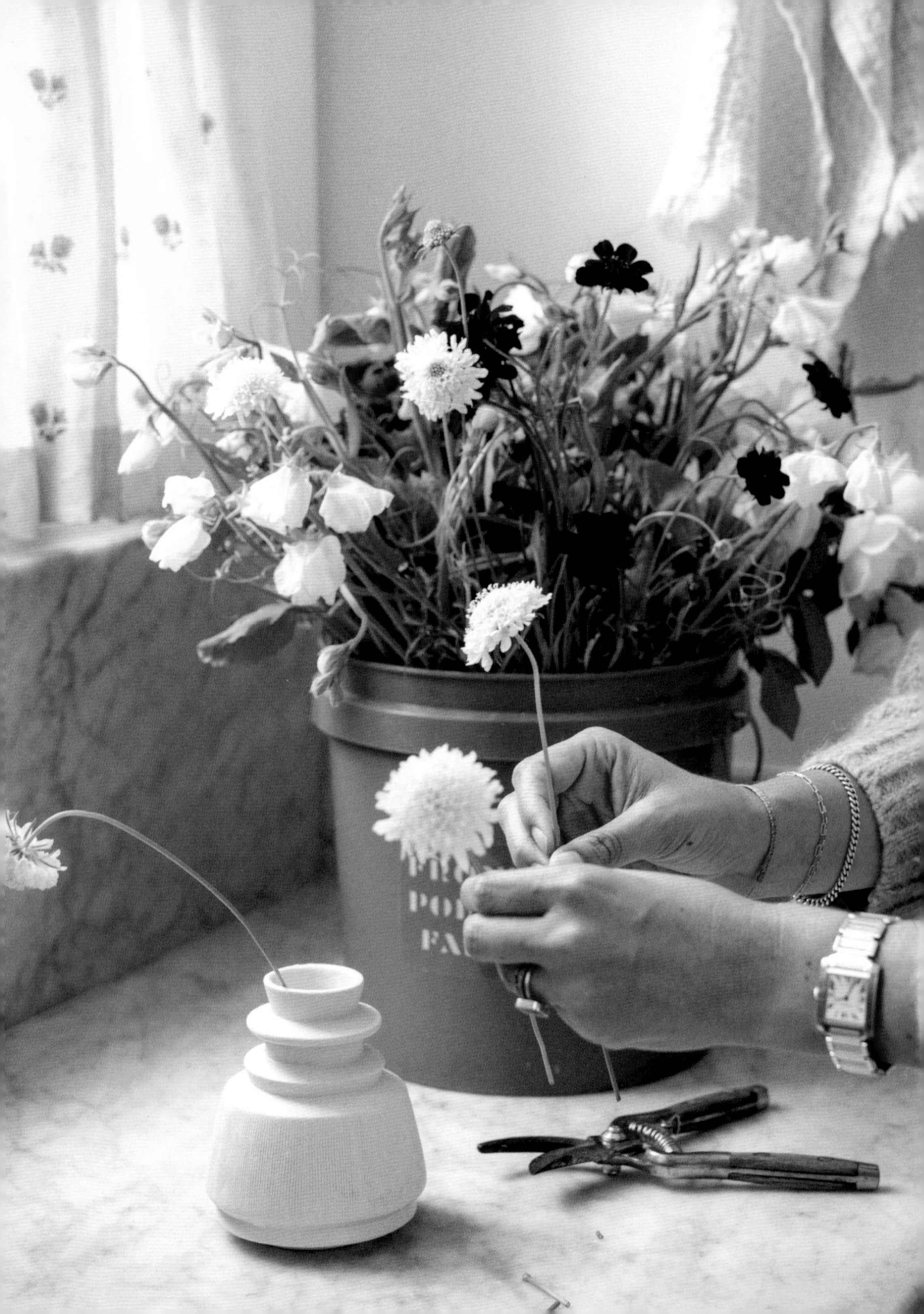

Personal Development

Cultivating creativity, curiosity, and growth is a crucial part of human development and evolution. As children, we are encouraged to play, explore, and try new things, but as adults it's easy to get trapped in stale and stagnant routines. In this chapter, we'll explore how you can ignite your personal interests and passions while also giving back.

Ready to create a more fulfilling, meaningful, and dynamic life? Let's dive in...

ADJUSTING VOLUME: PERSONAL DEVELOPMENT EDITION

Did you know that the more you improve yourself, the more you improve the world? Just by getting clarity on what you want and working toward becoming the very best version of yourself, you'll start to inspire the people around you, at the very least creating a less grumpy world around you. And for the skeptics who hear the words *personal development* and reflexively roll their eyes, I promise that it doesn't have to involve chanting in a circle, walking barefoot over glowing coals, or making extended eye contact with strangers. The version of personal development I recommend is grounded in turning *up* the volume on the things that light you up inside and dialing *down* the volume on old, tired stories and limiting belief systems that are dragging you down. Let's get started!

Banish the Blame Game

What if, starting today, you took full, 100 percent responsibility for your life? That means total ownership over your health, your relationships, your career, your finances, your messy fridge, your uninspiring wardrobe—all of it. It's so easy to complain, finger-point, and cast blame. But, here's the thing: None of it will get you closer to what you want. It turns out that blaming other people for your unachieved results (even if justified—seriously, though, why does my family insist on shoving mystery tinfoil balls into my perfect fridge?) will not advance your cause. It will likely just lead down a path of more negativity. I want to encourage you to do something very difficult. Stop complaining. Stop blaming. Stop finger-pointing. Make the decision to just stop it and put all of that wasted energy into creating the results you want. Trust me, it takes just as long (if not longer) to pick up the dirty socks your husband left out on the couch as to lecture him about leaving his socks on the couch again. Likewise, you could spend years of your life moaning about how much litter gets dumped in your neighborhood (especially if, like me, you live between a major hospital and a supermarket—both high-capacity litter generators) or you could put on some gloves, grab a trash bag, and get the job done yourself. I used to come in the house every day grumbling about the curbside litter in front of our house, and now each weekend I take five minutes and clear the trash from my trash-filled block. New mantra: Less complaining, more taking care of business.

TRY IT

For the next week, challenge yourself to banish all blame from your vocabulary. Each time you're tempted to blame someone for something–anything–channel your energy instead into doing something small and positive yourself that will get you closer to the results you want.

Do More of What You Love

I always begin my home-organizing sessions by asking my clients: What do you really love that you wish you had more time for? I lead with this question because it's absolutely fascinating to learn about what lights people up inside (we're all such unique and spectacular little snow-flakes). The answer eventually guides me in how I set up their homes. My client Phoebe loves drawing people in hats. She's even started a small drawing club for other people who want to learn how to draw people in hats. You simply can't make this stuff up. My client Claudia feels most alive when she is solving very complex crossword puzzles. And get this: My daughter's friend Maya loves open-water swimming so much that she swims for hours and hours straight, sometimes through the middle of the night, in icy, shark-infested water while a little boat follows her to make sure she doesn't drown. This is what she does *by choice. For fun.* And at just sixteen years old, she's already broken multiple world records and raised over $75,000 for pediatric cancer research. *Just by doing what she loves* (I mean, she got *stung on the face by a jelly-fish,* and just kept swimming!). My point is this: All of us are born with wildly varying interests and passions (Periodontists. Podiatrists. Proc-tologists. Bless these people). When you fully embrace the things you are drawn to, and integrate them more fully into your life, you'll not only become more pleasant to be around, but you'll also have a greater impact, and inspire others to do the same. Go on, do more of what you love, share your gifts, and shine brightly like the rare diamond that you are. The world is waiting.

TURN ENVY INTO INSPO

Envy is defined as a painful or resentful desire centered on someone who has something that you want but do not have. While envy is generally considered a negative emotion, I think that it can be used as a helpful and constructive tool. If you pay close attention to the circumstances that lead to you experiencing feelings of envy, you will be able to identify *exactly* what you are craving more of in your own life. An instant shortcut to self-discovery. Now you can put your awareness to good use! Instead of wasting all your precious brain energy coveting what your friend/neighbor/colleague has, get to work figuring out how to create it for yourself. Off you go.

TRY IT

Consider:

- What would you do for free and for fun?
- When do you lose track of time and find yourself in a flow state?
- What sparks your interests and makes you feel more vital and alive?
- What's one tiny way you can infuse more of what you love into your day, week, or month?

Get close to what you love and do it as much as possible. Starting now.

Give Your Thoughts an Upgrade

One of the most game-changing things I learned during my life coach school training was that your *thoughts*, not your *circumstances*, produce your feelings. This means that no matter how objectively challenging

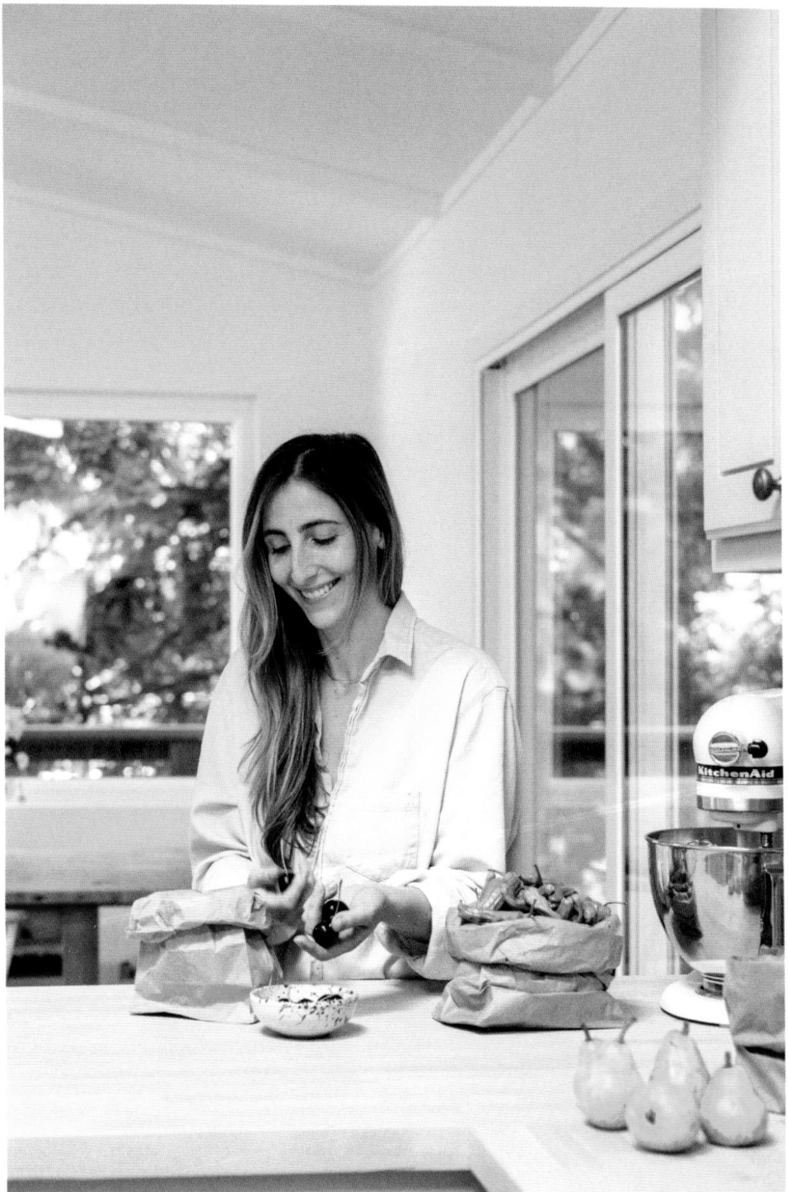
KitchenAid

your circumstances may be, you always get to decide how you want to think and feel about them. This is very good news! In a whole sea of possible thoughts, we get to cherry-pick the ones that will best serve us, *no matter what is coming at us.*

When you choose to replace a negative thought with a more productive one, your entire mood and mindset will shift. It's kind of like magic. Context is important, and the world we live in is not equitable or fair in many ways, especially when it comes to power and privilege. I believe that positive change is possible for anyone, but I want to acknowledge that for those who have faced personal or systemic discrimination, this work may require a greater level of muscle and faith.

Say you get laid off from your job and find yourself thinking, "I can't believe this is happening to me." That thought has a high probability of leading to feelings of *despair*, which is fine if you want to have a brief pity party before moving on. Totally understandable. But, if you want to feel *motivated* instead, you could try test-driving a new thought like this: "I was hired before and I will be hired again, but now I get the opportunity to find a job that's a better fit for me." Same exact circumstance, but just by altering a single thought you can move from despair to motivation. That's powerful. Here's the kicker: Most of us have tons of subconscious thoughts swirling around in our brains, oblivious to what those thoughts are creating in our lives. It's up to us to start paying attention to what we are thinking, as curious, nonjudgmental observers, so we can make the choice to replace our low-level, unproductive thoughts with new and improved thoughts. Here's how this works:

- Step one: Identify your current (possibly subconscious) thought patterns.
- Step two: Decide which unproductive thoughts you'd like to upgrade.
- Step three: Identify new high-level thoughts to purposefully practice.

Reminder: The only way to shift a thought or belief system is to identify and practice a new one again and again until it feels second nature.

Warning: You will almost certainly want to change your given circumstances to feel better; e.g., *I just want my job back! If I hadn't lost my job, I would feel just fine right now.* While this may be true, it won't get you where you want to go unless you have a magical ability to turn back time and alter reality (if only!). Instead of arguing with reality, focus on how you *want* to think about your given circumstances, because how you *think* will determine how you *feel*. If you want to feel better, this may be some of the most important work you ever do in your life. Simply put: Change your thoughts, change your life.

TRY IT

Pick any circumstance in your life and then decide how you want to feel about it. Next, identify and test out a new thought that will help create your desired feeling. Make sure the thought is believable to you or this process will feel like a silly affirmation exercise. You can't reasonably leap from "I hate my boss" to "I love my boss." Instead, try a more reasonable shift to something like, "My boss may be going through difficulties of her own right now." Sometimes a tiny little baby step thought can make a big difference in shifting your overall mood and mindset. Remember: No matter what you come up against, you always have the agency to choose what you think and believe about it.

Ask Helpful Questions

It sounds like common sense, but when you ask questions, your brain takes it as a cue to get to work and start answering them. If you're in the habit of asking yourself questions that lead down a dark road, such as "Why do I never make any progress on anything?" or "Why is my house always such a disaster?" or "Why does my partner never help with anything?" it may be time to switch it up and focus on open-ended, solution-oriented questions. Instead, try: "How can I set myself up to make better progress?" or "What steps can I take to feel better in my house?" or "How can I enlist my partner to participate in all the things that need to be done?" Asking better questions will help your brain come up with better and more helpful answers. Even if you're stuck in a major rut, you can jump-start your journey to thinking differently about your life and circumstances just by upleveling your questions.

Here are some of my favorite powerful questions to ask. You can use any of them as a journaling or meditation prompt.

- What am I doing, or not doing, to get the results that I want?
- What am I doing that isn't working?
- How can I best direct my time, energy, and resources right now?
- What am I willing to give up to get what I want?
- What do I love that I don't do enough of?
- How are my current habits standing in the way of living the life I want?
- What would I regret not doing?
- How can I lead a more generous life?
- How can I reconnect to my passion and purpose?
- What was I born to do, learn, create, or contribute?
- What do I want my legacy to be?

Shift the Narrative

Our brains are bombarded with an immense amount of information each day, and they need to work as efficiently as possible to process it all. *Confirmation bias* refers to our brain's tendency to *confirm* our preexisting beliefs while *ignoring or downplaying* information that contradicts or disproves those beliefs. It's clever really—like a mental shortcut. If you believe you are a victim and always have bad luck in life, your brain will get busy looking for evidence that this is true. *I never find good parking spots. People always cut ahead of me in line. I always get ignored at work meetings.* Same, same, same. Conversely, if you believe that good things always find you, your brain will go on a fact-finding mission to prove that and will stockpile evidence in support of that belief. *I beat the traffic to work. My boss remembered my anniversary. I got the biggest slice of cake at the party!* Once we understand how confirmation bias works, we can use it to our advantage, deciding which beliefs and stories we want to reinforce on purpose. If perception creates our reality, it behooves us to edit unproductive belief systems and reshape narratives that point our brain in a more positive or constructive direction. To prove this, I'm going to share two different stories about my life. Both of them are 100 percent true.

STORY ONE

My life has been punctuated by grief, trauma, and loss. I had a lonely childhood. My parents were a mismatch from the start and split up when I was just three years old. I don't have a single memory of the two of them together other than when they sat me down to announce their divorce and talk about who would keep the cat. I longed for a sibling, and rarely saw or enjoyed gatherings, parties, or rituals with my relatives, who lived across the country in New York. Eventually, my father remarried and had a son, but our age gap was so large that I barely got to know him before I left for college. After another difficult divorce and multiple failed relationships, my father struggled on and off with crippling bouts of depression. We were very close, and while I did everything I could think of to help him, he ultimately chose to end his life by overdosing on pills. I was the one who found him and called the police. Despite being a new mother with a six-month-old baby and a toddler, I was responsible for cleaning out his home, planning his funeral, and resolving his estate because I was the only relative who lived near him. My life has never been the same since losing him.

STORY TWO

My life has been defined by creativity, community, and travel. I was raised in the San Francisco Bay Area by parents who were brilliant, creative, and loving. I made friends easily and cultivated an incredible community through school, summer camps, and my participation

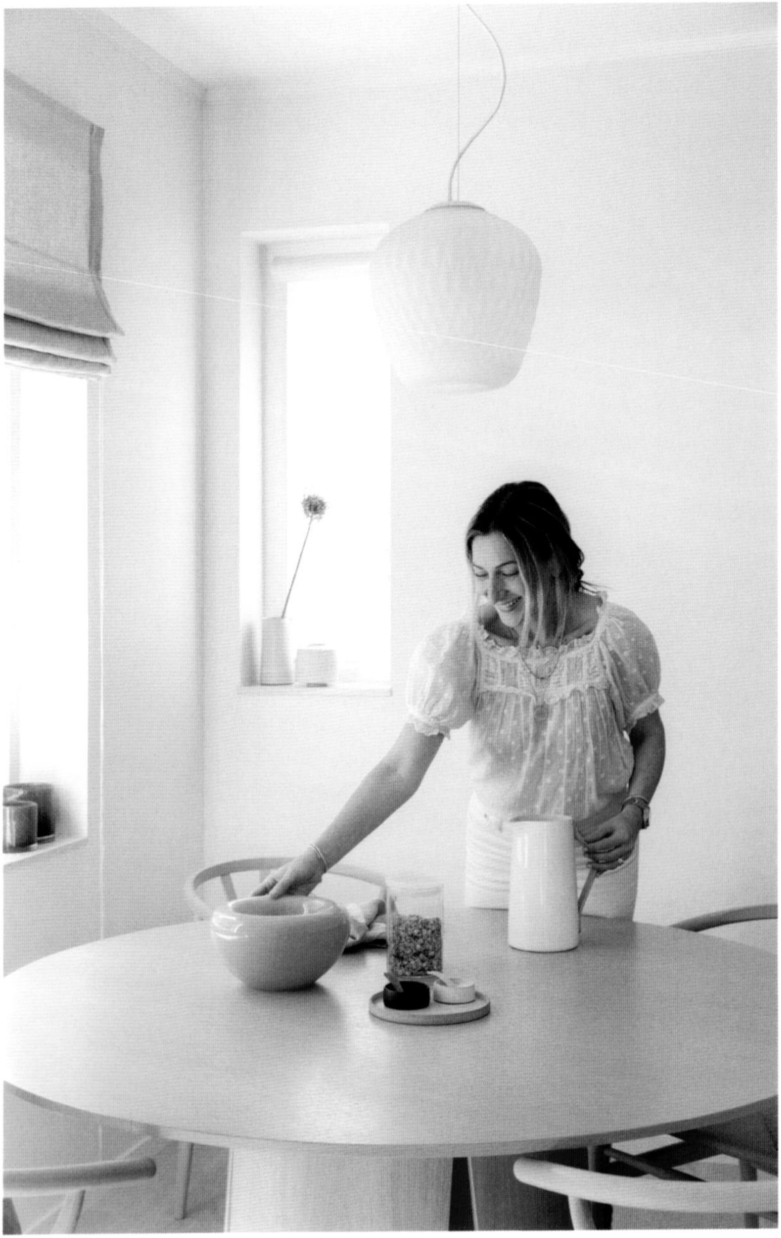

in the theater arts. My parents encouraged and supported my love of travel, and in high school and college, they helped me coordinate a summer exchange program in Spain, an artist's residency in Italy, and a year abroad studying drama in the UK. After graduating from college, I lived and worked as an actor and event producer in incredible cities like London, Chicago, Los Angeles, and San Francisco, before starting my own business as a home organizer, author, and speaker. I am married to a wonderful and supportive man, have two incredibly dynamic, beautiful, and hilarious children, and my brother (despite being much younger than me) has become one of my best friends in the world. I feel privileged and grateful every day to have built the family of my dreams and to get to do meaningful work that I love.

———

Now, as I said before, both of these stories are true, but one of them feels a lot more hopeful than heartbreaking. When I tell myself the first story, it makes me want to curl up in a ball. The second story leaves me feeling grateful, energized, and motivated.

Craft your stories carefully. The stories you tell about your life will inform how you continue to live it.

TRY IT

What story do you currently tell about your life to yourself and others? How do you speak about your childhood? Your family? Your finances? Your career? What belief system is your brain super cozy with that you want to shift or change? Remember, you can always recraft these stories and reshape how you think about your past, present, and future.

Be Grateful Ahead of Time

You don't have to wait for your circumstances to change to start feeling better about your life. This might sound a wee bit California woo-woo, but stay with me here. Try being grateful *ahead of time* for the things you want but don't yet have. I'm challenging you to practice envisioning what you want so clearly that it feels like it has already happened: The book you wrote. The house you bought. The marathon you ran. The trip around the world you took. Clarify your vision and keep that vision super close. Think about it, write it down, daydream about it. Fill in the details in your mind and imagine them as if they were real. *Feel* what that would feel like. Bask in the glory of accomplishment. Cultivating a sense of abundance and gratitude *before* you have the things you want will help shift your energy and inspire you to start actually creating these things. Act as if you were already where you want to be, cultivate gratitude ahead of time, and you'll start feeling better today.

TRY IT

Feel grateful on purpose. Pick one dream or goal that feels out of reach and imagine that it is already as good as done. Flesh out the details in your mind of exactly how it would feel to accomplish that goal. Sit with that feeling and let it wash over you like a wave.

Give Back to Get Back

Years ago, when I was in a bit of a slump, my mom gave me some advice I'll never forget. She told me to direct my attention away from myself and toward helping others. Her wise words reminded me of the beautiful Jewish value known as *tikkun olam*, a term that translates to "repair the world." The idea is that we all have a moral responsibility to actively contribute toward the healing and improvement of our fractured world. This can include anything from supporting marginalized communities, advocating for human rights, cleaning up our environment, or working toward reducing poverty, discrimination, and inequality. At the time my mom's advice felt counterintuitive because I was anxious about money and not exactly feeling like I had a lot to offer, but I tried it anyway, and guess what? It worked. I donated a nice coat I never wore to a women's shelter. I cleaned out our pantry and dropped off a crate of canned goods to our local food bank. I sent a check to the crisis support service center

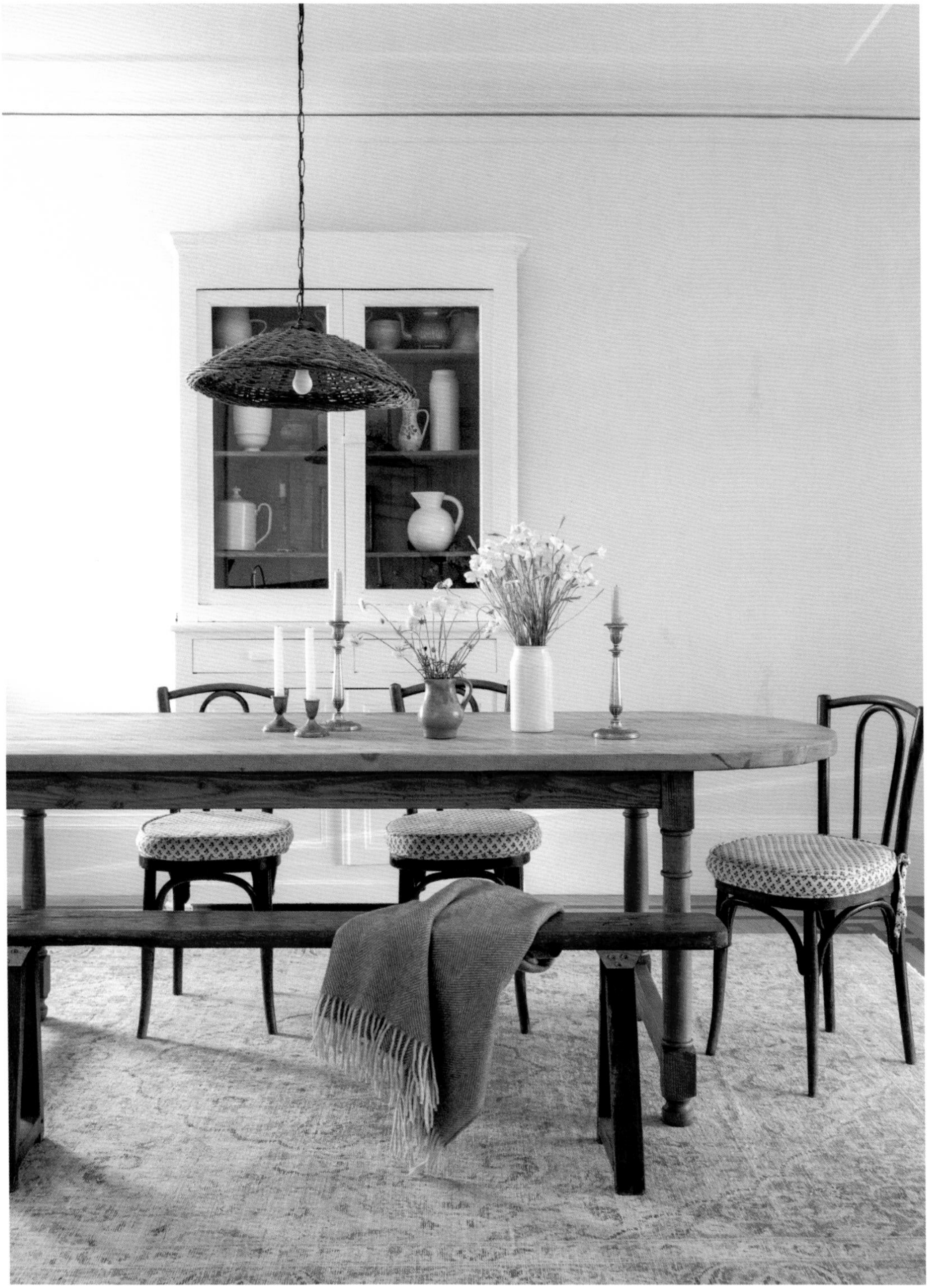

that had provided me with free counseling when I had lost my father. It all felt really, really good. These simple gestures helped shift my mind-set, boost my confidence, and strengthen connections within my local community. Engaging in acts of kindness, compassion, and generosity will help you take part in repairing some of the cracks in our broken world, while also leading to new relationships, and a deeper sense of meaning and purpose in your life. Find small and simple ways to serve, donate, help, and give back. You'll always get more than you give.

And Now for the Growth Part!

Self-awareness is a big part of personal development. Each of us has innate gifts, skills, and talents, as well as areas we need to work on or improve. Since self-improvement is time-consuming and hard, the challenge is to sort out which areas are actually worth improving first. For example, I've pretty much accepted that I don't like small talk, loud chewing, huge crowds, or overhead lighting. I'm a super-sensitive person and it would take SO much work for me to change these things. I do, however, think it would be worthwhile for me to work on my *extreme* impatience, as well as my tendency to assume that the people I love are dead in an alley somewhere if they don't answer the phone or reply to my texts right away.

TRY IT

Try owning all your stuff (good and bad) and identify which areas you'd like to work on improving, and which everyone should probably just get used to. By becoming more mindful and intentional about where you'd like to focus your growth, you can shift tendencies and traits that don't serve you (or have a negative impact on others) and be kind to yourself about the rest. Self-awareness is key! Remember, there is nothing worse than someone who thinks they are low maintenance who is actually high maintenance (and, yes, that is a *When Harry Met Sally* reference).

TINY WAYS TO GIVE BACK

Stop crying in the mirror and turn your attention to being more generous, helpful, and kind in even the tiniest of ways. Giving back reinforces the idea that you *are* enough, and you *have* enough, and we are all connected so you are not all alone in this hard, cruel world. Let's go!

- Offer to run errands for elderly neighbors who might need some extra support.
- Practice small gestures like paying for someone's coffee, holding the door open, or helping someone across the street.
- Dole out compliments like party favors.
- Pick up litter on your block or join a neighborhood or beach cleanup crew.
- Give away something nice that you never use to someone who would love it.
- Make a meaningful contribution (whatever that means to you) to the organization of your choice.
- Help spread the word about a cause or initiative that you believe in.
- Bring a hot meal to someone who is sick or struggling.
- Give blood (especially if you happen to be a universal donor and "baby hero" like my husband, who is beloved at our local blood donation center).
- Volunteer a few hours of your time to a school, shelter, or local organization.
- Vote and make sure that everyone you know is voting.

Become a Finisher

Starting something new is fun and exciting and full of hope, promise, and buzzy excitement. Finishing requires grit and patience and discomfort. Ever struggled to finish a course, a work or personal project, or even a book? You're not alone. Finishing is *hard*. I've made a whole career out of helping people stay on course so they can finish projects that are important to them. Here are some hot tips from a pro.

MAKE SURE YOUR GOAL IS WORTH FINISHING

My friend Hedy used to talk all the time about how she wanted to lose ten pounds, but she also put butter on her pizza. Yes, she liked the *idea* of losing weight, but she wasn't invested enough to commit to meaningful behavioral change. As the butter melted onto the cheese, I gently suggested that maybe she wasn't actually *committed* to losing weight. In the end she realized that food was a joy center and she had bigger fish to fry, and that spelled the end for operation-lose-ten-pounds. Before you spend your precious time trying to finish something, make sure it's worth finishing. It's perfectly okay to let go of the hobby you never took seriously, the business that never got off the ground, even the weight that you never lost, if these goals no longer resonate or hold value for you. We don't judge here.

DO ONE BIG THING AT A TIME

I have a rule that has served me very well: I give 100 percent to anything I do, and I only pursue one big goal at a time. Tackling one goal at a time means you can harness your full mental capacity, focus, and energy on that single task instead of diluting your efforts by spreading yourself too thin. I extend this rule to all areas of my life: If I'm reading a book, I won't buy another one until I'm finished. If I'm taking a class or a course, I won't sign up for any other courses, workshops, or trainings until I've completed the one I'm already enrolled in. When I'm working on completing a book, I say *no* to . . . basically everything else. There's only so much our brains can process, digest, and focus on, so when you take it one goal at a time, you supersize your chances of finishing.

KNOW THAT REJECTION MEANS NOTHING

I made an early career out of avoiding rejection. I quit when things got hard. I didn't tell my crushes that I liked them. I made it a rule to play it cool. And you know where that got me? Not very far. If you want to grow, change, evolve, and do big things in life, getting more comfortable with rejection is simply a must. Want to get a big book deal? Get ready for a lot of editors to pass on your project. Want to start a business? Spoiler alert: Not everyone will want to hire you. Want to find a life partner? You're going to have to go on a lot of first dates. Facing rejection is messy and awkward and vulnerable, but it also means you are building your resilience. Allow yourself to feel the sting of rejection when it does happen and then be super kind to yourself and keep moving forward. Rejection (and even complete failure) is often part of the necessary path to success. Anything truly worth doing is worth a little rejection along the way. Ouch, now onward!

STOP CHANGING YOUR MIND

Here's the thing: Most people don't fail because of lack of talent or aptitude, but because they don't stick with their goals or desired outcomes long enough to see success. I mentor a number of brilliant, talented, and creative women who block themselves from experiencing success because they constantly change their minds about their goals (Lily, I love you!). I'll watch them make a detailed plan to scale their home-organizing business, and then halt all progress because they've decided maybe they should pursue their love of photography. Then before they really dig in to the photography route, they'll get an itch to start experimenting with prop styling. Changing your mind is often an unconscious way of playing it safe. If you never fully go after your goals, you never have to face failure or rejection. My advice? Pick one goal to focus on for a set amount of time. Write down all your other brilliant ideas as they emerge and revisit them only after you've reached your original goal. Stay the course, my friends.

BE NICER TO YOURSELF—FOR THE LOVE OF ALL THINGS HOLY!

Relentless self-criticism is a poison that will get you nowhere fast, and there is literally no upside to beating yourself up. If you slip up, or don't follow through on something, don't use it as an excuse to submit to defeat. Pull yourself up off the ground, give yourself a sweet little pep talk and a big dose of grace, and then recommit. The sooner you start having your own back, the better.

MAKE IT MICRO

Humans are wired to seek growth, but most of us get easily overwhelmed and quit when we try to do too much too fast. Try trimming your goals down into itty-bitty baby steps. Whenever I write a book, I only think about the chapter ahead of me. If that feels too overwhelming, I'll set a timer and write a single paragraph. You'll work harder, and stay the course, if your goal feels attainable, so cut your goals in half. And if it's still too big, do it again. And again. Keep going until they feel manageable, and then get to work.

KICK PERFECTIONISM TO THE CURB

Please stop letting your dreams wilt and die in the name of perfectionism. I know so many people who are hiding their brilliance from the world because of the crippling fear of being imperfect. News flash, friends: We're all imperfect! And even if perfect were an actual thing (it's not), it would be dull as dirt. Stumble forward imperfectly toward the finish line, start embracing *good enough*, and then give yourself a well-deserved high five at the finish line.

TAKE CONSISTENT ACTION

Most of us get the relationship between confidence and success backward. You don't need confidence to pursue a challenging goal. You build confidence *through* pursuing a difficult goal. Instead of waiting to feel confident, start taking brave, repetitive action and confidence will follow. Once more for the people in the back—brave action first and then confidence.

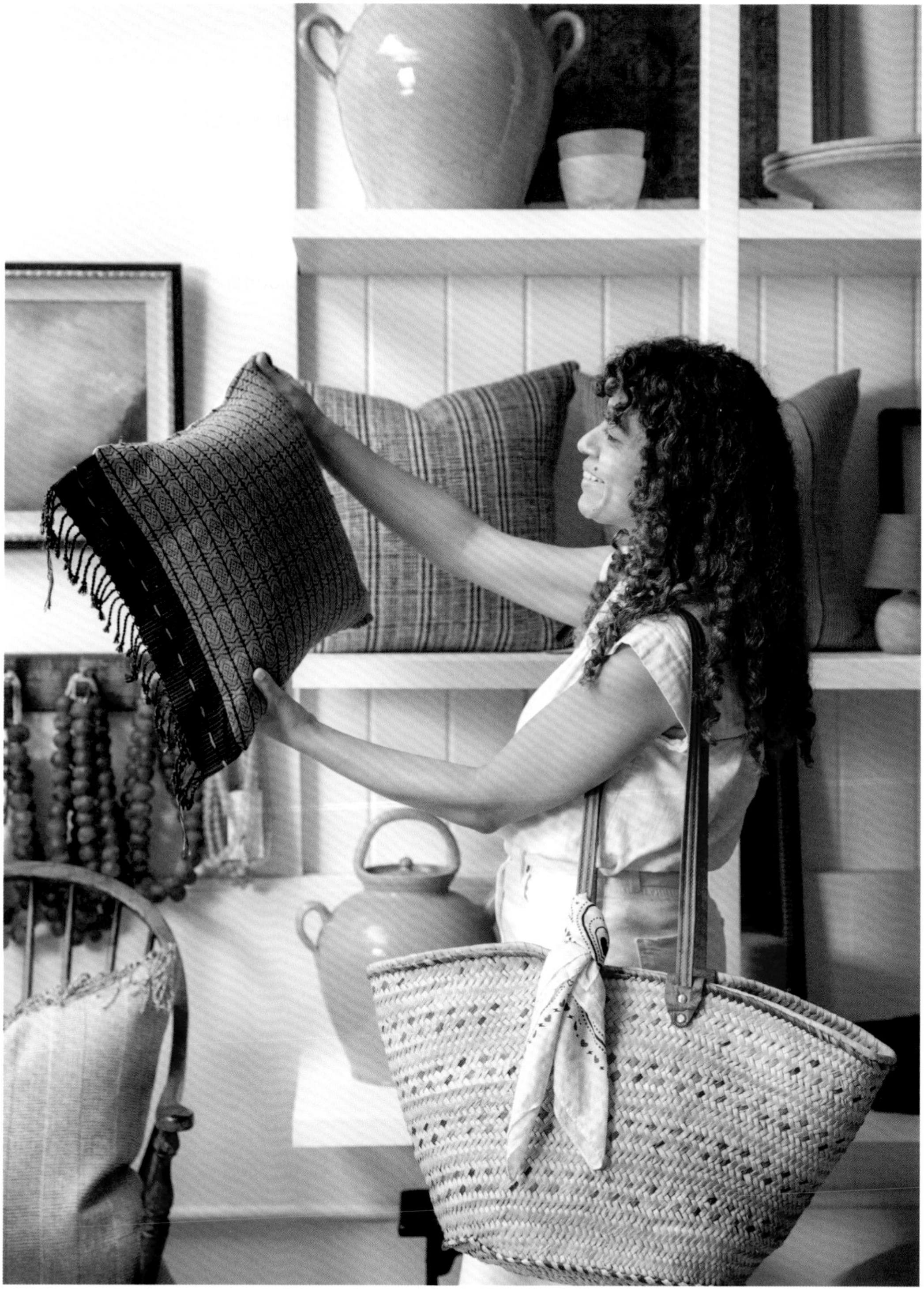

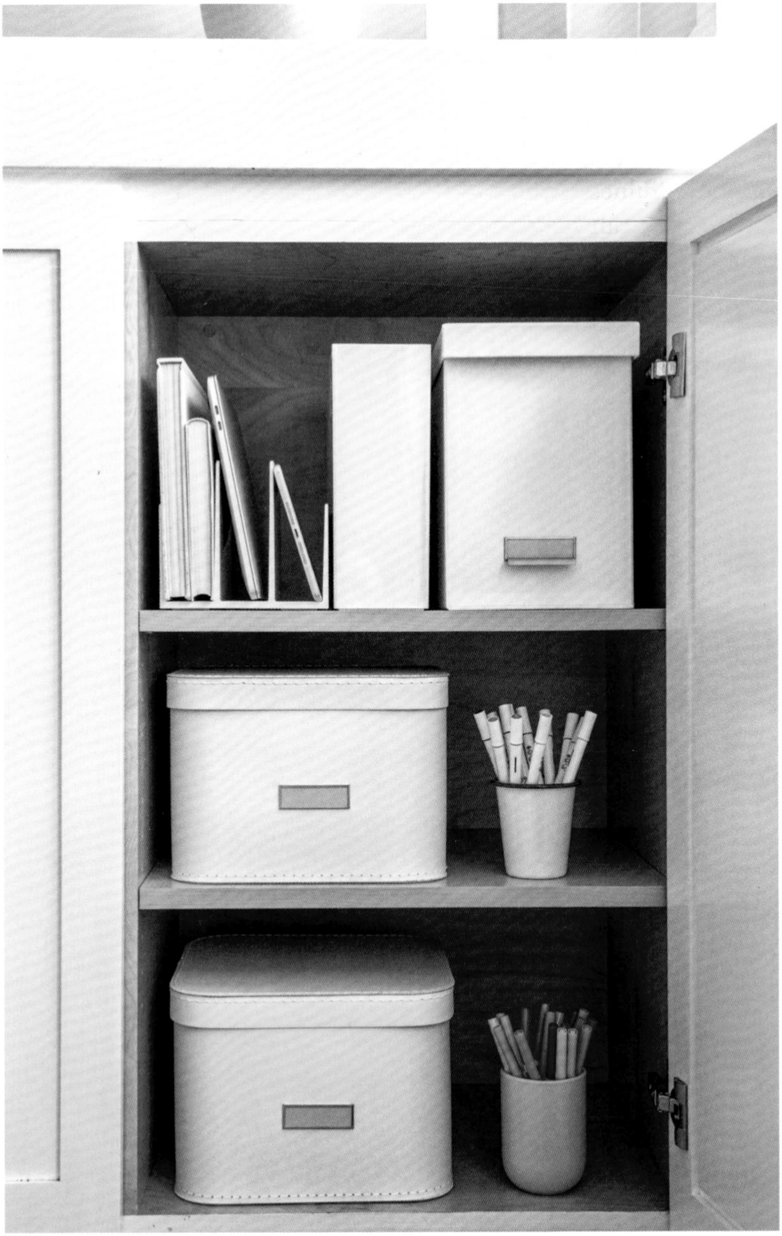

CREATING SYSTEMS: PERSONAL DEVELOPMENT EDITION

Personal development encompasses a wide range of activities and practices, including goal setting, self-reflection, continuous learning, and even mindfulness and meditation. Implementing systems or simple automations can help you infuse more personal development into your life with minimal effort.

Set a Stretch Goal

Each year, on December 31, I write down a stretch goal for the year ahead. I like to choose a goal that feels challenging, exciting, and a bit out of my comfort zone. If I feel a little bit nervous and exhilarated when I think about it, I know I'm on the right track. Past goals have included living abroad for a year, studying improv at the Second City Conservatory in Chicago, doubling my income, and publishing my first book. Setting a stretch goal each year ensures that I am continually trying new things, using different parts of my brain, and stretching myself to my highest capacity.

> **TRY IT**
>
> Try setting your own stretch goal for the year, or maybe even just the season ahead. Make your goal specific and measurable, while also defining success on your own terms. Your goal should be intrinsically motivated and rooted in your own values and priorities, as opposed to being linked to outside pressures.

Mix It Up, Shake It Up

It's easy to get stuck in stale, repetitive routines, so it's up to us to integrate more fun, curiosity, and adventure into our lives. When was the last time you dressed totally differently, tried a new type of cuisine, changed your route to work, or took yourself on a little adventure?

Cultivating curiosity as a regular part of your life will help you feel more present, engaged, and mindful.

TRY IT

Schedule a daily, weekly, or even monthly moment to step out of your comfort zone and engage with the world in a different way. You might just schedule a weekly appointment called "Adventure Time!" to make sure you regularly mix things up. Some ideas to get started:

- Read about a fascinating topic you know nothing about—wait, how *do* TVs even work?
- Identify a city you've never been to and plan a trip to explore it— you don't have to go far to experience something novel.
- Strike up a conversation with a stranger and gain a new perspective.
- Try a different route to work, errands, or school pickups and experience your surroundings with fresh perspective.
- Go to a show, concert, or museum you've never been to.
- Play tourist in your own city and take yourself sightseeing.
- Open your taste buds to a new experience by trying a new cuisine.
- Rearrange your furniture for an instant mental and environmental refresh.

Automate Giving Back

I believe that most of us want to do good, contribute to our local communities, and help people who are struggling, but life can get in the way of showing up the way we want to. If you want to make actively giving back a part of your life, try automating your preferred methods of philanthropy.

TRY IT

Experiment with any of the following ideas or come up with your own small wins:

- Automate donations–set up automatic donations to the charities of your choice to ensure consistent contribution without manual intervention.
- Use a roundup app to round up your everyday purchases to the nearest dollar and donate the spare change to charitable organizations.
- Set up a consistent day and time to volunteer or do community service, even if it's just once a season.
- Sign up to serve meals at a church or soup kitchen annually on major holidays like Christmas or Thanksgiving (or even non-holiday times).
- Participate in charity walks, runs, or challenges that you can fit into your schedule, combining philanthropic efforts with fitness goals.
- Participate in corporate gifting programs–many companies offer the opportunity to donate a portion of your salary directly from your paycheck and some will even match the gift.
- Link a cause you want to support in your email signature and on your social media accounts.

Schedule Travel Breaks

Traveling to new places exposes you to different cultures, languages, traditions, and belief systems. Exploring more of the world will broaden your perspective, shift your mindset, and help you appreciate diversity. I am hands-down the best version of myself when I travel. The second I land in a new city, I feel instantly more present, curious, and engaged. Since travel has always been at the top of my priority list, I've always found a way to incorporate it into my life–even on a shoestring

PLAN YOUR DREAM DAY

One day, many years ago, Jordan surprised me on my birthday by driving me to the Oakland International Airport. I didn't realize until he parked what was happening, but it ended up being one of the most delightful days of my life. We flew less than an hour to Los Angeles and spent the next twenty-four hours doing all my favorite things. (Jordan knew I was yearning for more travel, and I missed my friends since leaving Los Angeles.) We walked around different neighborhoods. We got the spicy tuna on crispy rice that I can never find outside of LA. We ate ice cream cones in the sun and had dinner with two of my best friends. I was struck by how just one glorious day could make me feel completely refreshed, inspired, and creatively recharged for weeks. Now, one of my favorite things to ask other people is what their dream day would look like. It says a lot about what they value. Some people are interested in high-intensity sports or hikes or physical challenges, while others just want to drink tea and do a massive puzzle in peace. And the thing is, most of what I hear from clients is quite simple and attainable with a little planning and intentionality. So, here's my invitation to you: Plan your own dream day for yourself. Here's how.

Imagine Your Dream Day Details

Would you stay home, go out, or travel somewhere new? What would you eat? What activities would you do? What would you wear? Would you enjoy your dream day alone or invite others? Brainstorm on a blank sheet of paper if that helps. Get as detailed as you possibly can.

Dream Big! But Not Too Big

Your dream day must be rooted in reality or else you won't give it to yourself. If you've just had a baby, or broken your leg, or your resources are limited, then zipping off to Paris may not be doable, right? But it is possible to scale that dream back or find a way to get even just a taste of what you are craving (playing some Edith Piaf while enjoying a glass of French wine or going to your favorite French bistro, for example). For me, if a day away to LA had not been possible, a day trip in town, coupled with a long phone chat with my friends, could still have provided the boost I was looking for. Identify what you want more of (solitude, connection, ease, nature, adventure) and then find something that fits your need that's still realistic, given your circumstances.

Sort Out the Logistics

The French writer Antoine de Saint-Exupéry said, "A goal without a plan is just a wish." So, let's turn that little daydream into reality, shall we? Don't despair if you're booked solid and you need to look months ahead; just find an empty day and block it off in your calendar. As someone who chronically overbooks myself, I like to write "FULL DAY OFF" in a bold color. If you have kids or pets, you'll want to make sure to line up the coverage and support you'll need for the day. If finances are tight, offer a babysitting swap to a friend so they can plan a day of their own sometime. Once your day is claimed, go ahead and book that mini trip or spa appointment or workout class or leisurely date with your BFF. Map out the hike you want to take or the bread you want to bake or buy seeds for the gardening you want to do. The more you prep and plan ahead, the more you can kick back and enjoy your day when it comes.

Be Fully Present and Enjoy

And now for the fun part! When the big day arrives, do your best to minimize distractions so you can be fully present for it. Set up an OOO if it's a workday, silence notifications on your cell. Self-care is not selfish; it's vital! Carve out that time you need, and you'll emerge from your dream day a much more relaxed and delightful version of yourself. Onward!

budget in college or while juggling a baby and a toddler. As a family, we've chosen to prioritize travel by cutting back on most non-essential purchases, driving older cars in a condition that might be embarrassing to others, and renting out our home to strangers on Airbnb. As a result, we've taken our kids to New York, Mexico City, Paris, London, Rome, Tel Aviv, and Tokyo, and before they go off to college, we plan to take them to Oaxaca, Bangkok, and Edinburgh for the biggest theater arts festival in the world. I get giddy just thinking about it. I recognize that travel can feel like an inaccessible luxury, but I encourage you to get creative if it feels important to you. Look into house or apartment swaps, try cashing in credit-card reward points for airfare, live/work exchanges, or just slowly save up for a big annual trip or smaller seasonal trips.

TRY IT

Even if you can't take extended or frequent vacations, consider integrating a weekend getaway or day trip into your monthly or seasonal calendar. Even a mini trip to explore a nearby city can provide a refreshing change of scenery and a little perspective shift for your brain.

Commit to Lifelong Learning

Cultivating a mindset of curiosity, adaptability, and continuous growth will ensure that you add depth, richness, and meaning to your life.

TRY IT

Here are some small ways to get your learning on:

- Diversify your information—follow a diverse range of thought leaders, authors, and teachers to expose yourself to new ideas, different viewpoints, and fresh perspectives.
- Try attending a new workshop, seminar, or retreat annually.

- Set up a coffee with a mentor or colleague who is willing to answer questions, share insights, and help you accelerate your personal and professional growth.

- Set micro learning goals—work on mastering a new skill, learning a language, reading a certain number of books on a specific topic—challenge yourself!

- Join a faith community; an affinity group; a book club; or a goal-setting, mastermind, or special interest group that provides structure, accountability, community, and support.

Find Your Folks

There are entire fields dedicated to supporting you on your personal growth and development journey. In addition to more traditional routes, like regular therapy sessions or analysis, you might consider booking a consistent time with a skilled life coach, intuitive, astrologer, sound healer, or art or drama therapist. For the animal lovers out there, check out equine therapy intensives or goat yoga classes. These are real things. Look them up!

TRY IT

Whatever route you choose, make sure to schedule and prioritize it so you can keep the growth coming. If you could benefit from therapy or coaching, you'll likely schedule weekly sessions. If you want to dip a toe into the alternative self-help world, you could try booking one specialist each season to see what resonates for you.

IMPLEMENTING HABITS: PERSONAL DEVELOPMENT EDITION

Implementing small, smart habit shifts can help ensure that you make personal growth, learning, and contribution a way of life.

Start or End Your Day with a Writing Practice

Spending even a few minutes each day writing down your thoughts can kick-start creative ideas and lead to greater clarity and self-awareness, boosting your overall mental well-being. Try spending the first five minutes of your day jotting down anything that's on your mind before you dive into the business of your day. Close your day with a quick summary of how you're feeling and what you'd like to do better or differently tomorrow. Think of writing as a way of cleaning out your brain each day. Don't concern yourself with punctuation, grammar, or sentence structure. Just put pen to paper and see what flows out of you.

Read All About It

In a highly scientific and peer-reviewed social media survey I conducted, 90 percent of my community said they wished they had more time for reading, and 99 percent said they spend more time than they would like on social media. Based on these staggering results, swapping screen time for curling up with a good book seems like the natural solution. If you struggle with social media addiction (my hand is up and I am also raising Jordan's for him because I see him scrolling), you might try deleting the apps from your phone for a few weeks and putting a good book in your handbag. You could also forgo watching the nightly news (or *The Real Housewives*) for a nice chunk of evening reading time. Short on time? Try reading on your daily commute (assuming that you're not the one driving, of course!), while waiting for your kid to get out of soccer practice, or even while standing in line at the supermarket. Reading offers a huge range of benefits that contribute to personal, cognitive, emotional, and intellectual growth. Commit to making it part of your daily life.

Rest Up to Rev Up

In a hustle culture that rewards us for skipping meals and working round the clock, it can be easy to forget that it's *rest*, not hustle, that's linked to greater creativity, productivity, and focus. Making rest a habit will help you:

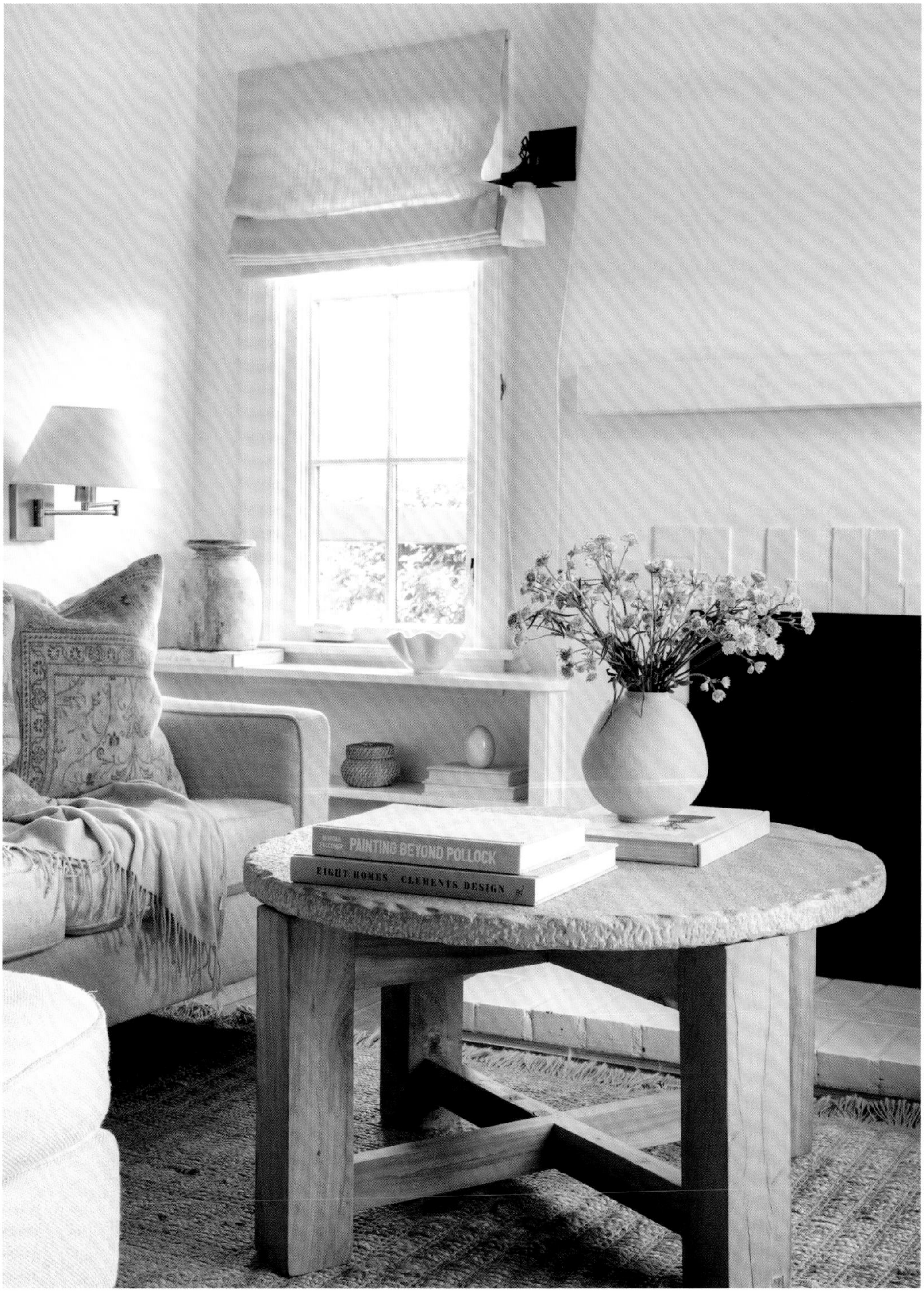
PAINTING BEYOND POLLOCK
EIGHT HOMES CLEMENTS DESIGN

- Recover, recharge, and repair, increasing immune function and overall health.
- Improve cognition, brain function, and memory, so your brain can process information, you can organize your thoughts, and you can make better decisions.
- Lower the production of stress hormones, like cortisol, promoting a sense of calm and reducing anxiety.
- Boost your creativity (most of my best ideas come when I'm taking a leisurely walk or daydreaming).

On board? Here are a few ways to integrate more regular bursts of rest into your life (not a great rester, so I'm writing this for myself as much as for you!):

- Plan breaks throughout your day. Try using the Pomodoro technique: twenty-five minutes of focused work followed by a five-minute break to eat a cookie, stretch, stare at the ceiling, or do anything that feels like rest to you.
- Integrate a daily mindfulness or meditation practice. Prioritize a few minutes of deep breathing when you wake up or during your lunch break.
- Engage your senses and daydream. Anytime, anywhere.
- Try a power nap. I am known as a "nap shamer" in my family, but I certainly can't deny the benefits of a quick burst of deep rest.
- Make a NOT-to-do-list. Identify activities and time wasters you want to *stop* doing to free up more time for leisure. Examples: checking email 24/7, doing things for your kids they're capable of doing for themselves (e.g., packing lunches–game changer), worrying about things that may never happen.

Remember that rest is not a luxury meant to be earned. It's a crucial part of health and well-being and will help you be more energized, creative, productive, and healthy.

Make Helping a Habit

Don't have time for regular volunteer work or the extra income to donate to charity? There are so many other ways to contribute. Pick up litter when you see it. Put away your phone and practice being more present in conversations. Do something small to surprise and delight an essential worker in your life (postal worker, nurse, teacher–whoever inspires you). Look for small opportunities to help and demonstrate kindness. My husband practically races to help open doors for people, pick up things that they've dropped, or help elderly people cross the street safely.

Banish the "I'm So Busy" Rant

Stop talking about how tired, busy, and overwhelmed you are. It will only make you feel more so. That's my TED Talk. Good night!

Choose Your Influencers Wisely

I heard this question on a podcast and it stopped me in my tracks: *"What are the influences that you are allowing into your mind on a daily basis? And what do you want them to be?"* When it's so easy to succumb to the mindless scroll, it's up to us to become more conscious and intentional about who and what we let influence us (otherwise you might find yourself watching a perfect stranger unbox their new 16-step skincare routine–oops). To become more intentional in this area, ask yourself:

- What specific qualities do I want in an influencer or leader?
- What kind of content do I want to seek out on purpose?

Allow your answers to inform the people you choose to surround yourself with, who you follow on social media, what podcasts, shows, and movies you consume, and even what you read. You might even want to create a mission statement for how you choose to be influenced moving forward. Here's mine: "I want to be influenced by creators, thinkers, leaders, and trailblazers who think outside the box, and I want to consume content that is educational, uplifting, and inspiring. Shorthand: more MasterClass courses, fewer *SNL* bloopers. What's yours?

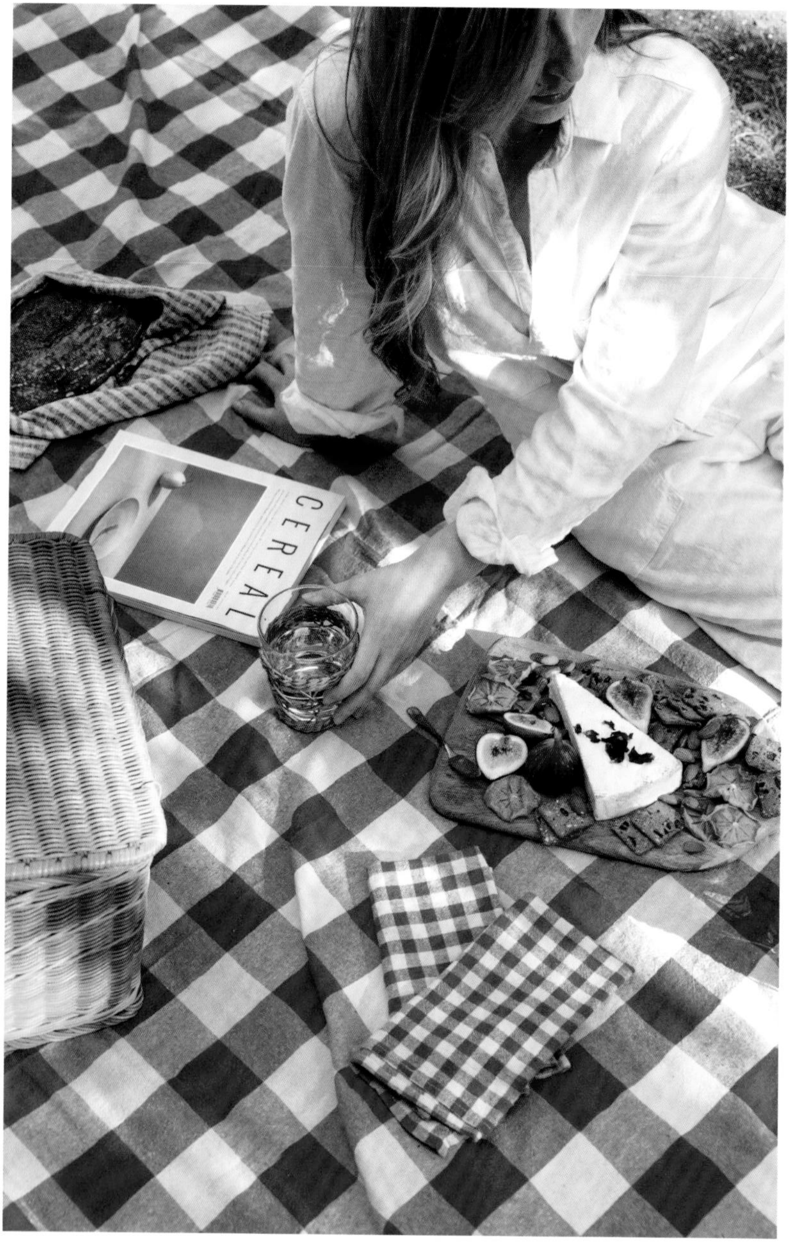
CEREAL

Do Something You Love Every Single Day

Integrate tiny, joyful habits into your life each day. You don't have to drop everything and plan a trip to Paris. You can just order a croissant with your morning coffee and eat it while enjoying your favorite book or magazine. If you don't have time for an art class, spend five minutes with your sketchpad between meetings. Make yourself a beautiful cheeseboard. Take your dog on a new hike. Get down with an ice cream sundae with your kids or enjoy a glass of wine and a chat with your best girlfriends. I guarantee you will become a significantly less cranky version of yourself if you do more of what you love, so please get to it.

March to Your Own Beat

The people I've always looked up to most are risk takers, not approval seekers (which is why I whispered "I LOVE YOU SO MUCH" when a woman in my power yoga class lay her body down during cardio and took a brief nap). We are wired to stick with the pack and fit in at all costs (once a survival imperative), but there is so much to be gained just by making a habit out of showing up as our most authentic selves and honoring what we need when we need it. There are so many ways to "do life." I have a friend who lives in a tree house, and a client who sold everything she owned and took her kids to travel around the world for a full year. My brother-in-law went to clown college. You do you.

Practice Showing Up

I'm not in the habit of quoting Woody Allen for obvious reasons, but his maxim that "80 percent of success is just showing up" really stuck with me. My friend Naomi says the other 20 percent is style and presentation—which is as much about feeling confident as it is about how you treat others *and* yourself—which I also love. Instead of waiting for some elusive "someday," show up fully and consistently today. Try the thing. Say the stuff. Take the risk.

THE BOTTOM LINE

Investing in continued growth, development, and contribution will infuse your life with more passion, purpose, and meaning, while also having a positive impact on others. Automation can ensure that you integrate continued learning into your days, weeks, months, and years, while tiny habit shifts will help keep you engaged in growth opportunities. There are plenty of approachable ways to actively enrich your mind, engage your curiosity, and create impact: Start small, and don't forget to celebrate your imperfect progress and minuscule victories.

YOUR PROMPTS

Ready to start living a more purposeful, meaningful, intentional life? Try the following prompts to kick-start your own progress and growth. Seriously, you got this!

- On a scale of 1 to 5, how would you rank your commitment to personal development?
- One thing you're interested in doing more of that has been deprioritized or neglected
- One small but critical action you will take to explore or reclaim a passion or interest
- One thing you can do to mix things up and step out of your comfort zone
- One mentor, friend, acquaintance, or colleague you'd love to learn from
- One tiny way you will integrate an interest or hobby into your daily or weekly life
- One way in which you'd like to give back, contribute, or volunteer
- One small action you will take to integrate more rest or leisure into your daily life

PART TWO WRAP-UP

At any given time we are all expected to wear multiple hats, but attempting to excel at being a top achiever at work, a committed partner, a mindful parent, a dutiful child, a loyal friend, and an active citizen is a recipe for near-certain defeat. Toss in trying to maintain a tidy home while serving healthy, balanced meals, and you'll probably just want to chuck a shoe at the wall. The truth is that if you're trying to do everything perfectly, it is nearly impossible to do anything well.

The definition of the word *priority* lies in its *singularity*, so the concept of juggling multiple priorities is quite literally paradoxical. Since it's not possible to completely drop the ball on many of the moving parts of your life (children need to be fed, bills need to be paid, work needs to be completed), you must practice prioritizing one singular goal at a time while committing to a baseline for the rest. Peace and freedom come from accepting our limitations and embracing purposeful trade-offs. Good enough has to be just that—good enough.

Some recent client examples:

- Ellie took a six-month sabbatical from her grueling corporate job to support her teenage son who was struggling with social anxiety and depression. She'd devoted herself to her company for many years, and stepping aside from work was not easy, but she only had one son, and the opportunity to be fully present for him was a no-brainer.
- Allie opted to embrace the "mess of life" in her home and let her kids eat cereal for dinner while digging in to finish up her dissertation. Despite longing for a tidy home and balanced meals, once she clarified that school needed to be her priority for this season of her life, it was easy to shrug off the makeshift suppers and finger paint and glitter on the countertops.
- Maria chose to pause all unnecessary spending for a full year to pay off her consumer debt and get her finances back on track. Her desire to reclaim financial stability trumped the (very real) desire to splurge on new outfits, weekend getaways, and even dinner and drinks with friends.

The goal is not to "do it all perfectly," but, rather, to identify the most important things right now and reduce your expectations on the rest without shame, guilt, or regret. I'll be right here alongside you, trying my very best, too.

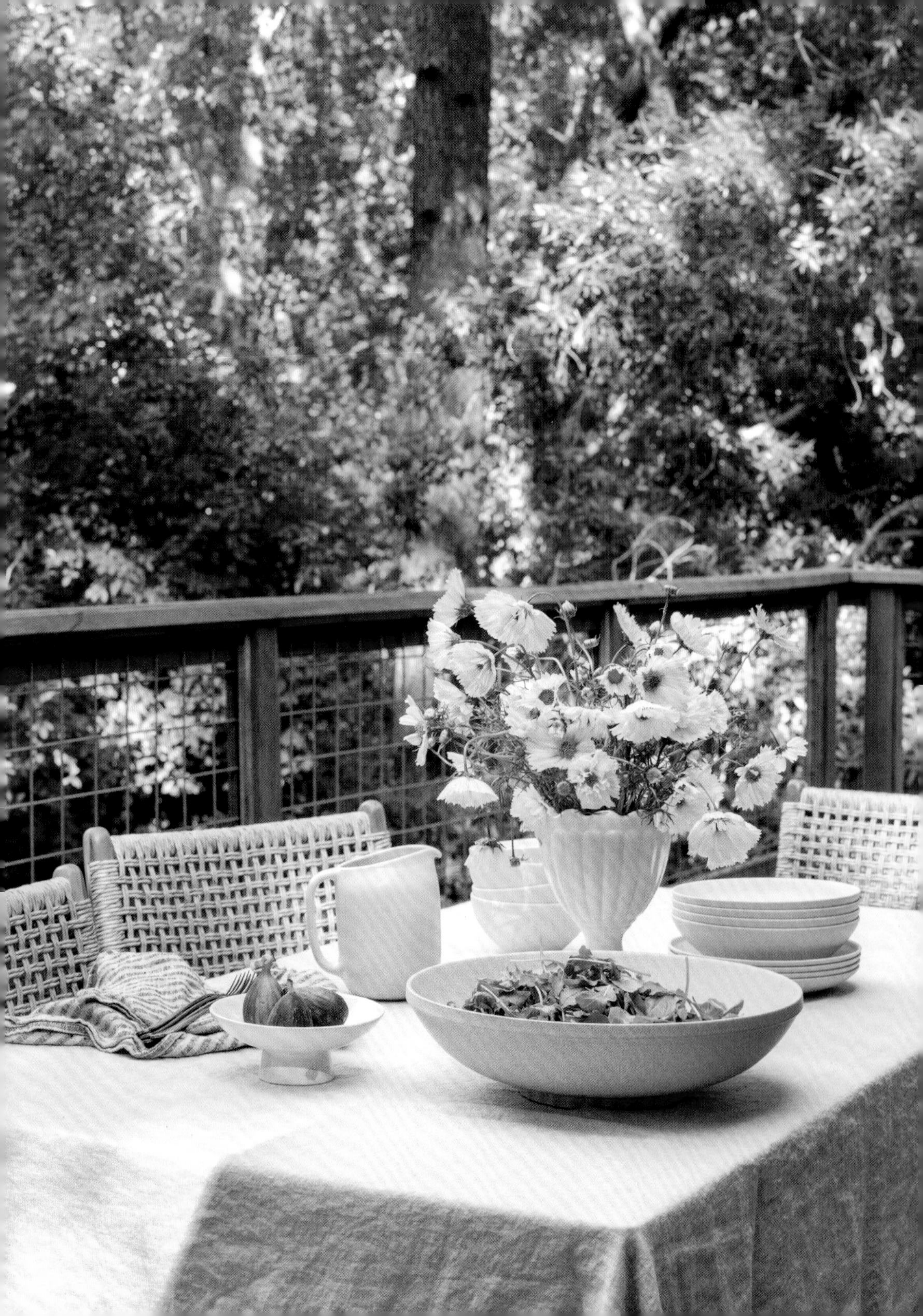

THAT'S A WRAP

When I tell you that *we are all in this together*, I mean it. I'm in this, too. Life is messy and beautiful and flawed and unpredictable. The aptly named *arrival fallacy*—the concept that once you reach a specific goal or milestone you will experience everlasting happiness and fulfillment—is, well, if you haven't already figured it out, a big old lie. Our goals will change. Our priorities *will* shift. The things that felt aligned and 100 percent true last year might feel constricting and ill-fitting this year. And you know what? That's okay. We will experience losses and unexpected challenges we couldn't possibly prepare for or imagine. We will have experiences—by design or by accident—that will ignite us in our centers and permanently alter our understanding of who we are. We can't control whether a taco truck crashes into our house (this happened to someone I know), your kid comes home from school with lice, or a natural disaster strikes close to home. In a changing world where so much is out of our control, we must claim control where we can find it. Luckily, there are so many things we *do* have agency over: our mindset and belief system; our work ethic; how often we move our body; what we eat or don't eat; what we buy or don't buy; how we treat each other; and what we read, watch, listen to, and consume. We get to say yes to plans and people and opportunities and responsibilities. And we get to say no, too.

The antidote to an overstuffed life is quite simply *less stuff*. Fewer energy-depleting plans. Less of making ourselves available 24/7. Less of running ourselves ragged. Less of buying things we don't need. Less of incessantly checking texts and emails. Anytime things start to feel too full and chaotic and stifling, you can choose to reduce mental overload and decision fatigue by ruthlessly editing your life, insisting on fewer distractions, and minimizing clutter. In a world full of endless pressures, responsibilities, opportunities, and demands, remember to take a deep breath and remind yourself that *less* is always available.

It's never too late to realign and reprioritize how you spend your precious time, energy, and resources. You can leverage the tools outlined in this book to help you edit, adjust, and recalibrate anytime things feel out of whack. Adjust the volume up or down. Create a new system to solve a problem. Integrate small, smart habits that will get you closer to where you want to go.

Since having it all is a myth, and attempting to juggle everything at once is a dead-end street, it's up to each of us to make peace with our limitations and redefine success on our own terms. It all comes down to this: Only you can give yourself the gift of an intentional and authentic life. Identify the things you value most, lean *way in,* and let the rest go.

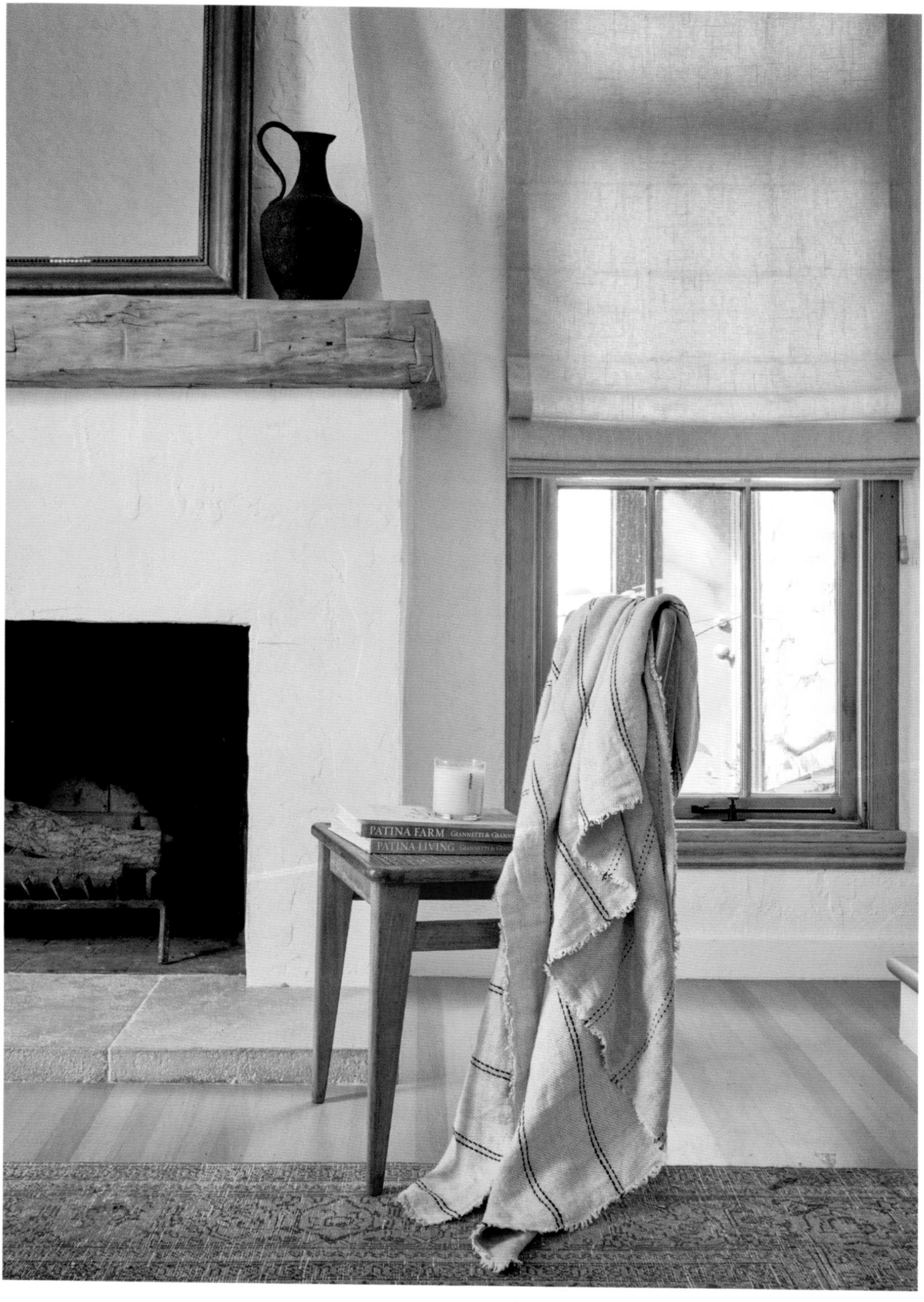
PATINA FARM
PATINA LIVING

THE PROMPTS:
YOUR QUICK-START GUIDE

I want to make it easy for you to integrate all the tools in this book into your life, so I'm providing you with a roundup of small, actionable prompts you can use at any time to improve your life on every level. The prompts are organized to align with the chapters in this book (Health and Wellness, Home and Environment, Relationships and Community, Career and Finance, and Personal Development), but you should feel free to jump around and pick any prompt that speaks to you. There are fifteen prompts within each category that can be completed in—yep, you guessed it—fifteen minutes or less (#15minwin). If you commit to trying one each day (or even one a week) they will compound to create major transformation and change. To the prompts!

HEALTH AND WELLNESS

1. Set a small health and wellness goal (daily vitamins, stretching before bed, a fifteen-minute walk each morning).

2. Move your body.

3. Hydrate: Reconnect with your water bottle or pour yourself a glass of water. Cheers!

4. Call a friend or loved one for a quick catch-up chat.

5. Select and *schedule* your weekly fitness classes, walks, or workouts.

6. Prep a few easy, nutritious snacks to fuel your body with sustained energy.

7. Try a mini digital detox. Take a break from screens, unplug, and get some fresh air. Don't forget to place your screens *outside* of the bedroom before you tuck in.

8. Schedule your annual wellness appointments, dental cleanings, specialists, and preventive care.

9. Make a list (or automate an online order) of weekly grocery staples (don't forget to double down on fresh fruit and veggies, and other healthy feel-good foods).

10. Take a sunshine break! Spend a few minutes in natural light. Sun exposure can boost your mood and provide essential vitamin D. Don't forget the sunscreen.

11. Organize a mini wellness station stocked with your favorite vitamins, supplements, and first aid essentials (no need to buy anything—you can repurpose a caddy, basket, or bin you already own).

12. Rest up (power naps are your friend—unless you're my husband, in which case I will wake you up and tell you I'm bored).

13. Review your product labels (cosmetics, lotions, shampoo/conditioner) to make sure they're filled with good-for-you ingredients. Toxins, bye.

14. Commit to a consistent bedtime each night. Tell your friends or family members for accountability.

15. Try out meditation or breathwork. Inhale. Exhale. Repeat.

HOME AND ENVIRONMENT

1. Make your bed, give your nightstand a quick tidy, and add something pretty or personal to rise and shine to—a favorite photo or object, garden clippings, or fresh flowers.

2. Declutter your entryway: Clear out excess shoes, coats, backpacks, and shopping bags to create a streamlined and welcoming space.

3. Gather up all loose mail and papers into one centralized inbox for review. Shred or recycle old magazines and newspapers (unsubscribe if you no longer want them).

4. Toss old or expired toiletries, makeup, and cosmetics.

5. Spruce up the bathroom: Open the windows, wipe down surfaces, replace used towels, bathmats, and hand towels with fresh ones.

6. Declutter a single drawer, shelf, or cabinet. Tackle a tiny organization project, like tidying up a kitchen junk drawer or editing your robust collection of novelty mugs (I see you!).

7. Refresh your fridge: Toss anything that's past its prime, give those sticky shelves a quick wipe-down, and add a box of baking soda to absorb odors.

8. Set up an "outbox" by the front door to corral shop returns, library books, and anything that needs to make it out of your house.

9. Wipe down countertops, tables, and other surfaces, and place dirty dishes in the sink (even if you don't have time to wash them).

10. Mix it up: Swap out or reposition decorative items or move around furniture for a quick design pick-me-up.

11. Stock up on a signature gift (candle, book, or favorite product) to have at the ready.

12. Ritualize setting the table: Dim the lights, break out the nice placemats, cloth napkins, and candlesticks, and play "fancy restaurant" in your own home.

13. Schedule a seasonal or big annual sweep to declutter clothes, toys, and housewares.

14. Locate your nearest e-waste and textile recycling centers so you can finally get those old sheets, towels, and busted electronics out the door. They'll even take all those orphaned cords. Sweet relief.

15. Fill a donation bag and drop it off. See ya'!

RELATIONSHIPS AND COMMUNITY

1. Plan your dream solo date or day and then schedule it. It's *you* time!

2. Reach out and tell someone that you love and appreciate them. Just 'cause it feels good.

3. Give someone a genuine compliment.

4. Listen up: When someone is talking, practice putting away distractions (I am talking about your phone) so you can listen actively and attentively. A true gift!

5. Practice kindness with strangers: Hold the door open for a stranger, pay for someone's coffee, leave an extra-generous tip.

6. Plan and schedule a walk or coffee with someone you want to see more of.

7. Assemble a group of friends for a meal, potluck, or gathering to celebrate something fun or for no reason at all.

8. Line up a fun date night for that special someone.

9. Invite a neighbor over for bagels or brunch.

10. Set up a weekly family meeting to check in and review meals, plans, and logistics so things don't get lost in the shuffle.

11. Give back to get back: Volunteer to help in your community—join a neighborhood or beach cleanup crew, serve a meal at a soup kitchen or shelter, bring a hot meal or care package to someone who is sick or struggling.

12. Make a meaningful contribution (whatever that means to you) to the organization of your choice. Make it in honor of someone special instead of buying them a gift.

13. Be a joiner: Sign up for a class, workshop, or activity that will connect you with others who share similar interests.

14. Initiate a conversation. Strike up a conversation with someone new, whether it's a colleague you haven't spoken to much, or someone you encounter in a social setting.

15. Help spread the word about a cause or initiative that you believe in deeply. Vote!

CAREER AND FINANCE

1. Clean out your wallet (adios crumpled receipts and gum wrappers!).

2. Disable the autofill feature that enables one-click ordering to save yourself from impulse buys you'll regret.

3. Organize all your login and password information in one secure place.

4. Centralize all your important physical documents and store them in a lockbox or safe.

5. Create a baseline budget so you can track your monthly spending.

6. Dust off your electronics. Use a microfiber cloth to freshen up your screens, cords, and chargers.

7. Clear off your workspace and declutter your office supplies. How many pens do you really need? Do you even staple things anymore?

8. Edit the apps on your phone and your computer desktop.

9. Unsubscribe from all the junk, marketing emails, online subscriptions, and solicitations you want to break up with. Scram!

10. Automate contributions to investment, retirement, and education accounts.

11. Make sure your LinkedIn profile and CV/résumé are updated and current. You never know when a new opportunity might come your way.

12. Schedule a networking coffee date. Send a quick message to someone in your network you'd like to connect with. Networking can open doors to so many new career opportunities and connections.

13. Invest in a work bag that makes you feel like a real professional.

14. Update your social media profiles (make sure to remove any unprofessional content that could negatively impact your career) and spruce up your email signature.

15. Set a small, achievable goal to improve your career or finances.

PERSONAL DEVELOPMENT

1. Pause and do something you love—right now!

2. Schedule something fun for yourself (a class, a spa treatment, a date).

3. Jot down three things you feel grateful for (repeat this enough times and you've got yourself a little gratitude practice).

4. Create a centralized hub for creative ideas and resources (Notes app, Google Doc, notebook).

5. Plan a get-it-done day to take care of the neglected (but important) things you just keep putting off.

6. Audit your influencers: unfollow social media accounts and unsubscribe from podcasts and other content that don't align with your bigger goals and values.

7. Challenge yourself to a "no complaints" day.

8. Make a let-it-go list.

9. Schedule time to do absolutely nothing.

10. Cancel something you really don't want to do.

11. Read.

12. Decide to try out that slightly scary thing you've always wanted to do (salsa dancing, zip-lining, stand-up comedy, solo travel) and schedule it.

13. Engage your curiosity and learn something new—a fun fact, a new word or phrase, a magic trick that will impress your kids.

14. Visualize your goals and imagine how you would feel if you achieved them.

15. Do something important that your future self would regret not doing. Say the thing. Write the letter. Take the risk.

FOCUS ON THE THINGS YOU CAN CONTROL

In a world where we have very little control, it's empowering to intentionally invest your mental, financial, and energetic resources in the things you *can* control—especially when the current news cycle just makes you want to curl up into the fetal position and weep. On my list:

My attitude, mindset, and actions

My work ethic

How I spend my time

How I care for my home

What foods I consume

Who I choose to spend time with

What I read, watch, and listen to

Who I choose to give my attention to

How I spend, donate, or invest my money

Who I vote for

How I treat myself

How I treat others

Making this list and choosing to focus on the many things I *can* control always helps me get out of a mental spiral. What's on your list?

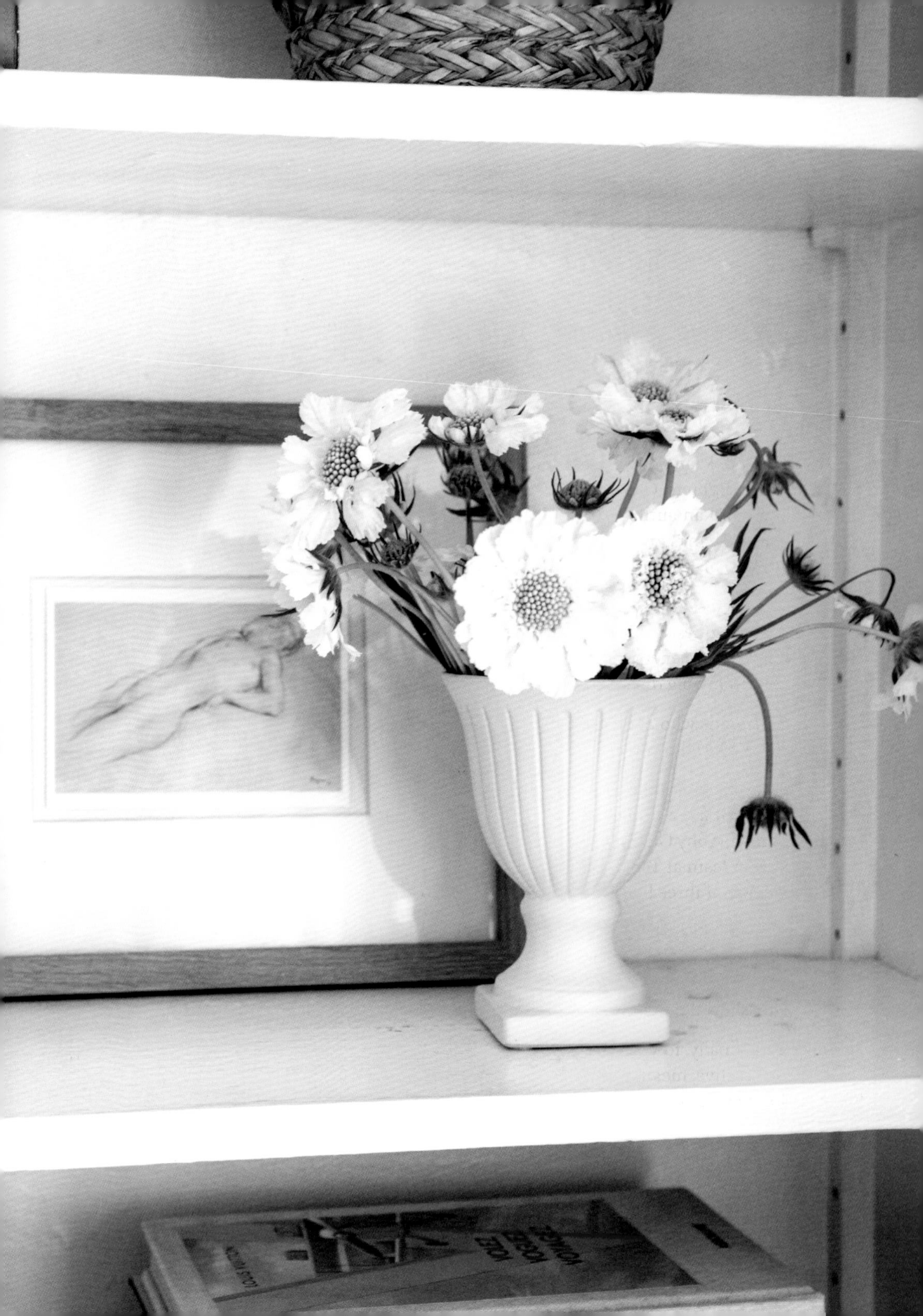

ACKNOWLEDGMENTS

This book, and everything I do, is dedicated to my husband, Jordan, and my two daughters, Chloe and Emilie. Thank you for putting up with me when I turn into an author-monster, shrieking, *"Nobody talk to me. I'm having an idea!"* Thank you for making me laugh harder than anyone and feel more loved than I ever thought possible. Home is wherever I'm with you.

To my mother, Linda, who inspires me with her resilience, intellect, and lifelong quest for growth, meaning, and self-improvement, and my father, Jules, whose energy, enthusiasm, and encouragement continue to propel me toward my big dreams.

To friends who are like family and family who are also my dearest friends—you know who you are.

Immense gratitude to my photographer, Vivian Johnson; agent, Julia Eagleton; editor, Kim Keller; art director, Betsy Stromberg; Dervla Kelly; Serena Sigona; Abby Oladipo; Mari Gill; Brianne Sperber; Jina Stanfill; and the entire dream team at Ten Speed Press who have been by my side through the completion of three books in a row.

Huge thanks to Anna Fiddler for her whip-smart editorial support, and the designers and stylists who graciously opened their doors and lent their talents to make this book beautiful: Caitlin Flemming, Chrissy Hunter, Paige Block, Brodie Jenkins, and Becca Meyer.

And, finally, to you—the readers of this book. It's not lost on me that I get to do creative, meaningful work that I love each day because of you. Thank you for your support. I'm so deeply grateful.

ABOUT THE AUTHOR
AND CONTRIBUTORS

Shira Gill is a globally recognized home organizing expert, bestselling author, and speaker. She has inspired thousands of people to clear clutter from their homes and lives, and developed a process and tool kit that apply to anyone, regardless of budget, space, or lifestyle. The author of *Minimalista* and *Organized Living*, Shira has been featured in more than a hundred print and media outlets including *Good Morning America*, HGTV, *Vogue, Dwell, Architectural Digest, Forbes, Real Simple*, and *The New York Times. LifeStyled* is her third book.

To join Shira's popular newsletter community or to find out about current offerings, visit: shiragill.com @shiragill

Vivian Johnson is a California-based interior lifestyle photographer with an eye for capturing lived-in spaces, architectural details, and interesting personalities. Her years as an award-winning photojournalist taught her how to tell a memorable story that truly captures the soul of the spaces people design and inhabit. Her work has been featured in publications including *Architectural Digest, Luxe Interiors + Design, California Home + Design, Dwell, Forbes*, the *Wall Street Journal, The New York Times*, and *Real Simple*. Vivian is the photographer behind several books including *Minimalista* and *Organized Living*.

visit: vivianjohnson.com @vivianjohnsonphoto

FEATURED HOMES

Caitlin Flemming Design is a full-service interior design firm based in San Francisco, with projects from coast to coast. She is the coauthor of *Sense of Place* and *Travel Home* for which she traveled the world to photograph beautiful homes and meet talented designers. She finds inspiration from the natural world and trains her eye for interiors through travel.

> Home featured on pages ii, 8, 33, 44, 49, 86, 113, 119, 122, 127, 134, 140, 145, 196, 209
> visit: caitlinflemming.com @caitlinflemming

Chrissy Hunter is an interior designer and lifestyle blogger based in Sausalito, California. Her company, Harlowe James, focuses on creating spaces and content that celebrate everyday moments. There is so much beauty in simplicity, and her goal is to capture that whenever possible.

> Home featured on pages iv, 3, 13, 18, 22, 25, 60, 71, 99, 102, 108, 133, 136, 157, 177, 242
> visit: harlowejames.com @_harlowejames

Paige Block is a freelance marketing creative based in West Marin, California. Her company, Here + West, works to empower small businesses with impactful digital strategy that feels visually inspired, intentional, and aligned.

> Home featured on pages vi, 21, 28, 77, 95, 116, 128, 151, 201, 228, 232
> visit: hereandwest.com @hereandwest

Brodie Jenkins is a Bay Area–based interior designer and indie musician. With a deep love of historic homes, she strives to create timeless, elevated spaces with warmth and originality. Her work is characterized by organic materials, soulful charm, and design that honors and enhances the architecture of each home.

> Home featured on pages 54, 91, 180, 235 (styling by Rachel Forslund)
> visit: @enchantedberkeley

Other Featured Interiors:

> Holly Blakey, pages 43 and 194; Sarit Sela, pages 59 and 206; Becca Meyer, pages 110 and 225; Marie Queru, pages 154 and 187; and Vintage Rug Shop, page 215

INDEX

ALSO BY SHIRA GILL

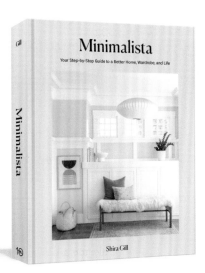

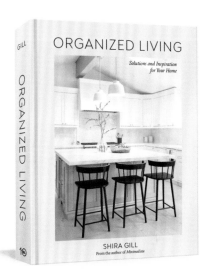

"Warm, funny, and direct, Shira builds you up while helping you edit down to the best version of yourself."

—STACY LONDON,
New York Times bestselling author of *The Truth About Style*

———

"Shira Gill is the funniest, wisest, most entertaining writer in the organizing game."

—ADAM MANSBACH,
#1 *New York Times* bestselling author of *Go the F**k to Sleep*

Copyright © 2024 by Shira Gill
Photographs copyright © 2024 by Vivian Johnson

All rights reserved.
Published in the United States by Ten Speed Press, an imprint of the Crown
Publishing Group, a division of Penguin Random House LLC, New York.
TenSpeed.com

Ten Speed Press and the Ten Speed Press colophon are registered trademarks of
Penguin Random House LLC.

Typefaces: Latinotype's Aestetico, Dieter Hofrichter's Ashbury, and
Commercial Type/Schwartzco Inc.'s Canela.

Library of Congress Cataloging-in-Publication Data
Names: Gill, Shira, 1977– author. Title: Lifestyled : your guide to a more
organized & intentional life / Shira Gill. Identifiers: LCCN 2023048129
(print) | LCCN 2023048130 (ebook) | ISBN 9781984863508 (hardcover) |
ISBN 9781984863515 (ebook) Subjects: LCSH: Lifestyles. | Interior decoration.
Classification: LCC HQ2042 .G55 2024 (print) | LCC HQ2042 (ebook) |
DDC 645–dc23/eng/20231030
LC record available at https://lccn.loc.gov/2023048129
LC ebook record available at https://lccn.loc.gov/2023048130

ISBN: 978-1-9848-6350-8
EBook ISBN: 978-1-9848-6351-5

Printed in China

Acquiring editor: Dervla Kelly
Project editor: Kim Keller
Production editor: Abby Oladipo
Art director and designer: Betsy Stromberg
Production manager: Serena Sigona
Prepress color manager: Nick Patton
Copyeditor: Diana Drew
Proofreader(s): Alisa Garrison and Robin Slutzky
Indexer: Elise Hess
Publicist: Jina Stanfill
Marketer: Brianne Sperber

10 9 8 7 6 5 4 3 2 1

First Edition